GAIA

GAIA

THE GROWTH OF AN IDEA

Lawrence E. Joseph

St. Martin's Press
New York

This book is dedicated to James Lovelock, Lynn Margulis,
and to everyone who gives them a good argument.

GAIA: THE GROWTH OF AN IDEA. Copyright © 1990 by Lawrence E. Joseph. All
rights reserved. Printed in the United States of America. No part of this book may
be used or reproduced in any manner whatsoever without written permission
except in the case of brief quotations embodied in critical articles or reviews.
For information, address St. Martin's Press, 175 Fifth Avenue, New York,
N.Y. 10010.

Library of Congress Cataloging-in-Publication Data

Joseph, Lawrence E.
        Gaia : the growth of an idea / Lawrence E. Joseph.
            p.   cm.
        Includes index.
        ISBN 0-312-05866-7
        1. Gaia hypothesis.   2. Biosphere.   3. Biology—Philosophy.
    I. Title.
    [QH331.J74   1991]
    550—dc20   90-28383
                                                                   CIP

First U.S. Paperback Edition: May 1991
10   9   8   7   6   5   4   3   2   1

CONTENTS

ACKNOWLEDGMENTS

Were it not for the sharp eye and great heart of my mother, Yvonne Joseph, this book and my dreams would be nowhere.

Only the heroic tenacity of Stuart Krichevsky of Sterling Lord Literistic, my friend and literary agent, saved my book from falling prey to the vagaries of contemporary publishing, and to my own bad writing habits.

Without the generosity of Laurence B. Shames, a writer whose touch of Picasso reminds his friends that happiness is our most important and least solemn duty, I'd never have gotten a start in the first place.

Judith Karolyi and Zenka Bartek, rare and wonderful birds, gave me seven months of uninterrupted writing in the perfect cabin in the woods, at the Foundation Karolyi in Vence, France. Without them and their colorful crew, my feeling for the living Earth might have remained citified and sterile. (Thanks also to the armies of ants that tried to invade my abode but were crushed.)

My editor Michael Denneny and his assistant Keith Kahla, a coupla world-class regular guys, have made it fun, exciting, and eccentric. Jim Fitzgerald, an editor, did me a great service.

Brian Cullman, a good friend and a superb cultural impresario, was the first one to tell me about Gaia; Randall Rothenberg, when he was editor at *The New York Times Magazine,* said with a straight face, "Everything in this draft [of the Gaia article] is good. Of course, we'll have to do it all over again."; David A. Weiss and gang will surely recognize that this book is written in the Packaged Facts format; Dean James Morton of the Cathedral of St. John the Divine, and Paul Mankiewicz of the Gaià Institute have been loyal supporters of Gaia and a real help to me.

There are also several people whom I would condemn, but why disgrace these pages with their names, especially when there are so many good people to thank:

My great friend John Colangelo and his wife Andrea for the ways they've welcomed me and mine into their lives; Christopher and Jane Buonanno, and of course little Chris and Arianna, a family who, headed by a man with a wild mind, truly make me feel like Uncle Larry; Jay Davis and Jack Atterstrom, guys among guys who take me ever so seriously; and Brown University, which feels like a friend, especially when I visit.

Playwright Mitchell Redman, whose capacities for friendship and startling insights are exceeded only by his knack for making me laugh; Ed Wetschler and his wife Carol, and Dave Lindner, his wife Suzy, and their daughter Sonya, who invite me in, calm me down and more often than not, crack me up; Richard and Marilyn Lester, great souls, solid friends, and fun collaborators; Janet and Avi Fattal, their daughter Danielle, and their son Jordan, who make me feel so easy and welcome, it's as though we were blood; the global Susan Becker, steadfast friend, colleague, and aw-shucks awe-inspirer; Stefanie Ramsdell, a phenomenon of nature and intellect, and a good egg; Kirsten Baker, a true goddess of Malibu, with "Oh Gaia" license plates; Jerry Mallow and his wife Francoise, whose help and hospitality are gifts from the blue; Scott Ste. Marie, Terry Lang, and their daughter Hannah, who uplift a great neighborhood; and Prospect Park, Brooklyn's best patch of Gaia.

GAIA

My father, Edward Joseph, and my grandmother, Hasiba Shehab Haddad, would be proud and happy, I think. Liz Berntsson, Robin Shine Ackerman, and Monica Fread (thanks, Mo) dwell in my heart. The Mirabitos and the Mayers are closer than blood. To Tom Azumbrado, wherever you are, you've got class. And Michael, may you rest in peace.

Once again, thanks, Mom. Without your love and hard work I wouldn't even have come close.

INTRODUCTION

FROM GODDESS TO THEORY

Daughter of Chaos and mother and lover of the sky (Uranus), the mountains (Ourea), and the sea (Pontus), Gaia, Greek goddess of the Earth, has been reborn through modern science.

The Gaia hypothesis is the first comprehensive scientific expression of the profoundly ancient belief that the planet Earth is a living creature. Formulated by British atmospheric scientist James Lovelock and American microbiologist Lynn Margulis, the Gaia hypothesis states that the Earth's climate and surface environment are controlled by the plants, animals, and microorganisms that inhabit it. That taken as a whole, the planet behaves not as an inanimate sphere of rock and soil, sustained by the automatic and accidental processes of geology, as traditional earth science has long maintained, but more as a biological superorganism—a planetary body—that adjusts and regulates itself.

Gaian scientists propose that the proper study of our immense planetary organism is not traditional geology, but that it

1

is geophysiology, the science of bodily processes as applied to the planet Earth. The distinction is crucial. If the Gaian vision of a globally integrated organism is correct, then the planet regulates and maintains itself through a complex system of corrective mechanisms and buffers, akin to the way that an animal body reflexively adjusts to compensate for changes in temperature, chemistry and other vital variables in its immediate environment. This quality of homeostasis, or "wisdom of the body," may mean that the climatic system is in many ways more robust and resilient than has been generally believed. For example, beleaguered systems such as the stratospheric ozone layer may have some capacity to heal and regenerate, though not necessarily over time frames convenient to humankind.

By contrast, traditional earth science holds that the Earth's climatic system is less biological than geological, significantly less responsive than a global body might be, and is therefore more fragile and susceptible to permanent disruption.

Geophysiologists warn that if the planet does function like a body, the Earth may have the equivalent of vital organs and vulnerable points. Regions of intense biological activity, such as the tropical rain forests and coastal seas, are seen as vital not only to their geographic regions but to the entire global environment, much as the liver or spleen is necessary to the survival of the body as a whole. Once destroyed, these planetary organs can debilitate the entire system, much as an injury to the spine can cripple one's body up through the neck and down to the toes.

"I feel like an eighteenth-century physician discovering the body!" Lovelock declares.

THE RENAISSANCE RUSTIC

James E. Lovelock, age seventy, an easygoing country scholar, is one of the only self-employed researchers ever admitted to Britain's Royal Society, an ancient elite that generally has been averse to renegades ever since one of its early presidents,

Sir Isaac Newton, took to persecuting those who would not conform. While it is tempting to shelve Lovelock as yet another admirable English eccentric, a renaissance rustic whose nap under the apple tree collected him quite a favorable conk on the noggin, he is a scientist and inventor whose work has achieved global significance, who accepts no boundaries, who concedes no professional turf, and who is deadly serious beneath the charm. Lovelock wrote:

> Most of us were taught that the composition of our planet could adequately be described by the laws of physics and chemistry. It was a good, solid Victorian view. . . . On this reliable and predictable planet of the hardcore geologists, the biosphere (the region of the earth and its atmosphere where organisms reside) was regarded as a bystander or a spectator, and was not permitted to enter the game. We and the rest of life were told that we were amazingly fortunate to be on a planet where everything is and always has been so comfortable and well suited for life.[1]

Lovelock has told me:

> Luck is the least of it. I think of the Earth as a living organism. The rocks, the air, the oceans, and all life are an inseparable system that functions to keep the planet livable. In fact, I now believe that life can exist *only* on a planetary scale. Can't have a planet with sparse life any more than you can have half a cat.

Lovelock fell silent after delivering this controversial tidbit, as though listening for the howls of protest that have echoed ever since he first presented his Gaia worldview almost twenty years ago.

An interdisciplinary wanderer through the jealously special-ized halls of academe, Lovelock holds degrees in chemistry and

3

medicine and has taught engineering, physiology, and cybernetics (the study of information-control systems) at various universities in England and the United States, including the medical schools of Harvard, Yale, and Baylor. He has consulted for the National Aeronautics and Space Administration (NASA) at the legendary Jet Propulsion Laboratory (JPL) on a number of occasions, designing instruments for the early lunar probes and, later on, life-detection experiments for the *Viking* satellites to Mars.

After a decade of technical articles and studies that began in the 1960s with his work for NASA, Lovelock introduced his Gaia theory to the general public in *Gaia: A New Look at Life on Earth*, published in 1979 by the Oxford University Press. Igniting a scientific, environmental, and spiritual movement that has burgeoned through scores of seminars, symposia, and songfests at home and abroad, the Britisher's opinions on Gaia have since been roundly in demand. Indeed, *The Greening of Mars*, coauthored with Michael Allaby and published in 1984 by St. Martin's Press, was a highly successful novel wherein humans create an earthlike atmosphere and essentially bring the red planet to Gaian life. In their scenario, the Martian atmosphere is filled with greenhouse gases that heat up the frozen planet, melt its ice crystals, and "shake" the oxygen out of the dominant gas, carbon dioxide. This book of "science faction," speculative work supported by scientific principles, launched three scientific conferences examining Gaian theory and the feasibility of Lovelock's plan.

Though most often referred to as a biologist or atmospheric scientist, with more than thirty credits in *Nature* magazine alone, Lovelock thinks of himself first and foremost as an inventor—to which a few score patents, handy new devices, and lucrative retainers from Hewlett-Packard, Shell, and other advanced technological companies attest. His most important invention, the electron capture detector, is invaluable for detecting minute traces of toxic chemicals in the atmosphere. By taking readings with this device on an ocean voyage halfway around the world,

Lovelock was the first to demonstrate that chlorofluorocarbons (CFC's) were accumulating in the atmosphere, thus providing the hard data for the international movement to ban these substances for the dangers they present to the stratospheric ozone layer and as potent greenhouse gases.

Several years ago this atmospheric scientist was named president of the Marine Biological Association of the United Kingdom, an oceanographic and marine life laboratory and research complex on the Atlantic coast at Plymouth. He since has written *The Ages of Gaia: A Biography of Our Living Earth*, prefaced and published under the editorial guidance of Lewis Thomas, editorial director of the Commonwealth Fund of New York City. It is a technical primer on Gaia theory and on the new discipline of geophysiology that has emerged. Well reviewed and featured in *the New York Times, Newsweek,* and many other publications, the advanced text culminates a lifetime of scientific creativity and two decades of studying the ways and mechanisms of the living Earth. It is by far Lovelock's finest work.

Perhaps most impressive, in triumphant contrast to the indifference that had long plagued his notions of the living Earth, Lovelock was to earn his due when the American Geophysical Union (AGU), the international association of geologists and geochemists, devoted the entire week of its 1988 biannual Chapman conference to debating and discussing Lovelock's Gaia theory.

MOTHER EARTH WITH A THIRTY-PAGE RESUME

Lynn Margulis, coauthor of the Gaia theory, is one of the youngest women ever elected to the National Academy of Sciences. Now fifty and a professor of microbiology at the University of Massachusetts at Amherst, Margulis's resume reads like a saga; it is a thirty-page, single-spaced barrage of awards (Guggenheim, NASA, CalTech, MacArthur Foundation), top scientific publications and academic honors. Most recently she was named in a

Newsweek cover story as one of twenty-five American innovators, a group selected from all professional fields.

Margulis's lab bustles with experiments, demonstrations, in-jokes, and lots of student overtime. And a large NASA photograph of the Earth captioned "Love Your Mother!" dominates all points of view.

> Life's pressure is felt all over the surface of the Earth, from the depths of the oceans to where the air grows very thin. Wherever and whenever something can grow and reproduce, suitable organisms will find their way and flourish. Lovelock tells about the wildflowers pushing through the rubble weeks after cities had been bombed out during the Second World War, and we've all stepped on weeds forcing their way through the cracks in the sidewalk. Any living creature can and will be killed, but life itself cannot be stopped. Not from any plan or intention, and assuming no "soul" or other mystical power, Gaia theory states that the net effect of this ancient, ubiquitous life force is the regulation of [the] local, and ultimately the global, environment.

Microbes are Margulis's passion, and her goal is to correct what she sees as the pervasive misconception that bacteria, amoebae, paramecia, and other single-celled organisms are primarily agents of disease. Margulis believes strongly that the biological microcosm provides a key, controlling influence in the global environment, and argues that the role of these tiny organisms has been underestimated because they are invisible without microscopes and other technological encumbrances. Usually they must be taken from their natural habitats and brought back to the laboratory for observation. Many species simply cannot be grown under laboratory conditions and thus must be killed for examination. Some can be grown only with expensive, artificial techniques that may keep them alive but that place them in thoroughly arbitrary contexts, as though a researcher wanting to understand human life plopped a person under bright lights, provided nutritionally sufficient but alien foodstuffs, and then took notes.

As a field biologist, Margulis searches the world for microbial communities worthy of study, plunging in with hands and feet to whet her mind. She has led her band of students, researchers, and instrument bearers to the lakes, lagoons, and other watery habitats of Baja, California, Mediterranean Spain, western Australia, the Persian Gulf, and the Atlantic coast in order to learn how microbes behave on their own turf and what they do to keep that turf comfortable. That is why she is known as the Wizard of Ooze.

> Microbes are the building blocks of the rest of life on Earth. And all organisms, from the microbial level on over to the visible world of plants, animals, and human beings, change their environment all the time. One hundred percent of organisms give off gas, transfer energy, and alter their surroundings 100 percent of the time.

The renowned microbiologist believes that the best way to understand the mechanisms and effects of life's continuous pressure on the environment is to study the organisms in their most fundamental, microbial form. She illustrates the Gaian argument of life's collective influence over the planet's system as thus:

> There is always a feedback loop between an organism and its environment, a continuously evolving cycle of interaction between the two. For example, imagine that you are in a room, and it gets hot. Your first response might be behavioral—you might fan yourself or remove a layer of clothes. The next level of response might be physiological—you might sweat. Then you

7

would probably act upon your environment, by opening a window or turning on the air-conditioning. In
short, you adapt to your environment, and you would
also do your best to adapt the environment to you.
That in a nutshell is how living organisms evolve with
and control their environment.

Margulis's most recent book, *Microcosmos*, cowritten with
Dorion Sagan, her son (from her first marriage, to Carl Sagan),
traces the evolution of life on earth from the original bacterial
takeover of the planet four billion years ago. Prefaced by Lewis
Thomas, the book propounds the theory that ever since the
earliest bacteria began to process mud, the Earth's organisms not
only have adapted themselves to their surroundings, as traditional Darwinism holds, but have also adapted their surroundings
to themselves—not with any plan, self-sacrifice, or global mentality, but simply as a result of their mutual interest in controlling a potentially hostile environment. In Margulis's view, sym-
boisis and cooperation have been as important to biological
evolution as the competitive struggle for survival that is the
hallmark of traditional Darwinist theory.

Lovelock calls Margulis "my best and staunchest colleague,"
and clearly they are the deepest of friends. He complains about
her reverence for academic rigor, particularly her participation
in the "accursed peer review" system whereby scientific papers
are evaluated for publication by teams of referees, and she
complains about his penchant for seductive speculations that do
not look nearly as good in the cold light of morning, especially
what she regards as his sometimes cavalier fondness for some of
the more spiritual aspects of Gaia. But they are as close as family
and partners to the core. Early on, Margulis, devout in her
rejection of anything but hard facts, vacillated over how closely
she wanted to be identified with Gaia. As the science of Gaia
has evolved, particularly Lovelock's, Margulis has grown more
comfortable with the whole enterprise, and now she is pleased
to be called a coauthor of the living Earth theory.

STEPHEN SCHNEIDER, HONEST BROKER

Stephen Schneider, forty-two, deputy director of the National Center for Atmospheric Research (NCAR), is a fast-talking ex–New Yorker who has a natural political bent; if he were to run for office, he would win all of the debates by burying his opponents in facts, statistics, and smart remarks—though he might be a difficult dinner companion. This commanding young atmospheric scientist is sought after by congressional committees, popular and scientific media, and international organizations for his opinions on the greenhouse effect, the stratospheric ozone, nuclear winter, acid rain, and now the Gaia theory.

For the past decade Schneider has played the role of supporter and constructive critic, encouraging Lovelock and Margulis to sharpen up and substantiate their positions while at the same time bringing into the debate skeptics, particularly geochemists and climatologists, who otherwise would have dismissed or overlooked the Gaia theory.

It is virtually beyond dispute that the Earth modifies itself due to a complex of organic and inorganic interactions. Lovelock once observed that there are biologists studying bugs on the ground who have noticed that methane was being released, but it didn't mean much to them. And that there are aeronomists studying the upper atmosphere who have noticed the methane but knew nothing about the bugs.

Though he has always played the role of devil's advocate, leveling sharp criticisms at Lovelock's work, Schneider conceived of, fought for, organized, and moderated the pivotal 1988 AGU conference on the Gaia theory.

The Gaia hypothesis is a brilliant organizing principle for bringing together people who don't normally talk to each other, like biologists, geochemists and atmos-

9

pheric physicists, to ask profound questions about how we got here and how the machinery works.

THE WORLD ACCORDING TO GAIA

Much as at the dawn of history, the idea of the living Earth today exercises a profound intellectual enchantment. The notion of our planet as an infinitely integrated superorganism has compelled world leaders from Mikhail Gorbachev to Pope John Paul II, Ronald Reagan to Archbishop Desmond Tutu, and United Nations Secretary General Perez de Cuellar to Norwegian prime minister Gro Harlem Brundtland to write on the theme of global interdependence in *The Gaia Peace Atlas*, published in 1988, which concludes by thanking Lovelock "for his continuing inspiration."

The nerve center of Gaian philosophy is the Lindisfarne Association, an international group deriving its principles from such early supporters as Gregory Bateson, the anthropologist and philosopher best known for his *Steps to an Ecology of the Mind*, and E. F. Schumacher, author of *Small is Beautiful*, and long dedicated to the development and propagation of a planetary culture based on broad Gaian principles. The group meets and publishes regularly, with the goal of translating the biological notion of the Earth as a single, coherent organism into political and cultural policy.

William Irwin Thompson, the founder of Lindisfarne, writes:

Part of the Gaian politics for the nineties is, therefore, to realize that we are all organelles within a planetary cell, and that it is a dangerous illusion to think that any national state can make it on its own, militarily or economically. Greenpeace can intrude into the politics of France, and Nestle can buy up Carnation in the U.S.A., Chernobyl can ruin the agricultural produce of Eastern Europe, and middle-class American college students on cocaine can sustain the Shining Path along the Andes.[2]

Thompson, a former cultural historian at the Massachusetts Institute of Technology (MIT) now living in Switzerland, is the group's intellectual ringleader. He reminds one a bit of Henry James, spinning the engrossing whirl of optimism and ennui that American expatriates seem to manage best, although, as H. G. Wells once said of James, at times Thompson's ponderings have all the elegance of a hippopotamus trying to pick up a pea. Lovelock and Margulis are longtime members of Lindisfarne, as are the likes of the influential Reverend James Morton, dean of the Cathedral of St. John the Divine in New York City; Mary Catherine Bateson (daughter of Gregory Bateson and Margaret Mead), former dean of faculty at Amherst College; Maurice Strong, former undersecretary of the United Nations; John and Nancy Todd, innovative ecological engineers, entrepreneurs, and publishers; the French biophysicist Henri Atlan; and two Chilean biologists, Francisco Varela and Humberto Maturana, founders of the study of autopoiesis, a word they coined to describe the self-organization and maintenance of living systems. All are loyal to Thompson and their shared intellectual cause.

"Ideas, like grapes, grow in clusters,"[3] writes Thompson, as if by way of explanation, in Lindisfarne's most recent book, *Gaia: A Way of Knowing: Political Implications of the New Biology.* This collection of scientific and philosophical essays is introduced, edited, and concluded by the same crusty sage who has authored such recondite explorations as *The Time Falling Bodies Take to Light, Pacific Shift,* and *Imaginary Landscape,* Thompson's latest.

"People like to hang out together because they feel their ideas growing fuller and richer on the vine,"[4] observes Gaia's master vintner.

THE GODDESS RETURNS

Certainly the most colorful and eclectic Gaian phenomenon has been the rebirth of the Earth goddess in the popular imagination. For every scientific symposium and scholarly lecture, there has been at least one festival, workshop, or art exhibition celebrating "the goddess" as a spiritual or creative inspiration.

Merlin Stone, author of the popular goddess manifesto *When God Was a Woman*, is a true impresaria of the goddess movement. One need read no further than her occasional "Letters from Merlin" to keep abreast of the latest festivals, films, books, and workshops on the goddess theme. Through Merlin, who hosted the New York City Open Center's Goddess Festival in 1989, one learns of a group of women who have come together on an island in the Pacific Northwest, now called Gaia Island, and one meets such artists as Diane Snow Austin, whose song "The Goddess Walks Again" has a rousing pop-hit style. Only after pressing does one also learn that Merlin has been commissioned by Olympia Dukakis, the Academy Award-winning actress (and cousin of the former Democratic presidential candidate), to write a play about the Earth goddess of ancient Greece.

Even macho Ted Turner has become a devotee, developing for his networks several environmental and Earth goddess projects around the Gaia theme. And the devoutly this-worldly Bob Geldof has worked to sponsor a series of environmental benefits in Gaia's name. But to the ardent faithful, like Otter and Morning Glory G'Zell, who describe themselves as priest and priestess of Gaia, this is all accommodation of an inevitable trend: "The winds of change are blowing," write the G'Zells, whose pagan ruminations bubble like a sacred brook. "And by the time the century turns we will see that once again the Goddess is Alive and Magick is Afoot."[5]

SO WHAT?

The jury on the Gaia hypothesis has barely begun to deliberate. If nothing else, Lovelock and Margulis are guilty of triggering an avalanche of inquiry on the coevolving relationship between life and the planet. Beyond that, responsibility for scientific proof of the iconoclastic theory rests squarely on their shoulders—a burden that would stagger Atlas.

But ultimately Gaia will be judged less on the accuracy of its postulates than on the value of its results. Atmospheric scientists curious about the relationship between cloud formation and the greenhouse effect have been led by Gaian theory to look for biological influences on meteorological events. Could it be, for example, that the dumping of toxic wastes into the ocean not only pollutes the water but inhibits the growth of marine algae instrumental in creating the cloud cover that helps cool the planet? And if there is such a toxic waste-greenhouse link, then what are the ramifications for environmental treaties and international law?

Environmentalists captivated by geophysiology's emphasis on how vast ecosystems interact with one another are encouraged to examine more closely the coupling between tropical rain forests and the warm coastal seas fed by their groundwater. In addition to the immediate impact of deforestation, what consequences will it have for the fishing industry and for the local weather of adjoining coastal territories? Already there are strong indications that the destruction of the Amazon has lowered the rainfall and increased the silt runoff into the Panama Canal, threatening to make the waterway impassable. What is the ecological domino effect, and how will the planet respond?

Nearly one hundred scientific and technical articles have been written on aspects of the Gaia theory since the AGU conference in March 1988. For the most part these researchers care less about any final yea or nay on Gaian theoretical assertions than they do about the hypothesis having led them to ask hard new questions of practical, sometimes vital, importance.

13

Regardless of its technical accuracy, many people find the idea of the living Earth spiritually compelling, beautiful. As philosophers, artists, and theologians have crafted the Gaian imagination, the concept has amassed a critical momentum and shows signs of becoming the focus of a cultural phenomenon. Whether based ultimately on science, fear, or wishful thinking, the Gaia movement and the reasons for its regenesis tell a great deal about the societies that give it root.

The goals of this book, then, are to critique the science of the living Earth theory and to explore its intellectual and cultural development—in short, to find out what the return of Gaia hath wrought.

I

JAMES LOVELOCK AND THE THEORY OF GAIA

"LOVELOCK, YOU ARE A FOOL"

Discovering a nest of gleaming technology deep in the countryside can be a delightful surprise, much like finding a flower bed in the middle of the city. Hard by the River Carey in St. Giles-on-the-Heath, a hamlet on the Cornwall-Devon border in southwestern England, stands the laboratory of James E. Lovelock, a white windowed cabin attached to his house and patrolled outside by half a dozen peacocks and peahens, gyrating shrubs of green and gold that honk a merry tumult at the slightest provocation. Inside, a phalanx of spectroscopes, chromatographs, radiation detectors, and microcomputers flickers and hums, each instrument carefully overstrewn with texts and monographs on mathematical physiology, biogeochemistry, and atmospheric physics. Set incongruously in a fragrant meadow, next to a beaming marble statue of Gaia, Greek goddess of the Earth, Lovelock's little lab seems like a probe sent to unravel the secrets of nature.

Lovelock, a slight, fit fellow with a shock of white hair, stout eyebrow bushes, and a friendly, playful intellect, has gathered a growing army of adherents who would argue that he has indeed discovered one of the Earth's deepest truths. Yet their leader shies away from any such claims and enjoys much more telling stories of how he got into this unique predicament in the first place. Out in the yard a libidinous peacock wails, so I draw my chair closer as the softspoken gentleman recalls one of his favorites: how it all began with his headmaster's warning when he left school in Brixton, in London, in 1938:

> "Lovelock, you are a fool to take up science. There is no place there except for those of genius or with private means." He knew well that I had neither of these, nor any prospect of acquiring them. . . . His words were well meant and at the time very true, for in the post-Depression years just before the Second World War, newly graduated chemists were employed for a year or more in some notorious industries at no salary on the excuse that they were acquiring industrial experience. But I was not only obstinate in my determination to do science of any sort. I was also incredibly lucky. My first employer, Humphrey Desmond Murray, was a kindly and tolerant man, and his business as a consultant chemist covered topics from the advanced organic chemistry of the synthesis of new developing agents in colour photography to the invention of invisible but detectable powders with which to mark bank notes for Scotland Yard. He provided what in those days was a princely wage, for an untrained laboratory assistant—three pounds per week. He also paid my fees to attend that splendid institution, Birkbeck College London, at which I was to attain a degree by evening class study."[1]

Although the young man went on to earn his master's and doctoral degrees, Lovelock remembers the early days of his apprenticeship to Murray as the best training he had.

16

My ultimate objective was to work like the artist or novelist. Most people regard science as different from painting or writing novels, but it's very much the same thing. Like anyone else who desires a bit of creative freedom, I wanted to be able to do scientific work without any constraints from employers or customers. Gradually I found that the work done to answer such questions as "I wonder if" almost always led to bread, as an invention or through publication, in only two or three years' time. No worse than the time span a novelist must contend with between the first idea and the first receipt of royalties from a book he has published.

While there are a few independent scientific consultants maintaining lucrative practices in the United States and abroad, as well as a handful of those fortunate enough to be able to indulge their curiosities unsupported, Lovelock is that rare creative, a truly independent practitioner who does science as a family business. Revenues from his books and, more important, his inventions, have been vital to the support of his wife Helen and their four children as well as to the rest of his creative research, paying most of the bills for the past twenty-five years. There has never been much to spare, but Lovelock feels that

the more money you've got, the less progress you make, because you tend to goof off. All Einstein had at the start was a pencil and paper and a small salary. When he came to Princeton, they forced him to take a higher salary than he wanted, so he didn't bother cashing all his checks. It's like artists starving in their garrets. There's a lot in that. Look at Darwin. He just bummed a ride on a ship.

Despite his self-reliant nature and work style, Lovelock's ability to find and collaborate with good people has sustained him as an independent for most of his professional career. Lovelock has the genteel habit of omitting the names of those whom he criticizes, however mildly, and of pronouncing very slowly and distinctly the names—like his first mentor, Humphrey Desmond Murray—whom he admires. The scores of university and corporate researchers with whom he has worked over the years, as well as the companies, such as Hewlett-Packard and Shell, that have retained him virtually without stipulation, have been willing to take the trouble of changing their routines and incurring the bureaucratic penalties because he is pleasant to work with and because when Lovelock succeeds, the collaboration will prove to have been well worth their while.

Still, the rogue and peasant researcher cannot resist the odd opportunity to pour some gall in the ears of the scientific establishment. In the preface to *The Ages of Gaia* Lovelock attacks the academic tenure system as perverse insurance against invention and initiative.

> In fact, nearly all scientists are employed by some large organization, such as a governmental department, a university or a multinational company. Only rarely are they free to express their science as a personal view. They may think that they are free, but in reality they are, nearly all of them, employees; they have traded freedom of thought for good working conditions, a steady income, tenure and a pension. They are also constrained by an army of bureaucratic forces, from funding agencies to the health and safety organizations. . . . Lacking freedom they are in danger of succumbing to a finicky gentility or of becoming, like medieval theologians, the creatures of dogma. . . . Fellow scientists join me, you have nothing to lose but your grants.[2]

Since his days as a stubborn schoolboy, Lovelock has enjoyed being a contrarian and an outsider. One of his favorite forms of subversion has been to agitate, at times abrasively, for a broader free-lance science subculture of kindred rebellious spirits. Yet hackles sprout like hives when Lovelock knocks academe, since many of those who choose university life consider it the moral alternative, where income and profit potential are foregone in favor of purity and scholarship. And critics are quick to point out that anyone who takes money from multinational corporations and governmental agencies like NASA can hardly proclaim himself free. There is an unarguable touch of hubris in Lovelock's give-up-your-grants emancipation proclamation, since most scientists would go bankrupt following that advice, and he knows it. But the Englishman also knows that almost none of his colleagues are going to make the leap he calls for, and that the few who have the gumption to try would probably be the best candidates. The way he sees it, in the world of science, academe is the establishment that needs some shaking up.

THE MOTHER OF HIS INVENTION

How does one man come to master the study of so many different branches of science—no field seems to have completely escaped his notice—when even the most brilliant of his peers, including the majority of Nobel laureates, with all their luxury of time and tenure, seem to restrict their inquiries to a few special disciplines? Upon first meeting Lovelock, my skeptical nose sniffed for fraud or dilettantism. Instead it should have picked up the scent that the Nobel Prize winners bear—the whiff of TNT.

Nostalgia for wartime always seems a bit traitorous, no matter how romantic or heroic the tale. Still, if it hadn't been for the push given to research during World War II—the crisis pressure to know how to do everything and get it done at once—the fledgling British scientist never would have matured so fast and so far. After completing his studies at Birkbeck College, in

19

1941 Lovelock landed a job at the prestigious National Institute for Medical Research (NIMR) in London. Ordinarily the NIMR would have been a place for relaxed, scholarly pursuits, but in wartime all of Britain's scientific institutions had been conscripted in the battle of wits and weapons against the Axis. Yet, quite in contrast to the stereotypical steel-gray image of stealthy spies and cryptic codes, the young scientist found an open and stimulating atmosphere.

> In those days concern about the security of scientific information was almost nonexistent and problems were openly discussed. I soon found myself participating in a bewildering range of subjects, such as the measurement of blood pressures under water, the spread of upper respiratory infections among a United States bomber crew at a midlands airbase and the measurement of infrared radiation from flash and flame.[3]

Lovelock believes that the life-and-death demands to produce immediate, practical results were what led him ultimately to work not only as a research scientist but as an inventor.

> My senior colleagues always said, "Wait until the war is over and you can see what real science is like." But when it did end, and the leisurely pace of normal research was reestablished, I found it to be dull and unprincipled in its pursuit of personal recognition.[4]

That complaint, however, seemed to apply less at the NIMR than generally, especially after its new director, Sir Charles Harington, took over after the war. So Lovelock stayed on in what proved to be a flourishing environment for the next fifteen years, from 1946 to 1961, working on everything from acoustics to zoology.

During that time, the Englishman and his family managed

to spend two years in the United States, under arrangement between the NIMR and Harvard and Yale medical schools. Lovelock recalls his postdoctoral research at Yale rather fondly, but the year as a Rockefeller research fellow at Harvard was hellish. In those pre-Sputnik days, American scientific research was terribly underfunded, both in research budgets and stipends paid. Having an unusual blood type, Lovelock sold a pint of it every few weeks to help support his family of five in an expensive city on only three thousand dollars a year. To this day the British scientist gets a special zing out of spearing the Cambridge, Massachusetts, "bastion of high-level conventional thinking" (which just happens to be the home of some of the Gaia theory's fiercest critics), as though each point won were payment for a drop of his rare blood.

Through it all, however, the young man seems to have had more than his share of fun in his work and excursions for the NIMR. At one point Lovelock was rather taken with the then-fledging medical science of cryogenics and, as he admits while trying to fight off a devilish grin, froze up quite a few little animals. "Hard as rocks they were. One could bang them about—quite stiff," says Lovelock. "Then we would warm them up properly and off they'd go. In most cases."

THE GREAT RADIOACTIVE NOSE

The most consistent theme of Lovelock's work with the NIMR, though, was the invention of a number of different kinds of detectors that could be used in conjunction with the gas chromatograph, which had been developed by Archer Martin, a senior colleague. Chromatography, essentially chemistry's reproduction of the olfactory senses, is the process of percolating complex gas mixtures through selectively absorbent substances, yielding layers, usually of different colors, that identify the components of the gas mixture and their relative concentrations. Master perfumers approximate this process with their finely

21

attuned noses, sniffing out the component fragrances of complex blends. And highly trained chefs steal one another's recipes with palates that discern the what and how much of key ingredients. Chemists substitute chromatographs for these bodily senses, gaining safety and computer accuracy at the expense of the more visceral pleasures.

It was during this postwar period at NIMR that Lovelock developed the electron capture detector (ECD), his greatest invention. Even were Gaia to fall to the critics, the Englishman has earned his spot in the history of twentieth-century science with the creation of this uncanny analyzer, essentially the world's first radioactive nose. Lovelock replaced the layers of selectively absorbent material normally employed in chromatography with a minute radioactive ionization chamber that has the capacity to respond to a variety of ionized gases. First developed in 1957, the palm-size device is still the most useful instrument around for sniffing out minute chemical traces in the air, water, and soil. Rather than testing for amounts in the parts-per-million range, which is as fine as the conventional gas chromatograph gets, the ECD can accurately identify and measure ionized gases present in concentrations as low as parts per trillion.

Some of the most lethal contaminants that pollute the global environment are present at the almost infinitesimal, parts-per-trillion levels that only the ECD can detect. And whenever the instrument has been used to detect these toxins, storms of controversy seem to envelop the inventor. By demonstrating in the late 1950s that pesticide residues were present in all species on Earth, from penguins in Antarctica to the mothers' milk in the United States, the ECD provided the hard data for Rachel Carson's 1962 landmark book on environmental hazards, *Silent Spring,* and helped launch the international campaign to ban the pesticide DDT. Lovelock's little analyzer has since gone on to reveal minute but hazardous quantities of other toxic chemicals, such as polychlorbiphenyls (PCB's) polluting the wilderness and peroxacetyl nitrate (PAN) adding to the poison of Los Angeles smog.

In the early 1970s Lovelock sailed from Britain to Antarctica and back, using the ECD to analyze the air and demonstrate that CFC's were accumulating worldwide. As explored in chapter 8, his research became the hard data basis for the international movement to ban fluorocarbon aerosols because of their potential harm to the stratospheric ozone layer—a controversy that has since resurfaced with the discovery of a hole in the ozone layer above the South Pole.

And Lovelock's ECD is still the basis, some thirty years after its invention, of the explosives sniffers currently found in airports throughout the world.

Lovelock considers himself an inventor, first and foremost, whose business is the creation of useful objects and ideas. "The Gaia Hypothesis is an invention, actually," he argues, explaining that a theory is not so much an idea per se as a generator of ideas, something that performs a useful function repeatedly, like a good tool.

And the electron capture detector has been remarkably helpful to me in my work on Gaia, and not only for the data it has yielded. It's a great little thing to trade, and that's important when you're trying to pry information out of specialists. Some of the academics are so committed to protecting their own turf. But who can turn down a chance to analyze the air?

THE MID-LIFE AMERICAN FLING

After fifteen years at the NIMR, Lovelock had achieved the kind of job security that he now likes to criticize. So in 1961 the British scientist practiced what he would go on to preach and packed up the family, which at the time included his wife and four children, and moved to Houston, where he had secured a professorship at Baylor University Medical School. Lovelock also had received an invitation from Dr. Abe Silverstein, the director of NASA, to be an experimentalist on the first lunar survey mission planned by the United States, so he spent most of the next two years shuttling between Texas and the world-famous Jet Propulsion Laboratory in Pasadena, California, where he shared an office with Carl Sagan. Lovelock recalls those years with fond regard for Baylor, the people of Houston, and, especially, the heaven-conquering ferment of JPL. It was there where he first conceived of Gaia, the living Earth.

The Englishman refers frequently to the need for a good, solid excuse to leave home; apparently he has taken some brain-drain, sell-out criticisms of patriotic ingratitude over his move to the United States. The charge nettles him to this day in a way not easily understood by most Americans—for U.S. residents there has been no comparable competing nation to "sell out" to. Referring to the insulting privation that he and his family had suffered several years earlier at Harvard, Lovelock says, "It is often forgotten that in the 1950s the standard of living and working of many scientists in the United Kingdom was much better than in the U.S."[5] He emphasizes that his consultantship at the JPL paid much more heavily in prestige than in income.

Some immigrants reserve their hearts, souls, and savings for the old country. Others renounce and denounce their past with sycophantic gusto. Lovelock's broad network of friends and colleagues in England and the United States suggests that he managed to hold onto his respect and affection for both old country and new. Ultimately Lovelock's decision to go to Houston in 1961 may have been less personal than political. Because America emerged from the two world wars as the most powerful and productive nation on Earth, the British scientist, from a country whose waning power was unable to support the long-term investment needed for basic scientific research, was compelled to relocate, even if at no higher a wage, or else fall behind.

Although Lovelock had planned to work for five years in

the States and then return to the UK with enough capital to start up an independent practice, he and his family found themselves back in England after only half that time, no wealthier than when they had left. Nonetheless, Lovelock had succeeded in picking up consultantships from Shell Research and Pye Unicam, and in 1964 the family settled in the remote village of Bowerchalke, in Wiltshire in south central England. A thatch-roofed cottage research laboratory was set up right next to the house.

NASA must have liked Lovelock's work as well, for in a rare gesture from the institution that had come to expect tribute as its due, they invited him to finish out his consultantship even though he had moved six thousand miles away from the JPL. This astonished the scientist, for only months earlier NASA had, in essence, fired him over his heretical conclusion that the *Viking* satellite probes—two unmanned spacecraft designed to land on Mars, to analyze the soil and mineral samples for traces of life and to broadcast television pictures from the planet surface—were a mammoth waste of time and money!

Lovelock's reasoning went as follows: If life were present on Mars, it would be detectable from its atmosphere. After a decade of examining the Earth's atmosphere with his electron capture detector, Lovelock and his JPL colleague Dian Hitchcock essentially decided to replicate that type of analysis at a distance of fifty million miles. Using a telescope tuned to the infrared and equipped with a spectroscope—an optical instrument that analyzes the chemical composition of distant objects by measuring the wavelengths and intensity of the light they emit—astronomers Pierre and Janine Connes had studied Mars from the Pic de Midi Observatory in France. They found that the Martian atmosphere was virtually in a state of equilibrium and was made up predominantly of carbon dioxide. Compared to the Earth's atmosphere, lively and complex as the carnival at Rio, Mars was as dead as the trash in the streets on Ash Wednesday morning. There was no trace of life.

These findings of Lovelock and Hitchcock were hardly

25

welcome news to NASA, which had built much of its budgetary case for the *Viking* probes on the grounds that there might be life on Mars. Carl Sagan and all the others who had fought so hard to fund the planetary exploration program were not about to give it all back just because of one salient insight. So NASA sent Lovelock packing back to his remote English hamlet, although they continued the incorrigible's consultantship for an extra six months or so. Much cheaper, the bureaucrats figured, than listening to all of his reasons for a lifeless Mars.

THE VIEW FROM MARS

Albert Einstein once asked himself what he would see if he rode around on an electron traveling at the speed of light, according to Jacob Bronowski's insightful recreation. When the great physicist closed his eyes, he managed to unravel the fundamental relationship between energy and matter, in the earth-shattering discovery now known as $E = mc^2$. Lovelock, in turn, speaks of a question he once posed to himself, an easy one next to Einstein's: If you were sitting on Mars, how could you tell that there was life on Earth? What would give it away?

"Utterly bizarre, that Earth atmosphere, unlike any other in the solar system," Lovelock thought from his imaginary Martian observatory. At first he was irritated with the uniquely difficult problems of how to penetrate his home planet's hyperactive gaseous layer to see through to the life inside. In polite contrast, the Martian atmosphere had settled down into a textbook chemical equilibrium, where everything that can react does react to form stable compounds, such as carbon dioxide, that stay at a comfortable, low energy state. Even Venus, suffering from her permanent hot flush, is at equilibrium and, like Mars, has an atmosphere of at least 95 percent CO_2. Yet somehow the gas that dominates the atmospheres of the two neighboring planets constitutes only 0.034 percent of our own.

Chemical equilibrium means that if you took some air from

either of those planets, heated it in the presence of rocks and soil from the surface, and then allowed it all to cool, there would be little or no change. All of the possible chemical reactions already have happened; all of the energy is spent, like the carbon dioxide that you exhale once your body has used up a breath of air. In vivid contrast, the same experiment on the Earth's atmosphere would yield a major chemical change, and the final product would be very much like the waste gases that cloak the flanking planets.

Lovelock explains that as far as we know, there are three types of gases that can be present in a planet's atmosphere: oxidizing gases, such as oxygen and carbon dioxide, which acquire electrons in a chemical reaction; neutral gases, such as nitrogen and carbon monoxide, which generally do not react; and reducing gases, such as hydrogen, methane, and ammonia, which give away their electrons. Understandably, oxidizing and reducing gases tend to react with one another, often with great volatility. Each of the flanking planets, one hot beyond lava and the other cold as dry ice, has an atmosphere containing only oxidizing and neutral gases. Jupiter and Saturn contain only reducing gases in their air. So there is no potential for the vibrant gaseous interplay that life demands.

> The Earth, our living Earth, is quite anomalous; its atmosphere has the reducing gases and oxidizing gases all coexisting—and this is a most unstable situation. It is almost as if we were breathing the sort of air which is the premixed gas that goes into a furnace or into an internal combustion engine. Ours is a really strange planet.[6]

In their minds, Lovelock and Hitchcock reversed the experiment conducted by their French colleagues at the Pic de Midi Observatory. Mounting a spectroscope on their imaginary Martian telescope to analyze the light radiating from Earth, they reasoned that one could take advantage of the fact that each element of nature emits light in a distinctive wavelength. Through their telescopic observations of Earth, then, they would see an atmosphere that defies all natural expectations: gases coexist when they should combine, and elements and compounds appear in gaseous form when they should remain solid and settled on the surface.

Lovelock was particularly struck by the oxygen—which because of its reactive power he calls the dominant gas of the Earth, even though it is not the most abundant. Why should there be so much free oxygen floating around—approximately 21 percent of the air—when this volatile gas normally reacts wherever and whenever and with whatever it can, especially with the violently reducing gas of methane? Or with carbon, to form the ubiquitous CO_2? Basic chemistry also predicts that the hot-blooded oxygen would react with the nitrogen—about 78 percent of the Earth's atmosphere, but only a few percent on Mars and Venus—and fall to the ground in the form of stable nitrate compounds. "It must take a lot of work to keep up such a wild disequilibrium," the Martian Englishman mused.

The extraterrestrial voyeur also had to admit that the Earth was gorgeous, with a style all her own. Lovelock writes:

> When first seen from outside and compared as a whole planet with its lifeless partners, Mars and Venus, it was impossible to ignore the sense that the Earth was a strange and beautiful anomaly. These dead planets are visually as well as chemically a neutral background against which the living planet Earth shines like a dappled sapphire.[7]

Many, many writers have rhapsodized on the orbiting Earth's lively beauty. Yet Lovelock understood what he saw only when he finally stopped looking, quit relying exclusively on the visual sense, and took a deep *Gedanken* whiff of the Earth's fragrant atmosphere. The man who had revolutionized gas chromatography with the electron capture detector, his great radioactive "nose," had imaginatively applied the very same principles of olfactory analysis to space science, and in so doing he had sniffed out the presence of the living Earth.

Lovelock's method has always been to analyze the air. This time he did it in his thought experiments, by analyzing the light emitted from the Earth's atmosphere with his imaginary Martian spectroscope. Interpreting the readings from a spectroscope requires a measure of experience and a dash of intuition, a process not unlike the way many of us go about buying cheese. If you want to know how a cheese tastes before you purchase it, the best way (short of trying a sample) is to smell it. If the cheese is behind a glass counter, the next best thing is to look at it and somehow judge by color, mold, and apparent moisture. If it is blue-green and crusty you can imagine that it will taste different than if it is white and fresh. This is roughly the relationship of spectroscopy to gas chromatography. When material experiments are impossible to perform, optical inspection of light in both the visual and nonvisual ranges is the next best thing. Sometimes the details are just too hazy and you cannot really guess much about the cheese. But one look at the fecund atmosphere of our Earth and Lovelock knew that Gaia was full and ripe. Unlike any other planet in the solar system, this one was bursting with life.

SEEING GAIA FOR THE TREES

When first formulating his idea, Lovelock considered calling it the Biocybernetic Universal System Tendency/ Homeostasis, or some other equally cumbersome scientific appellation. Would his theory ever have gathered the necessary critical mass of attention if it had been so drably named? Fortunately, William Golding, the British Nobel laureate best known for his novel Lord of the Flies, a friend and fellow villager in Bowerchalke, pointed out that anything living deserves a name and proposed that Lovelock name his theory after the noble Gaia,

29

Greek goddess of the Earth. Lovelock claims to have wrestled between poetry and professional propriety, but ultimately his frustration with the madness of the planet's chaotic system transformed to awe over the method behind it all. The Earth's atmosphere was not some veil that inconveniently cloaked Gaia's charms from his gaze, it was a natural extension of the life below, like a cat's fur or a snail's shell, as Lovelock used to say. Or even the skin of a goddess.

"I started to think and then to write about it [Gaia] in my early fifties. I was just old enough to be radical without the taint of senile delinquency," Lovelock recounts in *The Ages of Gaia*.[8] In fact, the early days of Gaia must have been more impressionistic than rigorous, since Lovelock left the Gaia theory vulnerable to attack when he carried the goddess metaphor too far. The living planet, he proposed, not only *maintained* the unstable combination of gases on which it depended for its very existence, but Gaia somehow *had determined to do so*. The goddess of the Earth, in Lovelock's earliest formulations, had a mind and a will of her own and could plan ahead, intentionally controlling her own environment.

It was this great error of intentionality that rendered Gaia ineligible for serious scientific consideration and made it a metaphor or poetic construction at best. Lovelock has gradually refined his theory to emphasize the automatic aspects of homeostasis, or what he calls the wisdom of the body. Fundamentally the Gaia Hypothesis finds the Earth to be more like a life form than an inanimate sphere, adjusting to internal and external changes much as an organism might react to threats and opportunities in the environment. A human being might sweat in response to rising temperatures; a flower might grow in the direction of sunlight—these are unconscious responses intended to maintain a healthy state.

Compared to our flanking planets, the Earth certainly does seem extraordinary, in some ways perhaps even lifelike, as Lovelock claims. But how, his scientific colleagues have demanded to know, did this gargantuan living system emerge and how does it work? It is one thing to observe that the Earth's atmosphere is actively influenced, perhaps controlled, by the living organisms that populate it. It is quite another to conclude that this behemoth hunk of rock, salt water, and gas has thereby been transformed, in the words of writer Geoffrey Cowley, *Newsweek,* from "an inert chemical ball into an immense, self-sustaining organism."[9] This leap of intuition, perhaps of faith, has been the source of most of the controversy as well as most of the color of the Gaia movement.

Lovelock likes to compare the Earth to a tree in order to clear this conceptual hurdle. This engaging but somewhat hyperbolic metaphor was first advanced by the physicist Jerome Rothstein, who spoke at the first large-scale Gaia conference, held in August 1985 at Amherst College by the Audubon Expedition Institute. Rothstein pointed out that the redwood tree, universally considered alive, is in fact about 97-percent dead. The only living parts of the tree are the needles and the thin layer of cells beneath the bark, not unlike the thin layer of life covering the surface of the Earth. The bark serves as a protective shell and transfer medium, much like the Earth's atmosphere and like the skin that covers our bodies. The rest of the redwood tree is lignin and cellulose, every bit as biologically inert as toenails, produced by the ancestors living beneath the bark, years or even centuries before.

"How like the Earth," Lovelock writes, "and more so when we realize that many of the atoms of the rocks far down into the magma were once part of the ancestral life from which we all have come."[10] Lovelock boldly asserts that the rocks, soil, and atmosphere of the Earth are either produced or directly modified by the planet's living organisms, observing that virtually all mineral samples that man has studied, even those dating back two billion years or more, bear life's unmistakable mark. The well-known process of carbon-14 dating, the most reliable method for determining the age of geological specimens, relies on the fact that there is always a certain amount of the carbon-

31

14 isotope, which is characteristic only of living matter, in even the most ancient samples.

Still, here Lovelock stretches the point almost beyond recognition. A redwood tree's ratio of living matter to inert matter is something on the order of one in thirty-three, perhaps as low as one in one-hundred in the oldest trees. By contrast, the Earth's life-to-mass ratio is more on the order of one in thirty-three billion. The planet's total mass is roughly 60 sextillion (6 followed by 23 zeroes) metric tons, while the total dry weight of the biomass, the sum total of all living things on Earth, is roughly 1.8 trillion metric tons (1.8 followed by twelve zeroes). Even assuming that the biomass is fully 90 percent water, which brings the total of living matter up to 18 trillion metric tons, there is a huge imbalance. The ratio of living organisms to total inert Earth mass is at least a billion times lower than it is for trees.

On the land surrounding his home and laboratory at St. Giles-on-the-Heath, Lovelock and his wife have planted some twenty thousand trees, taking advantage of an admirable British law that enables the government to subsidize up to 80 percent of the planting costs, under the condition that neither the landowners nor their heirs chop the trees down. "It's the closest you can get to taking it with you," chuckles Lovelock on a stroll through his proud new woods. Especially when contrasted to those stony, lifeless neighboring planets, this Englishman's forest only seems to strengthen the vibrant image of our blue-green globe and intuitively affirm his fantastic notion of a living planet.

As Gaia theory has moved from infatuation to analysis, certain fundamental tenets have gained acceptance in the scientific community. Probably the most important contribution from Gaia has been the notion that the evolution of living organisms and their environment is an inextricably coupled process, as opposed to the traditional assumption that organisms simply adapt to their surroundings without any significant impact or input of their own.

Deep in the Cornwall countryside, Lovelock and Gaia

themselves have coevolved. Far away from the scalding climate of academe and its acid rain of peer review, the living Earth theory has grown as a succession of promising observations, calculations, and evolutionary vignettes. That is how Gaia might have remained, a dazzling collection of intriguing ideas rather than a coherent and rigorous theory, had not Lynn Margulis, academician extraordinaire, come along and brought the sky-high goddess back down to Earth.

II

LYNN MARGULIS AND HER MICROCOSM

QUEEN OF THE MICROBE FESTIVAL

Dozens of pizza-colored microbes, with what looked like morsels of every conceivable topping on each, waltzed triple-time around the lecture hall screen. Suddenly one fat pie reproduced, both halves becoming whole and then whirling like pinwheels, as though tossed into the air by an invisible chef. Soon an army of corkscrews and question marks danced its way in, like an invading samba band. There seemed more harmony than clash to the chaos—like the collisionless crush of commuters at rush hour in Grand Central Station or the heavy traffic swirl around the Arc de Triomphe. Not exactly cooperation, but a reflexive respect for boundaries and space.

Much as Einstein quizzed himself on the subatomic perspective, Margulis wonders about the microbial point of view. She believes that microorganisms and their constituent parts are as fundamental to life as atoms and subatomic particles are to matter and energy. In Margulis's microbial cosmology, bacteria—single-celled organisms that have no nucleus—are the building blocks of life. Also known as *prokaryotes* (literally, "before nucleus"), bacteria were the earliest life forms, from which all other earthly organisms have evolved and through which, in Margulis's vision, biology can best be understood. Her thesis is that microbial eukaryotes—nucleated organisms such as amoebae, paramecia, algae, molds, and fungi—have evolved over the aeons from their bacterial ancestors, and that confederations of both classes of microorganisms gradually coevolved into plants and animals. For Margulis the difference between single-celled and multicellular creatures is analogous to the physicist's distinction between atoms and molecules—they are not fundamentally different, just more complex.

But rather than being prized as the building blocks of life, microbes, particularly bacteria, usually are feared or disdained as agents of disease, such as the infectious villains in Paul de Kruif's legendary book *Microbe Hunters.* Margulis insists that this research concentration on pathogens has obscured the many crucial roles the microbial world plays in global ecology as well as in the health of the human beings, animals, and plants that sustain the biosphere. To help set the record straight, Margulis circulates around the globe, lecturing in any of five or six languages at universities and research centers on the vitality and importance of the microcosm.

She traveled to Perpignan, a sleepy pocket of French Catalonia, squat between the salty Mediterranean and the snow-capped Pyrenees, for a day of ceremonies honoring hometown son Edouard Chatton (1883–1947), a great microbiological pioneer. "Chatton was one of the very first to realize that microorganisms aren't just germs and enemies!" Margulis exclaims, as though that were all the character reference anyone would ever need. Despite her sometimes brusque, scientific manner, Lynn Margulis is foremost a creature of the heart, genuinely astonished that anyone with mind or soul could look into the marvelous civility of the ultramicroscopic world and not be moved. The microorganisms displayed in her slides looked like the colorful, finely wrought artifacts of an advanced society.

And the moving pictures of spirochetes, flagellates, and ciliates looked quite like what Margulis maintains they are: home movies from a very different kind of civilization.

Judging from the "Ooh la la's" and "Ah joli's" that filled the auditorium, Margulis's film show of the ultramicroscopic world succeeded in enchanting an audience of bacteriologists and pathologists that normally despised the little buggers as germs. Declares Margulis, in her Spanish-accented franglais:

> There are over two hundred thousand species of microorganisms, perhaps a trillion trillion individuals overall, far outweighing, for example, the mammal population, including humans. The vast majority of these microbes do not cause any type of disease. Neither are they all decomposers. Every sort of nutritional mode exists among microbes, from parasitism to photosynthesis, and even forms of cannibalism, which is found about as frequently in microbial communities as in human society. Without the few pounds of anerobic bacteria in each of our guts, no one would ever digest food, and without the nitrogen-fixing bacteria in the soil, no food would ever grow in the first place. To think of all microbes as alike, or worse, as all disease germs, is to misunderstand them terribly.

THE GOSPEL OF SYMBIOSIS

The Chatton celebration's emphasis on the nonpathological aspects of the microbes provided Margulis an excellent opportunity to spread her scientific gospel of symbiosis.

> Symbiosis—the mutually advantageous association of two or more organisms of different species—is a worldwide pattern of microbial behavior. At the level of the microcosm, symbiotic cooperation is at least as important as "survival of the fittest" competition; in

order to compete—in order to get in the game in the first place—you have to cooperate. We now believe that the doctrinaire Darwinian view of "Nature red in tooth and claw" is naive and incomplete. Symbiosis means survival.

On the way to Perpignan, Margulis had stopped in northeastern Spain to visit Lake Cisó, one of her favorite sites for research into the mechanisms of microbial symbiosis. Possibly the oddest body of water in the world, the tiny upland lake is a giant bowl of bacteria, mostly sulfur-eaters that thrive on a steady underground supply of the yellow mineral. So dominant are these single-celled nonnucleated creatures that the lake has no fish; the most advanced critters are the relatively few flagellate and ciliate microbes that eat bacteria, and the occasional algae that blow in from time to time. Singular in content, Lake Cisó is also singular in style: the surface changes color dramatically, depending on seasonal shifts of bacterial populations, from clear to bright red to chocolate brown.

Margulis and many others who have studied what has to be one of the world's most thoroughly examined lakes concur that Cisó is very much like one big bacterial family. "Lake Cisó's microbial community can be thought of as analogous to a multicellular organism whose dimensions are determined by those of the lake basin," write Margulis and her colleagues in their essay "Microbial Communities."[1] Naturalists have long expressed the sentiment that lakes are like creatures in that they have life cycles; it is common usage, for example, to say that acid rain has killed a lake. Indeed, G. E. Hutchinson's well-known study of lakes, "Treatise on Limnology," provides ample scholarly backup for this holistic view. For microbiologists Lake Cisó serves as a concentrated microcosm that magnifies many of the organismic processes by which normal lakes operate.

Inside these limits, cells interact both cooperatively and antagonistically. They lower local hydrogen sulfide concentration for one another; they provide necessary organic compounds to one another; they shade one another, compete for resources, and excrete toxic wastes.[2]

Like a healthy body, or a city with a government that works.

Symbiotic associations frequently start out as casual, not required by any partner. Depending on environmental factors, eventually these partnerships progress to obligate relationships, which are required by all involved. "Many microbes have evolved to the point where they cannot survive alone, so they simply have to share. For example, those that can eat but not breathe have teamed up with others whose situation is the reverse," Margulis explains. "In other words," she adds with an inviting smile, "cooperation becomes habit-forming."

Unfortunately, some disease germs have proved frighteningly adept at the cooperative habit. Ever wonder how bacteria so quickly become immune to antibiotics? The traditional Darwinian succession—by which the weak die out and those with the appropriate mutations survive and reproduce—would have taken thousands or even millions of years to reach the current level of immunity, according to Margulis's estimate. But bacteria have developed the enzymes to digest penicillin and a host of other antibiotics in just a few decades. Modern microbiologists know that the reason single-celled organisms develop resistance so quickly is that they share genetic information in what essentially are tiny gift packages, called replicons. In a process made possible by the fact that these prokaryotic creatures have no nucleus, with their genetic material, therefore, floating freely throughout the cell, those bacteria already immune donate the appropriate genetic instructions on how to digest or repel the poison to other, vulnerable members of their species. Those that successfully adapt are likely to survive and pass the vital information on to successive generations. Gradually this immunization process spreads to other bacterial species and locales. For example, the enzyme that digests penicillin probably started out with bacteria in the soil and eventually reached the hospitals, where lots of bacteria are now completely resistant to the wonder drug.

Western science has long denied the inheritance of acquired characteristics, in what is known as the Lamarckian heresy. Cut the tail off mama and papa rat, baby rat will still have a tail—that's certainly true. But we now know that there *is* inheritance of acquired genetic material. Through viruses, plasmids, and the replicons that foster resistance to drugs, as well as a variety of other means, symbiosis, cooperation, and sharing must be understood as sources of innovation in evolution. From the level of microorganisms on up to the so-called higher organisms, including multicellular plants, animals, and even human beings, sharing is as essential to survival as struggle.

After the lecture Margulis swirled through the hall, opening windows and introducing everyone she knew or had just met and liked to at least half a dozen new people. In between congratulations, introductions, and quick interviews, she arranged lodging, transportation, and a few free meals, provided paper and pens for those who simply had to exchange addresses, fretted and made mental notes about the meeting she would be attending in Paris the next day, and generally had a good time. Margulis seemed at a loss only once, when this author asked her to leave me alone for a moment, as I was in the middle of a paragraph. After a moment's confusion she was genuinely delighted that things were going well, and she went off in search of some other situation to organize, amend, or improve. That's how Lynn Margulis's microcosm evolves.

THE TISSUES OF GAIA

James Lovelock's version of Gaia regards the Earth in relation to its flanking planets and examines the immense global systems of the atmosphere, the continents, and the oceans—the appropriate scale for a theory of the living planet. But how does coauthor Margulis start out talking about infinitesimal creatures and end up with a theory of the planet as a whole?

As a microbiologist Margulis believes deeply that she is studying the basis of all earthly life, the power and essence of Gaia. Ever since the billion years of molten hell following our planet's birth explosion finally cooled and the first single-celled bits of cytoplasm shimmered quietly in primordial coastal seas, the common need to regulate frequently hostile surroundings has engendered symbiotic cooperation among all life forms. Thus Margulis's fascination with the mechanisms of symbiosis meshes inextricably with the Gaia theory's theme of life's control over the environment. She believes that plants, animals, and microorganisms not only have adapted themselves to their local habitats but also have worked individually and collectively to make their home areas more livable, while conventional evolutionary theory simply regards organisms as exploiting their environment in the pursuit of self-interest, discounting the impact they have on their surroundings as incidental. For the two billion years (over half of biological history) that microorganisms and their communities were the only forms of life on the planet, on through the past billion and a half years of plants, animals, and the microcosm that still flourishes today, and for as long as terrestrial life survives, the Gaia theory sees the coevolution of life and environment as an inextricably coupled process.

Just as any group of pioneers would struggle, at times separately and at other times together, to tame a wild new land, each doing the best for himself and all pitching in when mutual interest called for damming a stream or building a windbreak, Margulis maintains that this is the most natural way for microbial societies to have coevolved with their surroundings. The field biologist's favorite example of this sort of Gaian environmental engineering is found at Laguna Figueroa, a site along the western coast of Baja California Norte, Mexico.

At Laguna Figueroa, three huge stratified microbial com-

munities thrive in the hypersaline tidal channels, where seawater
bubbles up beneath the sand dunes. These microbial mats,
averaging several acres each, operate by the same basic symbiotic
principles that obtain in Lake Cisó, but the processes of collaboration are far more complex. Each layer of bacteria in the mat
is like a layer of human skin, and just about as thick. On the
surface is a nonliving epidermal layer of salty evaporite sediment
that laminates the mat for protection. Just below are blue-green
and grass-green cyanobacteria, powerful aerobic photosynthesizers. Below them live purple anerobic bacteria, protected from
the air by the cyanobacteria yet close enough to the surface to
carry on their own form of photosynthesis. At the bottom is a
black layer of sulfur-reducing bacteria, like the ones thriving in
Lake Cisó, that convert seawater to hydrogen sulfide, the gas
that makes rotten eggs smell so bad. For the microbial community, though, the stinking gas is the breath of life, since both
upper layers use it for their photosynthesis. In all, up to two
hundred bacterial species, dominated by long, filamentous cyanobacteria, form quite a harmonious little community, each
group relying on the others to provide vital functions. These
multicellular layers are as complex and differentiated as animal
tissue, according to Margulis, who likes to call microbial mats
"the tissues of Gaia."

Fierce storms at the end of the 1970s overwhelmed the
microbial mats of Laguna Figueroa, but within five years the
communities were well on their way to reconstruction through
classical ecological succession—the sort of process by which a
forest, for example, renews itself after a devastating fire, but in
the mats' case, much quicker. By monitoring the reconstruction
of these mats, Margulis and her team of researchers were able to
learn firsthand how the microbial communities of Laguna Figueroa control their immediate environment. In addition to their
intricate joint ventures in eating and breathing, the microscopic
inhabitants modified their environment in key ways. First, by
desalinating the tide pools and varnishing the salt that they
precipitate so that it cannot redissolve, the microbes turn ocean

41

water into the fresh water they need to survive. Also, the mats secrete large quantities of a lipid substance that recently has been identified by satellite photographs to reduce the impact of the waves that crash on the ocean side of the lagoon. (It would be interesting to know if the production of this substance increased once the mats were fully reformed after the storms that had swamped them.) Not through any plan or conspiracy, as Margulis always takes care to remind us, but simply through automatic biological processes, the microbial community tries to keep its environment livable.

Eventually, of course, any collaboration must come to an end, and so it is with these mats. Much like human civilizations, new ones are built right on top of the old, abandoned sites. Stromatolites, microbial mats hardened by the precipitation of calcium carbonate, the stuff of seashells, are composed of numerous discrete, rocky layers, each one a former microbial community like the one at Laguna Figueroa. Just as archaeologists dig through ruins to study ancient human civilizations, Margulis digs through these domed columns of fossilized rock. She believes that stromatolites, some of which grew as high as thirty feet, covered much of the face of the Earth during the Proterozoic era (1.5 to 2 billion years ago) and were to the landscape "what coral reefs are to the present ocean: rich and beautiful collectives of intermingled, interdependent organisms."[3]

EVOLVING TOWARD ENDOSYMBIOSIS

One of the most fascinating varieties of microbial community is the one that may be currently eating your home. There are more than 500 species of termites today, 350 or so of the wood-eating variety, so prevalent overall that there are about three-quarters of a ton of these insects per human being. All termites harbor shockingly complex microbial communities in their hypertrophied intestines, called hindguts. Like little Lake

Cisó but even more convoluted, each hindgut contains up to thirty different species of microorganisms, with hundreds of thousands of eukaryotes and tens of billions of prokaryotes per milliliter of hindgut fluid. Only a small proportion of the microbes in wood-eating termites are specifically involved in cellulose digestion, but like all other microbial communities, it's a group effort. Other members of the team digest the corpses of their comrades, recycle wastes, and fix nitrogen from the air. The most important byproduct of termites' metabolism is methane, which, as is explored in a later chapter, is believed to be a crucial regulator of the global environment.

Margulis believes that this unique form of microbial intestinal community may have coevolved with the termites ever since the insects first advanced from the wood-eating roach some 1 to 1.5 billion years ago. The termites acquire their vital package of bacteria not through standard genetic inheritance but in a peculiar ritual whereby they feed on the anal fluid of their fellows. Yet when termites lose their intestinal microbes, they die:

> It's amazing, really, when you look at how deeply reliant some of the termite's microbial partnerships are. Or the eating-breathing partnerships in microbial mats, or at Lake Cisó. There are dozens more examples of just that kind of complete dependence between different species of microbes, all working and evolving together in the interest of maintaining their environment. Of course, these superspecialized little creatures didn't just pop out that way, they have evolved together over billions of years, each losing genes by the processes of natural selection, for the functions performed by the other, so certain is their mutual reliance.

But microbial symbiosis does not stop, says Margulis, at the side-by-side collaboration found in termite hindguts and microbial mats. She believes that over the course of evolution it often has happened that two or more species cooperate so closely that eventually their offspring lose redundant faculties and merge physically. This theory, the basis of Margulis's fame, is known as evolution through endosymbiosis.

THE CASE OF THE ERRANT GENES

Tradition has it that a cell's genes are supposed to be in its chromosomes, and if the cell has a nucleus, then that's where the chromosomes must reside. In the late 1960s, as a graduate student at the University of Wisconsin, Margulis learned of evidence that genes could reside elsewhere in the cell, but her repeated questions on what this genetic material was and where it came from always were brushed aside, with dwindling paternalistic indulgence. It is impossible, however, to brush Lynn Margulis aside. Fascinated by the implications that an additional, and quite probably different, dose of DNA was figuring into her inheritance, Margulis's curiosity got the better of her respect for authority, in what must have been a brief and lopsided contest. Where did this extra DNA come from? Was one parent contributing more genetic material than the other to their offspring? Perhaps some completely nonparental influence was creeping in. Whence all the funny business? Gregor Mendel, the father of modern genetics, would be shocked to learn what had wriggled into his pea plants.

Darwin's manly grand scenario for survival of the fittest traits would also have to be checked against these unauthorized new divers into the global gene pool. The orthodox linear reasoning (winner-succeeds-in-leaving-offspring, loser's-traits-disappear) seemed destined for some dramatic revision. But Margulis was discouraged repeatedly by her colleagues and mentors from pursuing this exciting, even revolutionary, line of work. "The message was plain," notes Evelyn Fox Keller, a mathematical biophysicist who writes frequently about women who have distinguished themselves in the field of science.

"Genes were assumed to reside exclusively on chromosomes, and accordingly, phenomena of non-Mendelian inheritance seemed aberrant, inexplicable and not worth studying."[4]

By 1960 Margulis, then twenty-two, had been married to astronomer Carl Sagan for three years, had had their first son, Dorion, and was pregnant with a second child, had received her master's in zoology and genetics from Wisconsin, and was ready for a change. Following her husband to the University of California at Berkeley she enrolled in the doctoral program in genetics, more intent than ever on solving the case of these extra, nonchromosomal genes. Ironically, soon after she arrived at Berkeley, one of her former professors at Wisconsin, Hans Ris, published a series of electron microscope photographs that provided the closest thing yet to conclusive proof that DNA could be found outside chromosomes. His micrographs of the algae Chlamydomonas showed that there were genes in the chloroplasts—the little bundles of chlorophyll found in the cells of most photosynthetic plants and animals.

Chloroplasts are now known to be autonomous and self-replicating organelles, or subcellular organs (as though, say, your pancreas somehow gained the ability to reproduce itself). Examination by electron microscope has revealed that these tiny blue-green packages bear an uncanny resemblance to cyanobacteria. Cyanobacteria are simple blue-green organisms now widely believed to have been the first life forms to brave the sunlight, using the hitherto lethal rays to metabolize water and develop the process of photosynthesis. Prior to the appearance of cyanobacteria, all microbes are believed to have avoided the sun's rays, surviving in the darkness by the lower energy, anerobic process of fermentation. As is explored in much greater detail in chapter 5, the robust, oxygen-loving cyanobacteria quickly conquered their fermentative underlings and spread like a film around the globe. They still fill the air today, causing mold and mildew and generally flourishing wherever hospitable surfaces are damp.

How, Ris wondered, did these tiny, utterly ancient oxygen-loving bacteria end up living inside other microorganisms, and

45

not as though they had been eaten up and digested, but doing rather nicely. They were the microbial equivalents of Vatican City inside Rome, or the United Nations in New York—independent enclaves completely interdependent with and surrounded by the larger entities. Ris thought it within the realm of possibility that somehow the cyanobacteria had been symbiotically incorporated inside the Chlamydomonas algae. That's where he stopped and Margulis's work began.

Declares Keller, whose proudly feminist works include the acclaimed biography of Nobelist Barbara McClintock, A Feeling for the Organism, as well as Reflections on Gender and Science:

> With a psychic gesture that felt like seizing her freedom, Margulis decided, in the mid-1960's, to dedicate herself to the task of substantiating not only Ris's interpretation, but the even bolder suggestion that intracellular symbiosis with bacteria is a universal characteristic [italics added] of plant and animal cells.[5]

Based on no more hard evidence than a few grainy micrographs, with no job and a degree greener than the chloroplasts she had studied, Margulis realized that her insurrectionary challenge to the orthodoxy of Mendel and Darwin never would get funded. So the newly single mother of two took a job with the National Science Foundation developing science programs for primary schools, cared for her children without the help of a father around, and plotted her challenge to the masculine establishment in the darkness of the night. For Margulis the price of psychic freedom was not having a moment to breathe.

THE PILLAR SUSTAINED

The original pillar of Margulis's theory—that in both plant and animal cells, the oxygen-processing cellular "power plants," chloroplasts and mitochondria, respectively, are the direct de-

scendants of independent bacteria—has now overcome all reasonable doubts and objections. Over the course of their evolution, the bacterial ancestors of these cellular power plants were
engulfed, but not devoured, by the ancestors of their hosts,
together forming tiny, Jonah-in-the-whale microbial communities. Unlike the biblical story, these symbiotic arrangements
grew permanent, as though the revolutionary oxygen-processing
capabilities of the swallowed prey were just too good to destroy.
Gradually, such redundant capabilities as the ability to gather
food were eliminated by the progressive pressures of natural
selection, until only the specialized functions vital to the cell as
a whole remained.

By this scenario Margulis explains the presence of the extra
mitochondrial genes that first attracted her attention. Some
bacteriologists have tried to minimize the discovery, arguing that
since human mitochondria contain less than 1 percent of a cell's
total DNA, her observations are likely to have no practical
medical value. Recently, however, Douglas C. Wallace and his
team of geneticists at Emory University have linked a specific
defect in mitochondrial DNA to a rare form of blindness called
Leber's hereditary optic neuropathy (LHON), which kills the
optic nerve, usually by the age of twenty. Mitochondrial genes,
it seems, determine production levels of ATP, the key fuel used
for all cellular functions, and when their DNA is defective, ATP
production usually decreases, causing certain cells to fail or
deteriorate. In human beings mitochrondrial genes are inherited
only from the mother. Wallace's discovery of their function
suggests a whole new mechanism for hereditary diseases. In fact,
the geneticist believes that a host of hitherto inexplicable heart,
kidney, and central nervous system disorders may now be explained by problems with mitochrondrial DNA.

Traditional microbiologists now grudgingly bow to the significance of chloroplast and mitochondrial endosymbiosis but
argue that this phenomenon can be explained away by the
parasite-host and predator-prey relations of natural selection—
that any sharing is entirely incidental to the single-minded

47

pursuit of self-interest. What Margulis sees as merger, the Darwinists would think of as acquisition. Debates like this frequently resolve to that all-purpose and quite possibly circular compromise, "enlightened self-interest." Meyer Lansky, the notorious mobster, provides an illustrative example of this conundrum. When asked how he had survived so long in such a dangerous business, he is purported to have replied that he always had made a profit for his partners. That, in a nutshell, is the argument for symbiotic evolution: in order to compete, one has no choice but to cooperate and share the pie.

Darwinists and other self-interest partisans might take some intellectual satisfaction in noting that in the end Lansky was rubbed out by a partner who wanted the whole damn pie, but Lovelock and Margulis have helped each other survive more than two decades of intellectual rubout attempts and now find themselves in prosperous positions. Much as the British maverick can call on an expanding cadre of scientists of the Gaian macrocosm, Margulis is the focal point for a new school of symbiotists, biologists who specialize in the study of mutually beneficial close associations. Built on her work and that of her colleagues, S. Sonea and M. Panisset, authors of A New Bacteriology, the new biological discipline is still relatively unknown in the United States and Great Britain but is growing much faster in Western Europe and Japan, where Darwin's theory of competitive natural selection never has been enshrined as doctrine.

In late 1988 a startling discovery lent weight to the symbiotists' version of how chloroplasts came to dwell inside plant cells. Prochlorophytes, single-celled plankton, were discovered thriving about 100 meters deep in the Atlantic and Pacific oceans as well as in the Caribbean Sea and the Gulf of Mexico. With more than 100,000 cells per milliliter of water, researchers now believe that these plankton are one of the world's two most numerous plant forms. Moreover, these prochlorophytes are remarkably similar to the chloroplasts that first launched Margulis on her endosymbiotic journey. Some scientists now suggest that prochlorophytes are essentially the missing link, or intermediate evolutionary stage, between cyanobacteria and chloroplasts.

THE DANCE OF THE SPIROCHETES

Since any seeming exception to evolutionary orthodoxy—like the symbiotic progression from cyanobacteria to chloroplasts—is liable to be dismissed as a fluke or, more likely, shelved as congruent with the traditional rules of natural selection in a way that as yet cannot be explained, symbiotists are searching for other convincing examples to establish symbiosis as a significant and consistent evolutionary phenomenon. Margulis has devoted much of the past decade to a more radical tenet of her theory, that all cell hairs—cilia, whipping tails, undulipodia, and other similar microtubules—are descended from spirochetes. Much as bacteria have become chloroplasts and mitochondria over the course of evolution, Margulis asserts that spirochetes have been endosymbiotically incorporated into plant and animals cells over the eons of evolution. But Margulis readily admits that she is still nearly alone in this judgment. Furthermore, she says, "If I think 'cell-hairs' come from spirochetes, the burden of proof lies on me."[6]

Advanced electron microscope studies have revealed that all cell hairs—whether they are found as the sperm tails of men, mosses, or gingko trees; lobster or cockroach antennae; the sensory cilia of inner ears or the locomotive cilia of the paramecium; the spindly axons and dendrites of neurons; the "dance" of the chromosomes in cellular mitosis; or almost anyplace else in nature—are composed of the same set of proteins and are arranged in identical "telephone dial" circle configurations of nine pairs of microtubules surrounding one pair in the middle. Few biologists dispute this rather extraordinary coincidence, but even fewer see any more reason to explain it by a special theory than they might need, for example, to explain why icicles form in the same crystalline patterns all over the world—that is simply the way nature does it. Conventional wisdom holds that for

49

reasons of natural economy or efficiency, cells usually make microtubules in these ten-pair protein arrangements for the purposes of locomotion.

With the same stubbornness that Lovelock first refused to accept coincidence as the full explanation for why there should be so much oxygen in the Earth's atmosphere when standard physics and chemistry predict that it should react into stable compounds, Margulis has never accepted chance as the full explanation for the uncanny similarity in the structure of microtubules. Instinct tells her that the dancing, whipping, propulsive movements of cell hairs and of spirochetes, which are believed to be the earliest bacteria with the ability to move at will, are profoundly related. Despite the fact that *no spirochete*, or any other microorganism, has ever been found to contain the evidentiary telephone-dial microtubules, Margulis has moved her laboratory from Boston University to the University of Massachusetts at Amherst to work with Canale-Parola, a renowned expert on spirochetes. She cleaves to her intuition that

> Predaceous, wary and incessantly moving spirochetes (like those in a latent syphilis infection) once tried to attack and eat our (immobile) bacterial ancestors but ended up as their intimate and essential companions. Growth, chemical communication and dancing have become they physical basis of learning, depression and elation. [7]

LIFE CANNOT BE STOPPED

The intrepid microbiologist and her expanding network of colleagues hope to establish endosymbiosis as the general theory of microbial evolution. They believe that individual cells, whether of the algae Chlamydomonas or of our bodies, are quite literally complex organisms whose components have evolved through 3.5 billion years of symbiotic encounters.

Now we see ourselves as products of cellular interaction. The eukaryotic cell is built up from other cells; it is a community of interacting microbes. Partnerships between cells once foreign and even enemies to each other are at the very roots of our being. They are the basis of the continually outward expansion of life on Earth.

Lynn Margulis believes that life cannot be stopped by any earthly means. That is the essence of her belief in the Gaia theory. She knows that neither she nor Lovelock can prove it yet, but it has long been their shared conviction that rather than thinking of nature as something "exquisitely sensitive to the depredations of man," as her ex-husband Sagan is fond of putting it, humanity's power is trifling when compared to the unfathomable resiliency of the plant, animal, and particularly, microbial world. Of course, human civilization may well destroy those parts of nature that are beautiful or essential to our own welfare, extinguishing species that by any moral or aesthetic measure deserve to flourish unmolested. But the ability to vandalize is not at all the same as the ability to control or conquer. Compared to the three-and-a-half-billion-year momentum of the microcosm, Margulis cannot help but snicker at the vainglory of our little species.

III

GAIA: GODDESS AND THEORY

A THEORY OF BIOLOGICAL RELATIVITY

"Gaia is not benign: she is generative—that is her only principle," writes Christine Downing in *The Goddess: Mythological Images of the Feminine,*[1] capturing the essence of both the ancient Greek goddess and the modern scientific theory that bears her name. Lovelock, Margulis, and the others participating in the Gaia discussion are not trying so much to determine whether the Earth is alive as whether the planet is ultimately more subject to the generative forces of biology than the automatic processes of geology. Does 3.5 billion years of continuous reproductive pressure to convert the Earth's elements and the sun's energy into living organisms, which grow and multiply whenever and wherever possible, mean that our planet is more alive than inanimate? Or does the vast mechanical power of such abiological systems as plate tectonics, volcanism, and continental drift dwarf life's collective contribution into a comparative pittance? And is it an either/or decision or is it a relative judgment?

Gaia, in fact, is a theory of relativity in that the concepts of life and death are no longer seen as absolute. Much as Einstein

52

demonstrated that there is no fixed point in the universe, no immutable standard (except for that pesky speed of light), Lovelock and Margulis have observed that the boundary line between life and the inanimate environment that most of us assume to be resolutely engraved somewhere cannot be clearly drawn. Just as matter and energy are radically different yet ultimately interchangeable phenomena, so too are the environment and living organisms ultimately functions of one another, two sides of some biological equivalent of Einstein's transcendent $E = mc^2$ equation, yet to be divined.

Scientifically—and theologically—the most practical question to ask about Gaia is not whether she is alive, but how alive is she? At the level of Lovelock's macrocosm, discussions about the nature of biological life seems most sensible as a matter of degree. If nothing else, Lovelock's example of the living redwood tree that is 97 percent dead focuses the question. Whether or not something is alive has less to do with its biological proportion than on the extent to which it behaves in a lifelike fashion. Lovelock is fond of pointing out that no scientifically and semantically rigorous definition of life exists; The Dictionary of Biology, he cites with glee, does not even have an entry under the word. In The Ages of Gaia he observes that "there is no clear distinction anywhere on the Earth's surface between living and nonliving matter. There is merely a hierarchy of intensity going from the 'material' environment of the rocks and the atmosphere to the living cells."[2] Life forms are so thoroughly integrated with their environment, in Lovelock's opinion, that it would be unwise to assume that even the core of the planet is immune to life's influence. And it would be at least as imprudent to assume that such a grand global organism, to whatever extent it exists, is without a certain divinity.

At Margulis's microcosmic level, the concept of endosymbiosis—where one single-celled organism incorporates another without destroying it, permitting the internalized creature to procreate as if it were autonomous—is a baseline example of the Gaian in-between. Is a chloroplast a living creature? It produces

53

vital energy and—central to all traditional definitions of life—reproduces itself and has its own DNA. But like any organ in any living body, the chloroplast is woefully incomplete; its capacity to eat, excrete, and otherwise sustain itself as an independent entity was lost eons ago. It is not surprising that biological interdependence has become one of Margulis's abiding themes.

> The consortial quality of the individual pre-empts the notion of independence. For example, what appears to be a single wood-eating termite is comprised of billions of microbes, a few kinds of which do the actual digesting of the cellulose of the wood. Gaia is the same sort of consortial entity, but it is far more complex. Consortia, associations, partnerships, symbioses, and competitions in the interaction between organisms extend to the global scale. Living and nonliving matter, self, and environment are nicely interconnected.[3]

Just as Lovelock relativizes the definition of life, Margulis has replaced traditional absolutist assumptions about what is (and what is not) an individual with much suppler ideas.

Like the curious consanguinity between the physics of the cosmos and that of the subatomic realm, where the spin properties of an electron are used to help deduce the shape of the universe, there is a bond between the macrocosm of Lovelock and the microcosm of Margulis that transcends simple analogy. Just as Newton's solid, reliable distinctions between matter and energy lose pertinence as the limits of the infinite or the infinitesimal are approached, the notion of discrete objects and waves dissolving into a speed-of-light blur, so too does Darwin's grand scenario of struggle among individuals seem to slip out of focus when life is examined at the global and cellular extremes. In biology as well as physics, distinctions between individuals are radically less important at the microcosmic and macrocosmic boundaries of nature than in the familiar worlds in the middle, where the visions of Darwin and Newton prevail.

IS NATURE REALLY MOTHERLY?

For most of the first decade of Gaian theory, Lovelock and Margulis's relativistic notions about life and the environment met with icy indifference and absolute rejection. Carl Sagan helped a bit by publishing an early article on Gaia in his journal *Icarus* in 1965, but neither that nor the flurry of articles Lovelock and Margulis wrote received much reaction from the scientific community, pro or con. Lovelock traveled on his shoestring budget from the hustings of Cornwall to scientific and environmental conferences, symposia, and colloquia in Britain, the United States, and abroad to spread the scientific gospel of the living Earth and perhaps enlist a few converts and stimulate a little research. Margulis worked behind the scenes, less involved with propounding the theory than developing research and using her academic credentials to help her collaborator gain influence and entree. There were a few helpful and encouraging responses, particularly from Lewis Thomas, the well-known philosopher of biology, but for the most part, the living Earth theory was belittled as spiritualism and metaphor or else ignored.

Lovelock and his theory were launched into prominence in 1979 , with the publication of *Gaia: A New Look at Life on Earth*. Just why that little book generated so much interest—it sold several hundred thousand copies and still is being reprinted—is not an easy mystery. Aimed at scientists and interested laypersons, the book combines complex, technical topics like the biogeochemistry of the oceans several billion years ago, worldwide production and consumption of methane gas, with lightly metaphysical musings about the earth goddess and her spirituality, and more than a few good chuckles to keep it all from becoming too dense or exalted. Yet some of that first-bash book's more poetic depictions of Gaia as a creature with will and intentions, its generally anti-Darwinist tone, the rather stark discrepancy between sweeping theory and sparse facts, along with a few scientific errors and unfortunate turns of phrase—all natural excesses of what the physicist Philip Morrison called "the exciting and personal argument of an original thinker caught up in wonder"—have forced Lovelock to spend as much time clearing up misunderstandings, some of them pretty outlandish, as he does presenting the legitimate scientific theory. There have been times when Gaia—book, theory, and goddess— must have been a terrible mistress to serve.

There was just one firm position for orthodox evolutionary biologists to take. Darwin's great vision of evolution—that species are not created separately but rather that there is a genealogical connection among all organisms that develops and diversifies over time—is one of the most heavily substantiated propositions in all of science. That is not at all contested by Gaia. But his theory of how evolution works—by the weeding-out process of natural selection, where the fittest organisms survive to reproduce and gradually crowd out weaker competitors—has had to prove its own fitness for survival against challenges from both thoughtful questioners and crackpots ever since the legendary Englishman proposed his evolutionary mechanism more than a century ago. In the eyes of battle-weary biologists, Lovelock's great motherly organism was just the latest in the eternal procession of piddling, if well-intentioned, attacks on the hard, cold truths of earthly survival. So their rebuttals sometimes seemed to have less to do with Gaia per se than with what the Darwinist community felt was merely some recycled argument for nature as being one big happy family.

"The Gaia theory thrives on an innate desire, mostly among laypeople, to believe that evolution works for the good of all. Profoundly erroneous," says Richard Dawkins, professor of biology at Oxford University and author best known for his widely admired book *The Selfish Gene.* The erudite Britisher is the paragon of modern Darwinian orthodoxy. An Occam's razor that slices away flabby, wishful thinking, his arguments have the seamless rigor of ideology, where each assumption has the strength of conviction and every debating point won is a triumph for the Truth. Dawkins, a passionate atheist who reveres Charles Darwin as the first man to bring intellectual fulfillment to the lives of nonbelievers, is a deeply civilized man who knows better than to make martyrs out of rogues. "I admit that I find myself involuntarily impressed with some of the facts that Lovelock has unearthed, like the constancy of oxygen levels in the atmosphere and so forth. He doesn't have any real explanations, but I do thank him for bringing it all up."

Andrew Knoll, a professor of paleontology at Harvard, dismisses Lovelock's theory as little more than a reaction to the extreme Darwinist orthodoxy that ruled evolutionary biology in the late 1960s, when Gaia first was formulated. Like Dawkins, Knoll thus far has declined to devote much time or effort to a comprehensive rebuttal, believing that a scholarly attack, no matter how devastating, would legitimize the heretical idea of a living Earth. Neither critic could have been very surprised, therefore, when an exhaustive critique from their colleague, evolutionary biologist W. F. Doolittle, plunged Lovelock and Margulis into the scientific debate they had worked so hard to stimulate.

> The good thing about this engaging little book by Jim Lovelock is that reading it gives one a warm, comforting feeling about Nature and man's place in it. The bad thing is that this feeling is based on a view of natural selection—that force which alone is responsible for the existence and characteristics of the biosphere—which is unquestionably false."[4]

Thus began Doolittle's now-famous Gaia critique, "Is Nature Really Motherly?" in the spring 1981 edition of *The Coevolution Quarterly*.

Ironically, the opening of Doolittle's critical article stands as the most radical pro-Gaian statement ever to make it into scientific publishing. The biosphere—that part of the Earth and its atmosphere in which living organisms exist—being a part of the planet, is at least as much a geological as a biological entity. Therefore, its "existence and characteristics" depend on a variety of geological forces, ranging from plate tectonics to volcanism to the wind and the rain, in addition to the forces of natural selection that Doolittle the Darwinist holds supreme. By attributing to the forces of life the entire character and dynamic of the surface of the Earth, from as deep in the ocean to as high in the sky that anything can live, Doolittle inadvertently argues that plants, animals, and microbes collectively dominate their environment. Perhaps he meant to write "biota," the sum of all living organisms, instead of "biosphere," but if so, the difference between the terms is telling. *Biota* is a hopeless abstraction. Never are all of Earth's living organisms gathered together anywhere without quite a lot of that pesky, inanimate environment holding things together.

Paul Ehrlich, the immensely popular population biologist from Stanford University, phrases Doolittle's concerns more adroitly: "Nonphysical parts of the biosphere do not evolve according to the fundamental mechanism of replication with variation and differential reproduction of the variants. That is the fundamental difference between geological and biological evolution." But the basic Gaian argument—that neither geological nor biological evolution happen independently, that this sort of coevolution is always and inextricably a coupled process that includes natural selection, geochemistry, and a myriad of other interdependent forces, perhaps guided or catalyzed by the liveliest force among them—survives even the rigorous living-nonliving distinctions set forth by Ehrlich and kindred critics.

Doolittle's five-thousand-word assault on Gaia, otherwise remarkably well researched and reasoned, turned out to be the break Lovelock and Margulis had been waiting for. It was formal recognition of Gaia's existence as a science. Each wrote extensive rebuttals that were published along with Doolittle's article, and both took every opportunity to send copies of the printed debate to whomever was interested. And in all of the excitement about the serious attention Gaia was receiving, neither scientist noticed Doolittle's gaping opening flaw.

GAIA V. DARWIN: THE CLASH OF CREEDS

There seems to be something almost theological about Darwinism. In fact, Darwinists of every stripe and degree have the curious tendency to express themselves in terms of faith and commitment. Though kinder and more liberal-minded than Dawkins and his purebred intellectual kin, Harley Cahen, a Cornell University biologist, proclaims a critique of Gaia in "Ethics and the Organismic Earth—A Skeptical View": "I'm a loyal neo-Darwinian . . . I believe that all organismic goals can be reduced to the elemental goal of maximizing genetic fitness."[5] In other words, I believe in one God, the Father Almighty, maker of Heaven and Earth. Or, as Ehrlich puts it, "Reading Darwin over and over again is like reading the Bible. You can find almost everything in there, including Gaia."

While enshrined as orthodoxy in England and the United States, Darwin's theory of the "survival of the fittest" (a phrase first used by Herbert Spencer and praised by Darwin as an apt description of the natural selection process) never has been as fully embraced in France, Germany, or, especially, Japan, where the collectivist principles of the biologist Imanishi hold sway. As Mary Clark, a biologist from San Diego State University (best known for her book *Ariadne's Thread*) explains:

> Scientific insight is often molded by social milieu. We
> in the U.S. see competition and violence in our lives,
> so we go out and look for it, and find it, in nature.
> There may also be substantial evidence for symbiosis
> and cooperation in nature, but it is the habit of science
> to ignore details incompatible with generally accepted
> models. The Gaia Hypothesis helps us to be critical of

59

the visions we have of the natural world, which are usually based on an individualistic, competitive world-view.

The thoroughly English Lovelock broaches the subject of natural selection with much the same trepidation with which an American liberal Democrat might respond to being branded "soft on defense."

> In no way do I want to join the mob that tries to pick holes in Darwin. I think he was the greatest. It may be, however, that the theory of evolution is incomplete. Darwinism sees evolution as occurring in a somewhat static world, one where the environment evolves according to the rules of physics and chemistry. It doesn't see any coupling between the evolution of the environment and that of living organisms. Instead of the narrow principle of adaptation, where organisms adjust to their environment and that's that, Gaia sees a tightly coupled process where the evolution of life and the evolution of the rocks, oceans, and atmosphere are so tightly joined together that they are really one single process. Natural selection is a key part of the Gaia theory. It is just that natural selection does not take place in a neutral environment.

Lovelock concludes that Gaia is complementary, not in conflict, with the theory of evolution by natural selection, but strict Darwinist orthodoxy precludes the existence of Mother Nature, whether cuddly or cruel. Unless the Earth were in direct competition with Venus and Mars, as Dawkins once suggested in his book *Extended Phenotype*, Gaia never could have come into being. His point is that a species of one organism—in this case, the living planet—could not evolve because there is nothing for natural selection to select from. According to Dawkins's strict Darwinism, the universe would have to be littered with dead

Gaias—planetary systems that failed to come alive—in order for ours to have evolved successfully.

When I once asked Dawkins if he really believed all of that quite literally, I was reminded of a flap that former president Ronald Reagan fell into early in his first term for quoting the Bible about Satan and the judgment day that was due. Reagan was not about to renounce the New Testament, the article of his faith, but neither did he seem to believe in the literal applicability of the Book of Revelations, as many of his critics had feared. Same with Dawkins and all of his dead Gaias. It is the rigorously logical extension of his creed, so he must point to their absence as one argument against Gaia theory. But he stops short of claiming that the presence or absence of dead planets constitutes anything like conclusive proof. Proponents of Gaia tend to ignore this rather dogmatic attack on their theory, although they could in fact point to Mars as possibly one of those dead Gaias that Dawkins's argument requires. The red planet seems once to have had liquid water and several other biologically conducive conditions, but the planet is now frozen over, lifeless, while Earth has survived to bloom.

THE GREAT REPRODUCTION DEBATE

For orthodox Darwinists the ability to reproduce is as essential to the definition of life as the Virgin Birth is to Roman Catholic dogma on the divine origin of Jesus Christ. To Dawkins and associates the Earth cannot be alive because it has not reproduced, and by definition, everything alive can reproduce. Except of course for mules, which are produced by the union of horses and donkeys, or Lombardy poplar trees, which are also dependent on the crossing of other species. Those must be the exceptions that prove the rule.

But how about elderly women, or men with a low sperm count? They certainly are alive, yet they cannot, at present, reproduce, and in some cases never could have reproduced. So, with freak exceptions like those understandably ornery mules, in order for something to be classified as alive it must be part of a species that is capable of reproduction. Gaia still does not seem to qualify. "The minimum requirement for us to recognize an object as an animal or plant is that it should succeed in making a living of *some sort* (more precisely, that it, or at least some members of its kind, should live long enough to reproduce),"[6] writes Dawkins.

Lovelock has two responses to the reproduction argument against Gaia. Pointing out that life has flourished on our planet for 3.5 billion years without interruption, he argues that "life is a planetary-scale phenomenon. On this scale it is near immortal and has no need to reproduce." His second response is more enchanting to the imagination: Gaia simply has not reproduced yet. (Since gestation periods do vary in rough proportion to the size of the animal—elephants and blue whales take over a year to deliver their young, while certain strains of bacteria can reproduce every few minutes—it is entertaining to note that compared to the eighteen-trillion-ton biomass of the Earth, even the largest mammals are no grander than a microbe. Judged by this crude time-weight proportion, Gaia barely has reached puberty.) The question of when Gaia might reproduce being moot, Lovelock's critics concern themselves with the even more fanciful question of how.

The Greening of Mars, as noted in the introduction to this volume, is a story written by Lovelock and Michael Allaby about warming up the Martian atmosphere through gas injection, melting the available water, and generally bringing the planet to life, in a process known variously as ecopoiesis, or terraforming. Dawkins and allies have argued that even if we were able to impart a self-sustaining biosphere to the dead planet, as a surprising number of NASA and other scientists think possible, this still would not constitute reproduction. But if humans were to land on Mars or some other planet or moon (Jupiter's Io is also mentioned) and stimulate the growth of a self-sustaining biosphere, Darwinists' objections to defining this as a reproductive process easily could devolve into technical quibbles. The Earth's likeness would have been imparted.[7]

Russell Schweikart, the *Apollo* astronaut who was the first person to walk in space without an umbilical cord to the craft, swept along by the magical, invisible connection of shared momentum, believes that Gaia may be nearing some sort of threshold analogous to giving birth. He observes that humanity's accelerating growth rate and demands for resources and waste processing are the same kind of burgeoning needs that tax a mother's ability to nurture a growing fetus. It is precisely the mismatch between the demands of the fetus and the abilities of the mother to provide, Schweikart notes, that triggers the birthing process. "This natural birth process, the first moment of life, is, ironically, a very close brush with death. And while there is violence, blood and a lot of anxiety, there is also the beginning of the full potential of life."[8]

Whether soon or at some point in the distant future, by the methods described in *The Greening of Mars* or by some other means entirely, the possibility that Gaia still may reproduce cannot be discounted. Margulis reminds us that the whole global system could conceivably reproduce as a single entity: "Reproduction occurs not only from organism to organism but hierarchically: molecules, cells, organisms, even communities—such as those comprising billions of microbes in the termite budget—reproduce."[9] Like Dawkins's dead Gaias, the reproduction argument against the theory of the living Earth seems more convincing as doctrine than as objective evidence.

GAIA BECOMES AN INDUSTRY

The reproductive power of Gaian ideas soon would astonish critics and proponents alike. Few books, especially those of the arcane scientific variety, spawn their own publishing houses. One of the most gratifying consequences of *Gaia: A New Look at Life on Earth* was that it inspired Joss Pearson to establish Gaia

63

Books, Ltd. Up a couple of creaky flights of stairs in an area of London so remote that taxi drivers lose their way, the spacious loft today overflows with a successful worldwide book-packaging business, all on Gaia-related subjects. But when they started in 1982, the Pearsons had little more than an absurdly ambitious first-book idea and lots of empty room.

While Darwinists may have been appalled by the heretical notion of a planetary organism, environmentalists and ecologists, the Pearsons reckoned, would be compelled by that grand holistic vision. Working with the same shrewd diplomacy that Lovelock has long used to disarm opponents, they went for quality over dogma and persuaded Norman Myers, a renowned environmentalist and winner of the World Wildlife Fund Gold Medal in 1983, to be editor of a Gaia atlas. Myers was by no means a convert to the theory, however.

> The Gaia hypothesis wouldn't be the first elegant and beautiful concept to fall on its face. Intuitively, I would like to agree with it. There's been too much plucking the flower to pieces. There's a sense of mystic togetherness with the apprehension that the planetary ecosystem works as a unitary whole. That feeling isn't anti-scientific. Just kind of right-brained.

Contributions were gathered from more than one hundred supporters and critics of Gaian theory—environmentalists, research scientists, and public policy analysts from the likes of Oxford, Stanford (including Darwinist critic Paul Ehrlich), Cornell, the World Bank, and the United Nations—and were organized into *Gaia: An Atlas of Planet Management,* a superbly illustrated trouble-shooting guide to the world's environment and resources. The book was dedicated to "Jim Lovelock, whose Gaia Hypothesis first alerted us to the idea that we might inhabit a living planet."

"The Gaia atlas generated a huge response among members of the Green movement throughout Europe and Japan," says publisher Joss Pearson of the oversized glossy book that has become an international bestseller. The Pearsons see Gaia as a life-style, a marriage of ecologists and conservationists to holistic healers and spiritualists. Books and manuals on such diverse subjects as endangered species, stress management, massage, and natural living have since been published under the Gaia rubric. "It has taken the Gaian principle to weld it all together," she adds, producing a bundle of letters from readers, many of them teachers and therapists, declaring that Gaia, the ultimate embraceable whole, had changed their lives.

"It may be that many people, possibly all people, can only think about complex wholes—think holistically—by using aesthetic or religious energy," says Mary Catherine Bateson, explaining what to Lovelock and Margulis was a puzzling and unanticipated response to their scientific proposals. As Bateson sees it, most people are overwhelmed by the complexity of the vast global system and need to feel some emotional or spiritual connection before proceeding intellectually. And the image of Gaia serves as just such a metaphorical invitation to deeper, more intimate understanding. Pointing out that Gaia culminates a great body of twentieth-century work on mental and physical systems, the anthropologist hopes that the living earth theory lives up to its fecund namesake goddess and gives birth to a world of new ideas. Finding the notion of a living Earth spiritually compelling or beautiful may, for many students of the planet, be the first thrill of a satisfying and rigorous intellectual journey, like the excitement of seeing the sunrise over the long, winding road ahead. "Gaia is the supersystem," Bateson concludes. "It is intellectually irresistible."

Like that endless debate about whether and to what extent mass communications direct or reflect social change, once a movement gets started, cause and effect are usually as impossible to distinguish as spokes on a spinning wheel. As Gaia Books capitalized on the trend it had promoted so vigorously, a bewildering array of Gaia organizations sprang up to help push or hitch a ride on whatever had gotten the living Earth ball rolling.

These ranged from the Liechtenstein-based Foundation for Gaia, irritably dismissed by Lovelock as inane, to the Gaia Institute at the Cathedral of St. John the Divine in New York City, which was founded and encouraged by Lindisfarne members and has offered seminars, lectures, and entertainment programs for much of the past decade. In short, over the course of the 1980s Gaia has become a guiding, galvanizing metaphor for that large, loose association of ecological, holistic, spiritual, and feminist activists described collectively, sometimes derisively, as New Age.

A GODDESS FOR THE NEW AGE

> Gaia is the one who gives us birth
> She's the air, she's the sea, she's Mother Earth
> She's the creatures that crawl and swim and fly.
> She's the growing grass, she's you and I.
> —from "Gaia Song"

The name of both a lively little hymn and an annual Christmas holiday festival, "Gaia Song" is the creation of the Commonwealth Institute of London, an organization that provides family-oriented cultural programs to the forty-nine countries of the British Commonwealth. Sponsored partly by donations from IBM, "Gaia Song" is a ceremony of music, dance, and responsive readings to cheer Gaia through the darkness of winter and on to a rosy future. Schoolchildren on five continents have been introduced to Gaia, song and theory, by the Commonwealth Institute.

"Gaia is like the myth of God, a mystery answering a mystery," observes Claudio Guillen, a professor of comparative literature at Harvard and at the University of Barcelona, explaining the contradictory allure. "It is a romantic metaphor that answers our need for oneness." God of humanity, Gaia of nature. God for men, Gaia for women. Gaia, God's wife. God, Gaia's husband. The great G-words paired and recoupled like recombinant DNA in the murky, high-nutrient soup of the New Age subconscious. Try as Lovelock and Margulis might to bring their living Earth brainchild up as a proper scientific theory, their budding princess, like most any other beauty, did not care a fig to be understood when she could be adored.

Goddess and theory demonstrated their combined drawing power in August 1985 at Amherst College, when a week-long conference, "Is the Earth a Living Organism?" sponsored by the Audubon Expedition Institute, had to turn away more than a hundred prospective speakers. They still wound up with a thirteen-hundred-page report of the proceedings, including presentations by Lovelock, Thomas, and even the maverick Nobel laureate chemist George Wald, a critic of Gaia theory. Science, environmentalism, and spirituality—the three elements of what publishers Joss and David Pearson call the Gaian life-style—were represented in roughly equal proportion.

"The concept of the earth being alive is more than a scientific theory," write Jim Swan and Thomas Hurley, editors of the Audubon conference proceedings.

It is a mythic theme, a metaphor and a primal symbol of the unconscious mind which periodically down through the ages has stirred minds and bodies to action. We know that we have environmental problems today, but we have not devoted a good deal of time to looking at their deep roots in the human mind. If we better understood how myths, symbols, and primal feelings about nature come about and are shaped, it seems likely that we could do a much better job creating more effective environmental education programs, as well as spreading an ecological ethic more generally throughout society.[10]

Faster than the theory of nature's dominance could be proved or even presented, Gaia had become a unified symbol for pantheism, an acceptably anthropomorphized object for the worship of all that lives. The Amherst gathering proved seminal, generating a network that has propagated Gaia conferences and festivals ever since, although few have offered the same scientific and philosophical rigor in their programs. That holism and Gaia are a natural match was amply illustrated by the Gaia Synthesis, a convention of several hundred alternativists held in April 1986 in Boulder, Colorado. Many from the Amherst conclave also spoke at this three-day event, but there the likes of Lovelock, Margulis, and company drew the line. Hard science had been spirited off the stage by a mile-high potpourri of geopsychology, perception, myth, sensuousness, Pueblo Indian perspective, etheric energy and economic theory of Gaia, plus a variety of musical performances, mimes, and dances.

Swan, one of the organizers of the Amherst event, also spoke at Boulder. He has become a key player in the New Age Gaia network. Most recently he was the coordinator of a gathering in May 1988 called Gaia Consciousness: The Goddess and the Living Earth. Sponsored by the California Institute of Integral Studies in San Francisco, where Swan is a faculty member, the program was, like the Boulder festival, light on science, heavy on religion—including scholarly presentations and panels on Judaic, Christian, Asian, shamanistic, and indigenous perspectives on the Earth goddess—and even heavier on general good vibes. Set in the forever-flowers district of Haight-Ashbury, it was an eco-feminist New Age blast.

GAIA V. THE COSMOS

Despite the swelling enthusiasm, Gaia and the New Age always will be something of an uncomfortable fit, in part because Lovelock and Margulis refuse to speculate about cosmic matters. Gaian theory is very specifically about the Earth and in no way declares the solar system, galaxy, or universe to be alive. For some folks, especially New Age ecstatics, this stymies the urge to exultation, the heady, wondrous rush of knowing that all of

GAIA

creation is life and love. The great physicist Heisenberg is said
to have illustrated the particle-wave duality of nature that is the
basis of quantum theory by maintaining that the universe is not
made of matter or energy, but music! Lovelock says simply that
he does not know much about the universe as a whole and that
the Earth is plenty big enough for him, accessible not only by
the imagination but "within the realm of the senses"—less
exalted, but all in all a more visceral creed.

The fact that Lovelock's theory first arose by contrasting
the Earth to other planets could have led Gaia in quite the
opposite direction from favorite New Age scientists and theories.
Austrian physicist Fritjof Capra, author of the illuminating *The
Tao of Physics* and, most recently, *The Turning Point,* has stressed
the similarities between modern physics and Eastern philosophies, arguing that modern society is now undergoing a "paradigm shift" away from the mechanistic and toward an organic
model of the universe. Margulis and Capra have appeared at least
once on the same stage, in a New York City seminar at the Bank
Street College on "The New Paradigm," sponsored by the Elm-
wood Institute of Berkeley, California. Clearly the most influential of the New Age scientists, Capra soared through the
emerging vision of reality while Margulis showed slides from her
last journey through the ooze. Her painstaking argument that
the surface of the Earth operates as an organism were greeted as
strictly ho-hum. Of course, everybody in the room had for years
known that the Earth is alive. So is the universe, now that you
mention it.

Yet much as Jesus, the son of God, personalizes and human-
izes a remote and awesome deity, the mother goddess Gaia seems
to embody a host of abstract yearnings about nature and the
cosmos.

"Sounds exactly like the origin of a religion to me," says
Richard Dawkins, deftly summarizing the state of affairs. "It
would be a privilege to witness the birth of a new religion,
though I'm rather hostile to the notion myself." Lynn Margulis,
who otherwise holds little truck with Dawkins, has been more

69

extreme in her disdain. "The religious overtones of Gaia make me sick!" she exclaimed at an interview in 1986. At the time, Margulis compared the New Age distortions of Gaian theory to the corruption of genetics into eugenics (the study of improving inherited human characteristics, chiefly by discouraging propagation among so-called undesirables) and then to nazism. "The whole set of values can get so distorted." The woman reddened at the thought of being branded for such an unnatural crime.

Twenty years more relaxed than his collaborator, Lovelock makes the proper protestations, calls himself a "positive agnostic," and handles it all with aplomb.

> For every letter I got about the science of *Gaia: A New Look at Life on Earth* there were two concerning religion. I was very surprised. I think people need religion, and the notion of the Earth as a living planet is something to which they can obviously relate. At the least, Gaia may turn out to be the first religion to have a testable scientific theory embedded within it.

THE HEALING HERESY OF NATURE WORSHIP

For a time it seemed that Lovelock and Margulis might not be able to reconcile their attitudes toward the spiritual aspects of Gaia, as if religious differences would come between yet another couple, but their friendship and collaboration ran too deep. And while Margulis would not count herself a convert, Lovelock's gentle, nature-loving spirituality helped them to find common ground. In *Ages of Gaia* he writes:

> Thinking of the Earth as alive makes it seem, on happy days, in the right places, as if the whole planet were celebrating a sacred ceremony. Being on the Earth brings that same special feeling of comfort that attaches to the celebration of any religion when it is

seemly and when one is fit to receive. It need not suspend the critical faculty, nor can it prevent one from singing the wrong hymn or the right one out of tune.[11]

In the past year or two Margulis has loosened up considerably and made her peace with living Earth spirituality. "Gaia is less harmful than standard religion. It can be very environmentally aware. At least it is not human-centered," she concedes, summarizing what may become an emerging criterion for contemporary spiritual devotion.

Reverence for the natural world certainly seems to meet the spiritual demands of the current environmental crisis. Once the object of fearful, wondrous worship, before humanity rose to challenge and despoil, the restorative powers of nature may be invoked to save us from self-destruction. Or, as Lovelock and Margulis prefer to put it, before nature destroys us for forgetting who's the boss. But as either humankind's master or its sacred ward, isn't nature worship profane by the standards of traditional, human-centered Western religion? Isn't Gaian spirituality as heretical an idea to Christian, Moslem, and Jewish theologians as Gaian science is to Darwinist nonbelievers?

"Gaia is a great organizing principle for bringing people into religious experience, though perhaps not always to Christianity," observes James Morton, Dean of the Cathedral of St. John the Divine and a member of Lindisfarne.

It is a sad commentary that nature has not been part of Western theological processes since the Middle Ages. Modern theology must reincorporate the Earth. Recently, there has been a resurgence of contemporary creation theology that sees its task as within nature, as opposed to the fundamentalist creationists, who are explicitly against the notion of evolution. Unlike the fundamentalists, contemporary creationists do not believe that man is above nature, or that nature is just a

71

commodity for our use. Rather, we are of nature's stream.

The distinctly upper-crust New York clergyman, a large, graying, distinguished man with sparkling blue eyes, has been at his environmentalist crusade for more than a decade, well before giving Lovelock his first book party in the United States and helping to found the Gaia Institute.

Morton, a very practical man known for his political savvy, explains that Gaian spirituality might have been rejected as heresy back in the days when religions mostly vied with one another for adherents. But in an era like ours, the biggest competition to religion comes from apathy, alienation, and secular pursuits. Proudly reminding me that Lovelock has preached Sunday sermon at the cathedral several times, Morton knows religious energy when up it bubbles; he has worked hard to capture the excitement of New Age spirituality for his cathedral. Pointing out that St. John the Divine had commissioned Paul Winter to compose "Missa Gaia," a full-scale choral mass blending high Episcopalian pomp with sonorous earth tones, Morton concludes that

> the living Earth principle gives us strong images and metaphors that require an inclusive way of understanding, a religious way of comprehending the greater whole. After all, the word "religion" does mean, at its roots, to knit together. Not at all unlike the Gaian idea of global interdependence: environment and organisms knit together as one. In this way Gaia may prove less a set of specific beliefs than a way to reincorporate faith into daily life.

There Gaia might have stayed, an enchanting speculation born of solid scientific argument, promoted by a philosophical vanguard, and buoyed by countercultural affections, a stock player on the intellectual whole-grain circuit, evolving steadily or perhaps sinking into oblivion. But just as W. Ford Doolittle's thoughtful criticism helped to make a contender out of a hitherto chump, and Norman Myers's discerning skepticism gave the Gaia atlas such a prestigious range, the single most important event to date in Gaia's giddy, girlish life, the American Geophysical Union's 1988 Chapman Conference in San Diego, could have killed her. And it very nearly did. No matter how brilliant the insights of Lovelock, Margulis, Watson, and the others, scientists are human and often trust less to their own judgment than to official symbols and cues. The fact that 150 of their most respected peers from top universities and research institutions around the world were willing to spend a full week debating the pros and cons of Gaia theory meant that the debutante truly had come out into the world and was ready for some serious proposals.

IV

THE GREAT GAIA
SHOWDOWN

THE 1988 AGU CONFERENCE

A question of fundamental intellectual importance to the geosciences is whether the earth's climate
is regulated. The Gaia Hypothesis, introduced by Jim
Lovelock from England and Lynn Margulis from the
United States, surmises that interaction between the
biota and the physical and chemical environment is of
large enough intensity to serve in an active feedback
capacity for biogeoclimatologic control. On the other
hand, geochemical arguments have been advanced to
explain many of the environment changes over geological time, regardless of the contribution of life. Clearly,
the possibility of active climatic regulation systems and
the relative importance of feedback processes between
organic and inorganic components need to be examined in a frank, interdisciplinary setting.[1]

74   This formal working statement, written by Stephen Schneider
of the National Center for Atmospheric Research, Glenn Shaw

of the University of Alaska, and Penelope Boston of NASA, served as the basic proposal for the American Geophysical Union's Chapman Conference on the Gaia Hypothesis, held in San Diego in March 1988.

"It was an epochal event—a veritable United Nations of scientists in one large room, debating a single idea: the Gaia Hypothesis," writes J. E. Ferrell of the *San Francisco Examiner*.

> Microbiologists challenged atmospheric scientists. Oceanographers listened intently to volcanologists. Population biologists argued with geologists. Meteorologists, marine biologists, geochemists, geophysicists, botanists, space physicists, exobiologists, mathematicians and computer scientists wrangled, guffawed, laughed, drank, ate, quibbled and quarreled through five long days.[2]

Along with the AGU, NASA, the National Science Foundation (NSF), and the Mitre Corporation of McLean, Virginia, cosponsored the conference of 150 scientists who had traveled from dozens of universities and research centers around the world. The University of California, the Scripps Institute of Oceanography, and Harvard (albeit mostly as loyal opposition) were particularly well represented, as were the Max Planck Institute and several other universities of West Germany, Japan, Sweden, and of course Lovelock's England. And what Gaian event would be complete without cameo appearances from the likes of Brother John from the Bay Area's Institute of Immortalism, to balance off all of the left-brain karma.

"The AGU almost voted this conference down," said Schneider, shaking his head as he took in the sights of what also had become quite a media bazaar. Given week-long coverage by the two international arbiters of hard science, *Science* and *Nature* (a rare concurrence), the southern California conclave also had reporters from *New Scientist*, *Smithsonian*, *National Geographic*, and a host of general interest print and electronic news services

75

and independent producers, including representatives from the Middle East and Asia.

"A lot of people objected to its religious aspects, and wanted to take the world *Gaia* out of the title," Schneider recounted.

There's also a bit of ego, and some turf is involved in the debate. Some geochemists feel that Lovelock has taken a few geological observations about global systems, labeled them "Gaia," and presented it all as new findings to biologists and the general public. And some others think that Lovelock is flaky for calling the Earth alive. He is not flaky; the guy is brilliant. But thus far, the case for Gaia is way overstated, and now he and Margulis have to back it all up.

Rarely has there been a more tempting opportunity for Lovelock's critics to nail the eccentric Englishman and send Gaia to an early grave. Many would-be Gaia hunters had traveled to the conference, turning killer questions over and over in their minds: How does Gaia know when to react, over what time scales, and at what rate does this system operate? Is its perspective seconds, years, millennia, eons? Does Gaia operate continuously or by intervention? If only someone could catch Lovelock acknowledging that Gaia has a perspective, "knows" anything, or intervenes purposefully, he'd nail him, since that would mean he was saying that the planet has some sort of a mind, which is completely unproven and probably is unprovable and therefore is in the realms of religious mysticism and other weak-minded pursuits. But the wily old Brit never would fall for it. Lovelock probably would claim that Gaia has operated continuously for the past three and a half billion years and that like any other system, it is more active at some times than others, particularly when it is being perturbed.

What does the global system do when it is perturbed? Perhaps they could force Lovelock into a bad misstatement with questions along that line. Does Gaia ever overcompensate, or is this regulatory system perfect every time? If it is not perfect, what reasons are there to believe, for example, that a hundred-thousand-year ice age is Gaia overcompensating for a hot spell, when there is the much simpler explanation that an ice age is just an ice age, neither a correction nor a mistake? Who needs all this oscillating back and forth, all the overshooting? Isn't this whole theory unnecessary?

CIRCULAR REASONING 25,000 MILES AROUND?

Two contradictory criticisms of logic have dogged the Gaia Hypothesis—one, that it is too circular, and two, that it is not circular enough: whatever happens in the climate or environment, there always seems to be a Gaian response to explain it all away.

With this citation the *Oxford English Dictionary* defines circular reasoning: ". . . for he is proving the being of God from the truth of our faculties, and the truth of our faculties from the being of a God." The same logical flaw has frequently been attributed to Gaia—for Lovelock proves the existence of Gaia by the truth of an environment hospitable for life, and the truth of an hospitable environment by the existence of Gaia. Stephen Hawking calls this sort of logic the anthropic principle, which he paraphrases as, "We see the universe the way it is because we exist." And as Schneider challenges, "Does life optimize the environment? If you define present conditions as optimal, then all you've got is circular reasoning."[3]

Lovelock responds to the charge by explaining that life, as we define the carbon-based phenomenon, can exist only under a very limited set of circumstances, conditions that are not simply coincidental to the Earth's existence but that by necessity have been actively maintained. Life as we know it, for example, requires water, usually in the liquid form. Certainly the planet's surface temperature must be below the boiling point, or its water would boil off into space (as appears to have happened on

Venus). Mars may have several kilometers of frozen water on its surface, but that does not seem to have prompted life to emerge—although it is conceivable that certain ice-melting organisms could draw energy from the sun and melt down the water they need. For all practical purposes, Lovelock writes, "the existence of life and pre-life chemicals requires a temperature range of between 0 degrees and 50 degrees C. The Earth could not have been frozen, nor could it have been hot enough for the seas to boil."[4] As demonstrated by the Faint Young Sun Paradox, the sun is widely believed to have strengthened some 30 percent since the Earth was created, and according to standard physics and chemistry, the planet's surface temperature should therefore have risen above the boiling point. Instead our planet has held remarkably steady, actually cooling slightly in the face of the mounting heat. Lovelock proves the existence of Gaia by the truth that without active and continuous intervention over the past 3.5 billion years—the process that he calls Gaia—an environment hospitable to life would not exist.

It is easy to imagine creatures thriving in the vast ocean of liquid nitrogen that is said to flow on Triton, Neptune's moon, as though liquid, water or otherwise were the key to lifelike existence. Could there be great electric eels taking instinctive advantage of the supercold superconductivity that we humans award Nobel Prizes for? Perhaps one day some such discovery will radically amend our current assumptions about life in the solar system. But the first question Lovelock would ask is what those monster eels were doing to keep their environment nice and subzero cozy.

NASA biologist Penelope Boston aptly summarizes the contention that Gaian reasoning is not circular enough.

> The essence of Gaia is the negative feedback cycle, or what can be thought of as the Gaian switch. As a climate change occurs, there has to be a corresponding feedback in the biological system causing the change.

Bugs produce gas, gas has climatic and environmental effects, but does this result have a direct effect on the bugs?

In other words, the loop must be closed. Lovelock knew that this question would arise again and again, because no Gaian feedback system between life and the environment has ever been fully demonstrated. Not surprisingly, Boston concluded that "the most useful result the conference proposed would be to come to terms with the question 'What do we consider proof of Gaian feedback between organisms and physical systems?' "

The question of proof is a Catch-22 for any new theory. In order to get funding for research, it is often necessary to show that the theory is legitimate. And in order to prove that the theory is legitimate, research is required. Circular reasoning, establishment style. In the name of survival, Lovelock has become adept at ducking the Catch-22 diplomatically:

> I don't really care whether the Gaia Hypothesis is right or wrong, so much as whether it causes one to ask valuable questions. This is where science has really gone off the rails in recent years. Science is never right or wrong absolutely. This is a dreadful misconception. It's always making guesses and trying to refine them. Look at Newton. He made a damn good guess. You can still navigate all the way around the solar system using Newtonian mechanics, except possibly between Mercury and the sun. You hardly need Einstein at all. A bloody good guess.

Lindisfarne colleague William Thompson chimes in:

> The concept of proof is naive. Heuristics [rules of good judgment] are more important than the final outcome. The heuristics of the Gaia Hypothesis will lead to new insights, new abilities and relationships

that formerly were not seen. This is overwhelmingly valuable.

Twenty years of interesting questions are what led to the Gaia conference, but now the 150 scientists who attended wanted more. They wanted to be shown at least one system where Boston's bugs-gas-environment-bugs loop was indisputably closed. Or as some of the AGU elders confided, they would have been just as grateful to find no evidence and declare the Gaia theory unprovable once and for all.

THE GEOLOGISTS V. GAIA

"I'd hoped it would all go away," groaned Heinrich D. Holland, a geochemistry professor at Harvard University. The gentle, slyly charming man has the habit of saying, "If we had enough time, I could convince you . . . The Earth is *not* homeostatically controlled. Look at what controls oxygen and carbon dioxide in the atmosphere—a complicated system of physics, chemistry, and some biology."[5] To the Harvard geologist, living organisms are mere intermediaries in global processes that would go on anyway; the impact of life on the planet's atmospheric system, in Holland's view, is relatively trivial compared to the state of the Earth's crust. It's an argument over what is the bottom line.

Holland's attitude toward Gaian theory has become progressively more constructive due to a personal affection for Lovelock and a growing respect for his work. The only speaker other than Lovelock to get an ovation before presenting, Holland was clearly everyone's favorite Gaia critic; his very presence at the AGU conference did as much for Gaia as the attendance of the theory's supporters, if only because his participation demonstrated of itself that Gaia was at least worthy of profound scientific debate. As a result of the conference, Holland seems to have bent his opposition of life's climatological importance a bit: "The biosphere is one of several factors in regulating the atmosphere, more important in some cases than others. But it does not control. If this be Gaia," added the savvy diplomat with a beau geste of magnanimity, "then make the most of it."

Maverick Nobel laureate George Wald, professor emeritus at Harvard with Holland, is crusty and proud of it. Known for his support of a variety of peace-related and Third World causes, Wald is a frequent lecturer where liberal-minded crowds are gathered, including the 1985 Amherst College conference on Gaia. Unlike his suave colleague, Wald declined to attend the AGU meeting, and he minces no words in expressing his disdain for the living Earth theory. "Gaia is a buzzword for bringing in the customers. Somehow it commands attention to what is essentially old news. I teach my students that the stars are alive. Planets are dead ashes, hangers-on of the sun."

Carl Sagan has compared Gaia to UFO's, noting that both hypotheses have strong religious appeal and that the world would be a much more interesting place if either proved correct. Sagan is right. In an almost Darwinian reflex of mental reproduction, human imagination hungers for life and imputes it wherever plausible. How much more intriguing to think of the Stonehenge, the Bermuda Triangle, or sacred Mount Fujiyama as emanating some sort of life force. And how much more compelling is the great Mother Earth than a behemoth hunk of rock, saltwater, and gases spinning in the void. If scientific facts were determined by popular vote, both Gaia and UFO's would likely be elected true. Why not give life the benefit of the doubt?

Robert A. Berner, a Yale geologist and critic of Gaia, also warns against being led astray by the earthy temptress. "The scientific attraction of Gaia is that it prompts everyone to look for feedback mechanisms, preferably negative, which are neat and satisfying to find," he says. That's why the arguments made by geologists like Walker, Berner, Sagan, and even Wald should be considered and reconsidered, because they suffer from an emotional disadvantage. Geology is a subject holding little enchantment for most people; hair grows faster than continents

81

drift. The much more captivating notion of a great planetary organism circling around the sun, sustaining and adjusting its body much as we keep ourselves physically healthy and content, is enchanting to many, but it could well be dead wrong.

Perhaps coincidentally, the AGU Gaia conference seems to have accelerated a holistic tendency in contemporary geology. At the AGU's annual meeting, held about six months later, all of the talk was interdisciplinary and about the need to draw together the disparate parts of the geosciences.

> According to Don L. Anderson, the legendary seismologist from the California Institute of Technology, more people now are starting to appreciate that you have to treat the earth as a system; you can't just look at part of it. Geomagnetic people [those who study the earth's magnetic field] used to just look at the core and not worry about the mantle, but we now know that they are interconnected. Likewise, until recently, the interrelationship between the buoyant, continental lithosphere [the outer part of the solid earth] and the mantle had been ignored, except in a few older papers.[6]

Peter Olson, a Johns Hopkins University geologist, agrees that an interdisciplinary attitude is emerging but despairs that research is just too complex: "The fact that there are physical problems and chemical ones, the fact that the data are seismological while the inferences are geodynamical [means] no one person can handle the whole thing."[7]

"GEOLOGY" IS THE STUDY OF "GAIA"

Lovelock's strategy for getting the AGU to let Gaia "handle the whole thing," as an organizing principle for the bewildering array of earth science disciplines and subspecialties, was to avoid presenting his theory as a radical new solution. Instead Lovelock sought to demonstrate that his ideas are descended from geological orthodoxy and thus are quite honorably old. So on the opening morning of the conference Lovelock mounted the stage, surveyed his audience, and wrapped himself in the flag.

The idea that the Earth is alive is probably as old as humankind. But the first public expression of it as a fact of science was by James Hutton, the great Scottish scientist known as the father of geology. Hutton, who taught us that the planet's crust is not some rigid, crystalline structure but a slow-moving fluid dynamic, said at a meeting of the Royal Society of Edinburgh in 1785 that the Earth was a superorganism and that its proper study should be physiology.

Take a shot at Gaia and you are taking a shot at the whole honorable history of geology, Lovelock dared the itchy assassins in the crowd.

Hutton went on to compare the cycling of the nutritious elements in the soil, and the movement of water from the oceans to the land, with the circulation of the blood. But his ideas of the living Earth died out because of the rapid scientific development and specialization that have taken place over the past century and a half. Since his time, geology and biology have evolved as completely separate sciences. It is now time to reject the apartheid of Victorian science and reintegrate the study of what truly is a living Earth. After all, the etymology of *geology* does trace back to Gaia.

New theories invariably are fleshed out with historical precedents to prove that their ideas are orthodox—proponents now date their Gaia as far back as Pythagoras, whose mystical love of numbers led him in the sixth century B.C. to deduce that

83

the Earth was spherical and alive, an idea rediscovered in the seventeenth century by Johannes Kepler, the German astronomer who heard the music of the spheres and thought our planet a great round beast. But in James Hutton, Lovelock has rediscovered an even weightier predecessor. The Scottish geologist was the first to demonstrate that the Earth is not thousands of years old, as had been held from biblical and Homeric times all the way through the eighteenth century, but that it is virtually immortal, with a history so fathomless that it has "no vestige of a beginning,—no prospect of an end."[8]

Through a convoluted mixture of theology, philosophy, and field observations of key fossilized rock formations, the great Scottish geologist discovered that the processes of geological uplift and upheaval restore the land surfaces of the Earth, undoing the damage done by wind, rain, waves, and so forth. Previously it had been assumed that the Earth's history was simply the story of erosion—that weather depleted land surfaces, washing whatever shook loose into the seas to disappear forever. What Hutton learned was that after enough run-off from the land had piled up as silt and sediment, the weight of it all generated enough heat on crustal layers below to start a churning process whereby some of what had sunk in earlier centuries or milennia heaved back up to the top. Scientists at the end of the eighteenth century were not equipped to calculate how long it had gone on, but Hutton sensed that the planet's age was in the billions of years.

Instead of a hapless orb, steadily losing the relatively little land mass it had into its vast waters, Hutton came to believe that the Earth was, as Stephen Jay Gould describes it, a self-renewing world machine. In his latest book, *Time's Arrow, Time's Cycle*, he charges that Hutton has been overrated by historians of science because the vision of an eternally churning world machine caused the Scottish geologist to lose the sense of time passing in the traditional linear, day-after-day fashion, which the Harvard paleobotanist calls time's "arrow." Gould asserts that Hutton's discovery of the immensity of the Earth's age was so overwhelming that eventually the discoverer refused to believe that time passes at all—that Hutton saw time only as the endless cycle of geological uplift and restoration, as though so entranced by the eternal repetition of the seasons that he paid no notice to the passing years.

Not surprisingly, Gould, a critic of the Gaia theory, pays scant attention to what Lovelock sees as Hutton's culminating insight, which is that the Earth should be regarded as a living organism. By theorizing that the planet is a living entity Hutton satisfies both of Gould's temporal modes. Organisms replenish themselves and restore their surfaces against the ravages of the elements very much in the cyclical manner of the hypothetical self-renewing world machine. But no one, certainly not Hutton, who also had trained as a physician, would assume earthly creatures to be immortal; from birth to death, time passes straight as an arrow. In the case of living organisms, time frisbees, but not forever.

SCIENCE V. THE HISTORY OF SCIENCE

As Lovelock and Margulis quickly learned, most of their scientific colleagues at the AGU conference were all too sharply aware of the passage of time. Unlike scholars in the humanities and social sciences, who not only prefer proof of intellectual ancestry but often require it before they will accord an idea serious consideration, physical scientists sometimes dismiss the history of their discipline as little more than a chronicle of what has been outmoded and left behind. For example, there are probably as many art historians as there are professional fine artists in the United States today, but historians of science, compared to the number of working scientists, account for barely an asterisk. In the what-have-you-discovered-for-me-lately world of science, pedigree rarely pays the dues.

Margulis followed Lovelock with a stinging attack on the antihistorical, antibiological prejudices of the current U.S. sci-

85

entific establishment, with a few barbs pointed at conference cosponsors NASA and NSF. But just as Schneider had succeeded in organizing the AGU conference by circulating a formal statement, Margulis, along with her protégé Gregory Hinkle, submitted an up-to-date summary of the Gaia Hypothesis that stands as the most precise formulation so far:

> The Gaia Hypothesis states that the Earth's surface conditions are regulated by the activities of life. Specifically, the Earth's atmosphere is maintained far from chemical equilibrium with respect to its composition of reactive gases, oxidation-reduction state, alkalinity-acidity, albedo, and temperature. This environmental maintenance is effected by the growth and metabolic activities of the sum of the organisms, i.e., the biota. The hypothesis implies that were life to be eliminated, the surface conditions on Earth would revert to those interpolated for a planet between Mars and Venus. Although the detailed mechanisms of Earth surface control are poorly understood, they must involve interactions between approximately thirty million species of organisms. Microorganisms, animals, and plants, all of which grow exponentially, may affect, for example, radiation absorption; polymer production; gas exchange; hydrogen ion concentration in solution, color, and albedo alteration; and water relations. Thus they store within themselves potential mechanisms of Gaian function and are probably of crucial importance to modulation and maintenance of the Earth's surface conditions. Potential for exponential growth, especially of microbes, coupled with community potential provides reserve mechanisms for qualitative changes of many processes with profound environmental consequences.[9]

Lovelock is in basic agreement with the above interpretation, but he does not limit his vision to the Earth's surface. Rather, he sees Gaia as the planetary whole, right on down to the molten core. This is a disagreement of long standing between the two collaborators, and it is probably the largest difference they have, theoretically and rhetorically, although it is mostly a matter of degree—kind of like defining the fruit as with or without the pit, except that in this case the pit takes up most of the room. In practical terms, however, most knowledge about the Earth is limited to its surface and atmosphere, so when it comes to questions on the science of Gaia, the two old friends stand hand in hand on the stage.

GAIA GETS THE
INTENTIONS KNOCKED OUT OF HER

Pro and con debates bristled for the entire week of the AGU conference, usually in polite tones. However, one lengthy, articulate attack launched by a young Berkeley theoretical ecologist named James Kirchner stands out as one of the most effective, certainly the most vicious.

Kirchner challenged the very validity of Gaia as a hypothesis and even as a topic for discussion. Observing that a confused variety of logically distinct theories had been offered under the single banner of the "Gaia Hypothesis," the young scientist argued that "many impassioned debates may result simply from a misunderstanding of which of the multiple hypotheses is on the table at any one time."[10]

In the interests of clarity, Kirchner went on to propose—and trash—five separate Gaian hypotheses: (1) influential Gaia, the formulation that life is but one participant in the global system, was dismissed as old news; (2) coevolutionary Gaia, simply the assertion that life and environment evolve as a coupled system, also was condemned as unoriginal and potentially misleading; (3) homeostatic Gaia, the traditional, strong

Gaian notion of biotic control of the global environment, was shunted aside as ill-defined and circular; (4) teleological Gaia, the early implication that Gaia operated with intent and purpose, was criticized as a "transparent tautology"; and (5) optimizing Gaia, with life's collective purpose specified as creating a perfect planet, was denounced as tautological and internally contradictory.

Kirchner stunned the audience. Some were aghast at his stinging, dismissive manner; many were impressed by the deft analytical dissection, especially those who sympathized with his anti-Gaian intent. Everyone was eager to see how the senior British scientist would respond to the young Turk's taunts. Virtually all of Kirchner's attack had been based on *Gaia: A New Look at Life on Earth*, ignoring Lovelock and Margulis's voluminous revisions and clarifications since the book's publication in 1979, most of which Lovelock had summarized in his opening address, which Kirchner also had ignored. (Later, when pressed, the young sciolist did not deny his selectively adversarial scholarship, remarking simply that misconceptions still lingered from the early days and the service he performed was to dispel them.)

Lovelock could have ticked off counterpoint after counterpoint, particularly on Kirchner's charges concerning circular reasoning and Gaian intentions. Instead the elder statesman raised his hand from the audience, mounted the stage, thanked the young man for a most stimulating analysis and defended Gaia only to the extent that it had led him to discover the atmospheric gases dimethyl sulfide and methyl iodide, and sat down. A forty-five minute excoriation answered by no more than ninety seconds of pleasantries. Lovelock, by denying nothing, stunned the multitude. Kirchner was taken aback and mumbled something about Lovelock's graciousness.

Several days later Lovelock explained his approach:

Young Kirchner's attack was rather invigorating. I saw no point in making the obvious logical arguments about his attacking old material, because those who cared enough about the subject matter knew that already, or would come to realize it over the course of the meeting or thereafter. Or they might remember that they had known how extensively Gaia has been revised, and that they had forgotten it in the heat of the debate. To counterattack wouldn't have much point, would it? Much better to wave your hat and get out of the way.

Kirchner's attack on Gaia was ultimately less concerned with the theory's logical viability than with the intellectual integrity of its formulator, which is one important reason why Lovelock's graciousness was so effective in response. Yet the challenge provoked interest and debate for much of the conference, leading to useful delineations of the varying "strengths" of the Gaia theory. In fact, he succeeded nobly in his avowed purpose of dispelling the misconceptions that, despite all of Lovelock's recent work on Gaia, had indeed lingered for a decade. As *Science* magazine put it, Gaia "got the intentions knocked out of her"[11] and thereby became a scientifically respectable mode of inquiry. Whatever his own intentions, Kirchner stands as a valuable contributor to the development of Gaian theory.

GAIA: WEAK, STRONG, INTENSE, AND OBVIOUS

The case against Gaia remains stronger by far than the case for Gaia. Though a public opinion poll might confirm Gaia's greater appeal than the conventional geological explanations of the Earth's system, a jury verdict based on the facts as presented at the AGU conference and since would, at best, be hung.

Fortunately, it is no longer a yea or nay situation. The debate prompted by Kirchner's attack on the logical rigor of Gaia led to the delineation of the relative "strengths" of the

89

Gaia Hypothesis, depending on how it is worded. Lovelock complained about it afterward, but the theory always has been difficult to formulate precisely, and the wording has been updated periodically over the years. So despite Margulis and Hinkle's fastidious submission, the phraseology of Gaia is fair game for revision, though Lovelock does not recognize these distinctions.

There were three basic choices: life collectively (a) influences, (b) modifies, or (c) controls the global environment.

Weak Gaia, by which life simply has some influence, is undeniable, and because it attributes such an insignificant role to the planet's living organisms, it is essentially the choice of the critics. This version appeals to those who do not think that life is crucial to the operation of the planetary system. At the outset of the conference, a "weak Gaia" would have been the most popular formulation, had a poll been taken. Opponents Holland and Kasting sum up the opposition consensus as thus: "The biosphere is one of several factors that affect the composition of the ocean and the atmosphere. Its effects are more important in some cases than others, but there is no compelling reason to suppose that the biosphere controls the whole system."

The most notable exception even to this modest concession is an article in *Nature* (which, ironically, has published some of Lovelock's most important work). In "Is the Earth Alive or Dead?" the best that reporter David Lindley can manage is a nod to the Gaians' "subversive victory: they provoked a meeting at which people in one discipline talked to people in others, and discovered they had mutual interests."[12] Then the British journal inaccurately concludes that Lovelock is moving away from his theory in favor of "more controversial ideas to worry about."[13]

Moderate Gaia—the biota modify the environment and make it significantly less extreme—was a good bargaining position between the Gaians and the traditionalists. This formulation appeals to those who feel that life collectively may be important, but not regulatory, to the global system. *Science* magazine, *Nature*'s American, even-more-orthodox arch-competitor, has published next to nothing by Lovelock but nonetheless landed close to the moderate Gaia position. In an upbeat article entitled "No Longer Willful, Gaia Becomes Respectable," Richard A. Kerr writes,

> Life may not control climate, for example, intentionally or by chance, but it surely participates in the climate system, everyone agrees. Life also clearly affects the composition of the sea and the air. Recent discoveries prompted by the Gaia hypothesis may even lead to the elucidation of new links between life and its surroundings.[14]

Kerr concludes that "now that Gaia has been cloaked in more fashionable garb, there should be more testable links between the living and nonliving worlds."[15] By the end of the conference, this version of the theory actually may have been the most popular, at least in its upbeat, what's-next outlook.

Strong Gaia holds that the biota collectively control the Earth's environment and that they effectively run the show. "Living organisms must regulate their environment in order to survive," declared Lovelock in his opening address. Aside from Margulis and Lovelock's protégé, ocean biologist Andrew Watson, and several others, some of whom were reluctant to be identified, there were few converts to this extreme. There was, however, a good deal more respect for this as a tenable, nonmetaphorical position. Not surprisingly, none of the scientific journals covering the AGU meeting has adopted this stance, although *New Scientist*, the adventurous British journal, starts its generally glowing article by heralding the new era: "It was, by common consent, the coming of age of Gaia as a subject for respectable scientific inquiry."[16]

Many of those who attended the conference, critics and supporters alike, dwelt on how fascinating they found the interdisciplinary scientific exchange. How unlike so many other meetings, where presenters would deliver their papers, take their criticisms, and leave. Most of the journals remarked on this intensity of the conference's intellectual fusion; even *Nature* managed a "stimulating." Each session was packed from beginning to end, including the last one on a very sunny Friday morning. During the breaks, opponents huddled together, ignoring their food, trying to reach rapprochement—much preferable to ideologues retreating to one another's predictable company. Lovelock is masterful at this sort of consensus-building because he gravitates to those critics he respects. For example, as a result of one such tête-à-tête, he and hard-line geochemist James Kasting are planning to coauthor an article for *Biophysical Review Letters*.

Preference for a particular "strength" of the Gaia Hypothesis seems to vary not only with where one stands on the various geological and biological issues but also, quite literally, with where one normally sits. Out in Lovelock's verdant hamlet in Cornwall, a strong Gaia seems the natural and correct hypothesis. So too must it when mucking around in those microbial mats of which Margulis is so fond. Conversely, most scientific laboratories are designed expressly to keep nature out, except in processed little pieces. So are San Diego convention halls, where the air-conditioning hums. It is not that scientists are unaware of the bias inherent in their surroundings, but their bravado of objectivity, the hallmark of this dispassionate profession, makes it very difficult for most researchers to admit that they could succumb to any consistent prejudice or subversion. Ironically, most of those scientists who consider themselves masters of their own surroundings argue that overall, life forms are mastered by their environment.

Lovelock acknowledges that the bucolic setting of his home and laboratory predispose him to attribute regulatory power to living organisms. Between the braying peacocks, the meadows, the thousands of trees, and all the rest of life that joins in, the biota does seem comfortably in charge. Of course, the English country gentleman is quick to argue that his environment is a much more appropriate place to study nature than are the big university laboratories and lecture halls where many of his colleagues and critics toil. It would be interesting to poll scientists on their opinions of Gaia and correlate the results with the amount of time they spend in the laboratory versus time in the field.

EVOLVING TOWARD GAIA

Much as Marxism started out as an impassioned and didactic analysis of inequity during the Industrial Revolution and then evolved backward through time into a class-struggle theory of human history that explained how nineteenth-century Europe had reached its sorry state, Gaia began primarily as a vision of a magnificent living organism and has grown roots as a theory of how life and environment have coevolved to become such a creature. Ever since what Margulis refers to as "the original bacterial takeover of the Earth," the biota have both consumed and constituted an increasing proportion of the global environment. Once barren, the surface of the planet now not only hosts life but is composed extensively of organisms and their remains. Not just in relatively purified forms, like the fossil fuels coal and oil, but deeply embedded throughout the environment. As Lovelock frequently points out, even the oldest rocks on Earth, dating back some 3.8 billion years, shows signs of organic content.

Gaia's pros and cons at the AGU conference and in subsequent publications have centered on two basic areas of inquiry: (1) the operating principles of the living Earth system, and (2) the specific roles of life in regulating the contemporary environment. But time and again, particularly when hard evidence is lacking, the debate wanders to the logic of evolution, in order to determine whether the situation in dispute ever could have come to be. Geological evolution and biological evolution have been separate disciplines for so long that the Gaia conference at times sounded like a swap meet for historical ideas. No consensus

93

on the evolution of the planet and the life it bears ever will be reached, because the topic is so broad and easy to speculate about and because throwing around billions of years like Monopoly money is, for committed Earth historians, just too much fun. Nonetheless, Gaia has helped to forge a new synthesis of disparate evolutionary disciplines, and from various stages in the planet's history have emerged coherent images—of cataclysm, horror, and miraculous recovery.

V

CATASTROPHE AND THE EVOLUTION OF THE EARTH: A GAIAN HISTORY OF THE PLANET

ORDER OUT OF CHAOS

Gaia's conception was so tumultuous that the canyon of eternity still rings with primal screams. Every minute of every day for the past 4.55 billion years, the Earth has been peppered by fragments from the same supernova star explosion that created it and the rest of the solar system. Though it has been impossible to determine whether the star ripped apart as it passed too closely to the sun's gravitational field or simply exploded because it had reached the end of life, studies of meteorites, moon rocks, and ancient terrestrial stones, all of which contain radioactive isotopes that decay with almost Swiss-watch precision, confirm the solar system's thermonuclear origins.

For much of the first billion years—known appropriately as the Hadean aeon, for the hellish volcanic upheaval and molten disorder that raged—the whole planet burned as a nuclear reactor, as the radioactive uranium, potassium, and thorium left over from the primordial bomb blast decayed. The element hydrogen consumed all available oxygen to form water in the center of the Earth, which grew so hot that it shot in geysers to

95

the upper atmosphere and vaporized. The water vapor, ammonia, methane, and hydrogen sulfide of the primitive atmosphere were laced with potassium cyanide gas and formaldehyde. All but the tiniest meteorites crashed right to the surface, unimpeded by what at that point was less a protective blanket than a gaseous sieve.

Gradually, primitive systems began to take shape. Called "dissipative structures" by Belgian chemist Ilya Prigogyne, who won the 1977 Nobel Prize for his work in this field, systems such as tornadoes and whirlpools formed, defined from the chaos by their distinct boundaries and coherent, rhythmical behavior. Like bicycles, which gain stability from their motion, dissipative structures show the markedly antichaotic behavior of increasing their level of organization as they absorb more energy, that is, by "dissipating" the energy available from the environment. For example, a whirlpool will spin sharp as a funnel when the stream that feeds it runs swift, no matter from which direction the water flows, but the whirlpool loses its shape when the water slows to a trickle this is quite unlike an ocean wave, which is a simpler, less-organized structure that usually is deformed and diminished by water flowing in from a tangential or opposing direction.

Prigogyne's scholarly goal has been to describe how order and life swirled out of the utter confusion of primordial Earth. In his best-known book, *Order Out of Chaos*, the chemist describes some of the mechanisms that convert randomness into the rhythmic, predictable order of dissipative structures. One of the most important of these processes is known as a "chemical clock." You know how sometimes rhythmic clapping will spontaneously emerge from an audience's random applause? Prigogyne has shown that chemical clocks work like this, switching steadily between general applause and rhythmic clapping, like a clock's ticking.

In the spirit of Kant, Voltaire, and the other philosophers of the eighteenth-century Enlightenment, who saw the universe as having been wound up and left to run by a clockmaker God,

Prigogyne has demonstrated that, at least at the molecular level, matter ticks methodically from chaos to order.

> Oversimplifying somewhat, we can say that in a chemical clock all molecules change their chemical identity *simultaneously* at regular intervals. If the molecules can be imagined as blue or red, we would see their change of color following the rhythm of the chemical clock reaction. Obviously such a situation can no longer be described in terms of chaotic behavior. A new type of order has emerged.[1]

A. G. Cairns-Smith, a geochemist at the University of Glasgow, describes the dissipative processes of crystallization, advancing the fascinating theory that early life evolved from rock and mineral crystals. Moved by the exquisitely complex, eerily lifelike crystalline structures that can be found flourishing like flowerbeds in undisturbed caves, the author of *Seven Clues to the Origin of Life* observes that crystals can appear spontaneously in solution, then grow and spread much as life forms might, until all of the available area is filled. With evolutionary doctrine so flawlessly orthodox that Richard Dawkins has become one of the theory's most enthusiastic supporters, Cairns-Smith contends that classical Darwinian natural selection existed even before life began, and that crystals competed with one another, developing to higher and higher levels of complexity in order to crowd out rivals for prime space on cave walls and other "fertile" areas. He concludes that these complex silicate structures were the original replicators, gradually giving way to a host of more efficient carbon-based organic replicators that eventually culminated in DNA.

FROM MEMBRANES TO EARLY LIFE

The most important organic dissipative structures to emerge in the prebiotic world were phospholipid membranes, complex fatty compounds insoluble in water and bound by the element phosphorous into intricate, semipermeable structures. These membranes generally are recognized as the precursors of life. Unlike other encapsulating structures found in nature, it is believed that simply by their makeup and structure, even prelife membranes could hold potentially reactive solutions close to each other without letting them merge, permitting certain chemicals in and water out, or the reverse, depending on the conditions of the immediate environment.

Possibly this extraordinary degree of purely chemical, non-living organization was accomplished with the aid of chemical-clock reactions switching in and out of synchrony to permit the alternating discharge and absorption of reactive chemical components. However it was accomplished, life could not have arisen prior to the existence of membranes. "The membrane makes possible that discrete unit of the microcosm, the bacterial cell," write Margulis and Sagan. "Most scientists feel that lipids combined with proteins to make translucent packages of lifelike matter before the beginning of life itself. No life without a membrane of some kind is known."[2]

The chemistry of the transition from prebiotic membranes to the earliest life forms has long been the object of speculation. Sherwood Chang of NASA Ames Research Center suggests that life began at the interface of liquid, solid, and gaseous surfaces, a juncture where there would be a lively energy exchange and where membranes and other dissipative structures easily could form. Peter Westbroek, a biochemist from the University of Leiden, declares simply that "life is located at the intersection of rocks, water, and air. It is a geochemical process."

In 1953 at the University of Chicago, Harold C. Urey, the great Nobel laureate chemist, together with graduate student Stanley Miller, tried to duplicate this "geochemical process" of life creation with their now-immortal experiment. For a week they bombarded a mock-up of the primordial atmosphere of ammonia, water vapor, hydrogen, and methane with electrical bolts meant to simulate lightning. Complex chains of molecules formed, broke up, and recombined by absorbing the jolts of power, successfully creating two protein constituents—the amino acids alanine and glycine—as well as several other organic substances previously produced only by life processes. Since then, almost every basic building block of primitive life has been produced under simulative laboratory conditions, but never has a living organism thus been chemically created by man.

After a billion years of random collisions, warmed by the sun and jolted by lightning bolts, the earliest microorganisms glistened in shallow coastal pools, and Gaia, to the extent she exists, was born. It was anything but a triumphant event. For the first billion years of her life, Gaia would have seemed a shy child. Virtually all Archaean life hid out in the mud to escape the lethal rays of the sun.

Margulis and Sagan devote a large portion of *Microcosmos* to this primordial era, and Lovelock also gives it a long chapter in his book. Once shelved as arcane, academic speculation with no practical value, studies of the early aeon of anerobic life are now being widely reexamined for potential clues to technological innovation. Fermentation, the basic metabolic process of early life, is the comparatively low-energy process of molecular break-down, and it takes place in the darkness.

The same decomposing process that bubbled from those bacteria embedded in the ooze today gives us products like wine, cheese, and soy sauce. And it promises, through genetic engineering techniques currently under development, to yield a new generation of microbes that break down and digest a grand variety of toxic substances. Suffice it to say here that after a billion years of fermentation, Gaia burst loose and nearly popped her cork for good.

THE OXYGEN METAMORPHOSIS

The greatest threat earthly life ever has faced came from a million-year flood of oxygen into the atmosphere. While the

manner and sequence of this conversion of the Earth's atmosphere from anerobic to oxygen-based are still disputed, with
varying emphases placed on biological and geological causes,
there is little argument that photosynthesis was the mechanism
for this change. "Before the advent of photosynthesis, there was
virtually no oxygen, maybe 1 percent of what it is now," observes
living Earth critic Holland.

The blue-green cyanobacteria that Margulis discovered to
be the ancestors of modern chloroplasts, and therefore of all
modern photosynthesis, were the first to emerge from the dark
fermentative womb of early life. By a trial-and-error process that
undoubtedly was very gradual, these bacterial pioneers learned
how to survive what to all organisms was deadly solar radiation.
Eventually they developed the ability to use these rays to split
molecules of water, which was as prevalent then as it is now,
into its hydrogen and oxygen constituents. The hydrogen then
was combined with the carbon dioxide that abounded in the
early Earth atmosphere, making sugars and carbohydrates. Not
surprisingly, a process that uses sunlight yields much greater
energy than a process that hides from it; photosynthesis generally
outproduces fermentation in its yield of cellular energy in the
form of ATP (adenosine triphosphate) molecules, by an average
ratio of about three to one. Just as in nuclear physics, where
particle fusion generates more energy than does fission, the
photosynthesis of new bonds proved more powerful than fermentative decay.

In a world covered with water, the cyanobacteria became
conquerors, rapidly covering the planet's damp land surfaces in
a tacky scum. Water stripped of hydrogen leaves a byproduct of
oxygen, a highly reactive element that sets out immediately to
find new mates. At first the oxygen was absorbed by metals as
rust, and by other gases, particularly methane, that abounded in
the environment. But after a million years or more of photosynthesis, where the oxygen producers gradually replaced the fermentative, methanogenic bacteria, the environment could no
longer suck up the poisonous O_2. As the fossil record indicates,

somewhere around 2.5 billion years ago oxygen flooded the atmosphere, exterminating anerobic life every bit as efficiently as global storms of chlorine, cyanide, or hydrogen sulfide, the preferred gas of those stench-loving anerobes, would kill us today.

Even the cyanobacteria were poisoned by the oxygen they emitted, much as any living organism can be killed by immersion in its own wastes. So in their second evolutionary coup, doubtless the result of milennia of working contact with the dangerous gas, the cyanobacteria essentially learned how to breathe the oxygen waste product of their own metabolism. Aerobic respiration, essentially controlled combustion used to break down carbohydrates into carbon dioxide and water, is marvelously efficient, yielding up to eighteen times as much ATP energy as does fermentation. "Cyanobacteria now had both photosynthesis which generated oxygen and respiration which consumed it. They had found their place in the sun,"[3] write Margulis and Sagan. A comparable achievement for humanity might be to learn how to purify the noxious gases our society emits, particularly the metabolic exhaust gas of carbon dioxide, and render them breathable air.

Gradually, other types of microorganisms learned the photosynthetic and respiratory tricks of the cyanobacteria. Most anerobic bacteria that did not adapt were killed off during the oxygen crisis. Those that survived did so by burrowing even deeper into their airless pockets; they still live today by avoiding oxygen, hiding out in such places as swampy stinkholes, termite intestines, and human guts, where they occasionally rebel. "The submission of the anoxic ecosystems to domination by the oxic was somewhat like the Norman conquest with the Archaean Saxons driven to a subservient underground position—the lower classes—from which, it is often said, they have never escaped,"[4] writes Lovelock.

By the end of the Proterozoic era, the atmospheric concentration of O_2 had soared from negligible to 21 percent. Margulis and Lovelock theorize that stromatolite microbial communities

101

proliferated during this era in a purely Gaian response to the flood of poisonous gas. Groups of anerobes like the ones found in the microbial mats of Laguna Figueroa teamed up with oxygen-loving cyanobacteria and formed multilayered confederacies. These bacterial colonies popped up in dome, cone, and cauliflower shapes in bays, lagoons, and warm coastal seas all over the planet. (This response of surface eruptions to the infusion of oxygen, Lovelock ventures, was not unlike the skin eruptions of adolescents undergoing the hormonal turmoil of puberty.) Without any central plan or forethought, this Gaian response was simply the result of the cyanobacteria's reflexive opportunism when faced with abundant new supplies of food and air. At innumerable locations around the globe, the microorganisms that had ignited the oxygen-pollution crisis gradually mitigated the problem they had caused by drawing down the powerful gas as they breathed.

The net effect of this global spread of microbial communities, the Gaian scientists believe, was the regulation and stabilization of oxygen some 2.5 billion years ago at the biota's "mute consensus" of 21 percent. Direct descendants of those cyanobacteria mildew your shower curtain if the bathroom is too damp, threaten the prehistoric cave paintings at Lascaux, and, according to Gaian theory, power the photosynthesis that helps maintain oxygen at the same 21-percent proportion today.

Lovelock's taste for the dramatic once led him refer to the radical metamorphosis of the atmosphere and environment as the oxygen holocaust, but critics quickly pounced on the flaw. "Why would Gaia nearly poison herself to death?" demands Schneider. How can a biological system that nearly asphyxiates itself be said to operate for the benefit of life? Lovelock has since softened his narrative considerably: "Between the Archaean and Proterozoic the appearance of oxygen as a dominant atmospheric gas was the primary event and marked a profound change in the Earth's geophysiological state."[5] Lovelock compares this to puberty, with oxygen playing the role of pituitary hormone.

The truth appears to lie somewhere between holocaust and

acne. A majority of the Earth's species seems to have perished from the deadly poisoning, a trauma less like the tribulations of puberty than like a near-death experience. Yet those who charge that this upwelling of poison disproves life's environmental control make the same mistake of intent usually leveled at the Gaians. The emergence of an oxygen-dominated atmosphere was the result of biological evolution, changing chemical conditions in the environment, and, as is explored in greater detail in the next chapter, a steadily strengthening sun. The biota simply reacted collectively to their relentlessly changing environment, and in a manner that ultimately transformed that environment. No decisions were taken one way or the other, but after a long, deep whiff of oxygen, shy-girl Gaia became a very robust woman.

LADY CATASTROPHE

Imagine a heroine haunted, plagued by inexplicable catastrophes yet stronger and more beautiful for each tragedy that befalls her. Her body has been impregnated with alien metals, leading us to believe that she has been shot at least five times, perhaps as many as 150 times, in her life, possibly even by the same dark, faceless assailant. Some of her most ghastly wounds appear to have been self-inflicted. Whatever the sources of her misery, we know that as frequently as every few months, life is nearly taken from this woman; fever and chills convulse her frame, phlegm chokes her lungs, and huge portions of her skin burn away. Yet to charge attempted murder or suicide would be quite beside the point, since within a week or so the good woman is invariably up from her sickbed, her body regenerated to a level of life and spirit higher than ever before.

Our planet is now believed to have been plunged since its birth into recurrent cataclysms of unfathomable horror, many as devastating as the oxygen crisis, each lasting for hundreds of thousands of years. Stephen Jay Gould believes that there have been at least five great episodes of mass extinction, possibly

103

many more, in which up to 90 percent of all species were extinguished. With his widely accepted theory of punctuated equilibrium, developed with colleague Niles Eldredge, Gould was among the first to recognize that catastrophe is integral to the processes of evolution: "For punctuated equilibrium, as its essential statement, accepts the literal record of geologically abrupt appearance and subsequent stasis as a reality for most species, not an expression of true gradualism filtered through an imperfect fossil record."[6]

Many other geologists now believe that catastrophes of comparable scale may have befallen the Earth one hundred times or more. Much as Hutton analyzed areas of fossilized sediment for patterns of deposition to discover the existence of geological upheaval, contemporary paleobotanists tracking evolution through fossilized plants and animals have discovered abrupt mass extinctions occurring on a what appears to be a regular basis. Enhanced by modern chemical analysis and radioactive carbon-14 dating techniques, there seems to be the beginning of a consensus that every twenty-six to thirty million years our planet suffers a fate a thousand times worse than if all the world's nuclear arsenals exploded at once. Or, as Lovelock describes it, equivalent in destructive energy to the detonation of thirty Hiroshima-size bombs exploded over every square mile of the surface of the Earth!

E. G. Kaufman of the University of Colorado at Boulder observes that these periodic catastrophies result in terrible mass extinctions that annihilate 50 to 90 percent of ecologically and genetically diverse global species within intervals of five hundred thousand to three million years. Explosions and catastrophes have been as normal to Gaia's development as fistfights in a Brooklyn schoolyard, and they occur almost as frequently; on a human life scale these attacks on the planet would happen every three or four months. And by most accounts, we are a bit overdue.

IMPACTERS VS. CONVULSERS

Two schools compete to explain the mass extinctions: the *impacters*, who believe that these catastrophes have been caused by impacts from objects flying through the solar system, and the *convulsers*, who hold that internal convulsions have been the cause. The impacters believe that the Earth is periodically smashed by comets or bolides (large meteors) while the convulsers argue that these catastrophes can be explained entirely by terrestrial causes, such as earthquakes and volcanoes. It is a surprisingly acrimonious debate. Although the constant shower of meteorites is commonplace in science, the notion of a "threat from outer space," even if unintentioned, seems to have disturbed some deep assumptions about security and planetary sovereignty. As if in addition to all other life's dangers, one suddenly has to reckon with the possibility that at any moment, boulders may come smashing through the roof.

The impacters clearly have the upper hand in the debate, because a collision or series of collisions is now widely accepted to have caused the mass extinction at the Cretaceous-Tertiary (K-T) boundary of geological history, after which the dinosaurs and about 50 percent of all other living species were extinguished. Luis and Walter Alvarez, the California father-son team of evolutionists, have made their case by pointing out that iridium, a metal found rarely on Earth but frequently in meteorites, is strangely abundant in a worldwide layer of rocks that dates from the K-T boundary. According to the younger Alvarez, who teaches at the University of California at Berkeley,

A very large impact has been documented as the cause of the Cretaceous-Tertiary mass extinction by evidence from iridium abundance, osmium isotopes [another metal found only rarely on the planet] . . . shocked

105

quartz (presumably distressed by the impacts), and the worldwide distribution of these diagnostic features. [7]

Judging by the size of other craters made by meteorites, the extent and severity of mineral stress and other physical indications of impact momentum, impacters assert that the K-T mass extinction was caused by the collision of a single planetesimal five to ten miles in diameter, or else a shower of bolides adding up to that size, traveling approximately sixty times the speed of sound—that is, 40,000 to 50,000 miles per hour. Alvarez cautions that while impacts also have been blamed for other mass extinctions, the evidence remains sketchy, especially for the currently popular belief that such impacts happen on a regular twenty-six to thirty million-year basis. Nonetheless, the impact theorists, including Gould, Kaufman, Michael Rampino of New York University, and James Lovelock, who with Michael Allaby coauthored *The Great Extinction*, a book on the subject, clearly have momentum on their side of the debate.

The convulsers demand to know just what in the universe sees fit to sucker-punch the Earth every thirty million years or so. Rather fervently represented at the AGU conference by Alan Rice from the University of Colorado at Denver, the convulsers argue that such clocklike regularity is much more likely a function of an internal geological process than of any repeat offender from the great beyond. For example, the subduction of the ocean floor, one of the processes that led to Hutton's discovery of geological renewal, is now believed to operate on cycles of about forty million years.

Rampino responds with the "Shiva hypothesis," a set of suppositions named after the great Hindu goddess of destruction and regeneration. Noting that comets pass through the solar system on a very regular basis, with Haley's comet predictable over the course of eighty-six years to within a few months, and that the Oort cloud, a nasty belt of comets and cosmic debris, hovers just beyond Pluto, the New York planetary scientist wonders if a vastly more powerful and destructive shower of comets might be circulating, perhaps set off by the motion of the sun through the Milky Way. Rampino's calculations suggest that the sun's journey through the galaxy might cause gravitational perturbations about every thirty million years, launching his hypothetical comet shower. Are Shiva and Gaia, Rampino muses, a coupled system?

THE BIO-DOMINO EFFECT

Some researchers have begun to question the impacters' working assumption that a collision with speeding planetesimals would set off such a chain reaction of geological and biological pandemonium. If one were as large as the Earth, what would it be like to have been hit with the planetesimals that caused the K-T catastrophe? Assuming that the object(s) were roughly the same density as the planet they hit, and working with Alvarez's estimated dimensions, one finds that the mass of the object that caused the K-T catastrophe was on the order of one billionth of that of Earth's, within an order of magnitude (degree of ten) lower or higher. The human equivalent of the impact, even factoring in maximum collision speeds of 40,000 miles per hour, works out to no more than getting plunked by a BB!

The scenario that emerges for the K-T and other catastrophes seems more like a chain-reaction collapse of large portions of the biosphere than a one-shot calamity. A domino effect. Impacters R. Turco and his colleagues describe the sequence to include environmental disasters such as the "deposition of shockwave and radiative energy, generation and dispersal of massive clouds of dust and soot, and production of large quantities of nitrogen oxides. These processes result in severe physical trauma, sudden climate change, and extensive pollution of the environment."[8] A host of explanations have been offered to describe the sequence of events that led to the extinction of the dinosaurs and the many other species, from frigid nuclear winter–type blackouts to unbearable warming from greenhouse effects.

107

But generally underrated is the reverse—the impact on the environment by the death of the organisms. From a Gaian perspective, the K-T and other mass extinctions could not have emerged simply from the impacts; rather, they resulted from a runaway cycle of initial environmental trauma, leading to the death of particularly vulnerable species, which in turn caused greater environmental instability, leading to more extinctions, and so on. For example, kill all of the flying and crawling insects in a field and eventually many of the plants and grasses also will die, which will lead to soil erosion, which will kill the subterranean microbiota that deposit humic substances into the groundwater, which will speed the flow and alter the characteristics of the river into which the underground waters flow. In order to explain the catastrophes that have shaped and organized the evolution of the planet, the impact of extinctions on the environment must be understood as a process inseparably coupled with the impact of the suddenly hostile environment on the species.

It would be fascinating to observe the effects of one of those hurtling planetesimals as it smashed into Mars or, particularly, Venus, since it is so similar to Earth in size. Like the difference between a hydrogen bomb dropped on an integrated ecological system like a rain forest or a metropolitan area, compared to one dropped on a desert like the one near Los Alamos, the effects of an impact on other planets would probably be absorbed more locally and would not provoke so complex a systemic response.

Planetary geologists agree that at least one earthly result of catastrophic impacts—that is, quakes and other seismic activity—would not occur on Venus. In fact, no planet but our own shows indications of any tectonic activity whatsoever. One of the world's leading seismologists, Don Andersen of the California Institute of Technology, once speculated in *Science* that plate tectonics may be the result of a planet's biological activity. The idea is a fanciful extension of Hutton's mechanism for geological upheaval: that the continuous rain of dead organic matter, such as seashells and plant and animal carcasses, washed into the ocean—the process crucial to the removal of carbon and release of oxygen from the carbon dioxide of our atmosphere—weighs upon the ocean floor, eventually warming the Earth's crust and lubricating the motion of the great tectonic plates. Truly movements in the bowels of the Earth.

LADY RECOVERY

Although most Gaian scientists reflexively oppose the convulsers' arguments, since self-induced near-death throes hardly fit in with the notions of a self-sustaining Earth, the mass extinctions plaguing the planet's evolution most likely have been caused by a combination of planetary impacts, convulsions, and other factors. Yet much as her human counterparts automatically replace virtually all of their bodily cells every six years, Gaia has always renewed herself with that same mindless vigor. The picture of Earth that emerges is less a global bomb site devastated over and over again, or a chronically spasmodic biosphere, than it is a responsive, integrated system in a perpetual spiral of disturbance and response.

"It is an illuminating peculiarity of the microcosm that explosive geological events in the past have *never* led to the *total* destruction of the biosphere," Margulis and Sagan write. "Indeed, like an artist whose misery catalyzes beautiful works of art, extensive catastrophe seems to have immediately preceded major evolutionary innovations."[9] Whether by external disturbance or internal disorder, it is as though Gaia were like a fruit tree periodically pruned back to the nubs, each time recovering from the near-death experience to grow stronger and fuller. Or as Thompson puts it, "catastrophe is the organizing principle for Lovelock's narrative of Gaia."[10]

Rampino wonders if Gaia actually is dependent on periodic extinctions and catastrophes for renewal and vigor.

The geologic record shows that climate may oscillate widely following impact perturbances, but that the environment stabilizes within a few hundred thousand years [about a day in human scale]. . . . At first, opportunistic species dominate the unstable post-catastrophe world, but the survivors of the extinction event apparently create a new working biosphere. Eventually, evolutionary radiation of surviving species begins to fill the vacant ecological niches. The periodic mass extinctions involve temporary but quite severe reductions in number of species. When looked at on a family level, however, the extinctions appear as minor setbacks in the climb toward greater diversity of life over the last 600 million years. Gaia (should she exist) seems quite resilient, but the details of the recovery of the biosphere are not yet well known.[11]

Why should such violence be required to accelerate and enhance the development of species? Maybe Newton's law of inertia—a body at rest tends to remain at rest; a body in motion tends to remain in motion—applies to evolution. If natural selection pressures were constant and perfect, plant and animal species might have evolved as rapidly and diversely as they have without those catastrophic kicks in the butt. But few creatures live in an area of perfect competition; even the most industrious will pass up a meal or some other opportunity in order to laze about a bit in the sunshine. And as any corporate trustbuster will affirm, even the most cutthroat competitors conspire to give one another a break once in a while; competitive environments often tend toward oligarchic stability, by a mutual agreement, frequently unspoken, to limit certain forms of competition in favor of maintaining the status quo. Could it be that all organisms, including human beings, habitually operate so far below potential that we require a taste of death to wake us up? Perfect competition presupposes an unlimited desire to survive and

110

reproduce, which of course is far from the only path to a satisfying life.

One of the greatest mass extinctions of all started several hundred years ago, due to the deadly convulsive impact of man, in what the renowned Harvard biologist E. O. Wilson calls "the death of birth." One of the most catastrophic losses of species in the Earth's history is now under way. Will the same evolutionary acceleration that has followed earlier catastrophes result from humankind's current plague? Possibly, but most likely we will have to wait a few hundred thousand years to find out for sure, if humanity has not made itself extinct along the way. Margulis and Sagan write:

> Life at the surface of the earth seems to regulate itself in the face of external perturbation, and does so without regard to the individuals and species that compose it . . . More than 99.99 percent of the species that have ever existed have become extinct, but the planetary patina, with its army of cells, has continued for more than three billion years.[12]

From the Gaian perspective, Earth history divides into three distinct eras: (1) the billion years before life began, (2) the billion years of anerobic life, and (3) the 2.5 billion years (thus far) of oxygen-loving life. Though Lovelock and Margulis firmly believe humanity's current importance to be transient and over-rated, one easily could argue that with the emergence of human civilization, a fourth stage has been entered. Humankind's permeation of the global environment, and now our growing ability to engineer new life forms, may yet prove as important to Gaia's development as did the early formation of microbes or the cyanobacteria that, during the great oxygen-pollution crisis, spread like a tacky scum around the globe.

VI

GAIA: MODELS AND METAPHORS FOR THE LIVING PLANET

SERENDIPITY OR SELF-CONTROL?

James Lovelock believes that the Earth's land masses, oceans, and atmosphere operate together as a mammoth cybernetic system, much like the thermostatically controlled system that probably heats your home. *Cybernetics,* a term coined by the recondite Harvard genius Norbert Wiener, derives from the Greek word for "steersmanship" and means the study of self-regulating systems, ranging from the simple devices that control refrigerators and furnaces to the immensely complex control mechanisms used in robots, or "cybernauts." The crucial difference with the planet's cybernetic system, according to Gaian theory, is that there is no "switch" or control box anywhere on the globe and there is no one to select the desired temperature or give any instructions. It would be as if your house's heating system were automatically regulated by the very building materials. As though the walls, windows, and doors somehow had the capacity to sense the outside temperature and absorb or reflect the sunshine to keep the interior comfortable. Hence the key Gaian term *homeostasis*—the tendency to maintain a state of

internal equilibrium through a complex of interdependent systems, such as the way our bodies maintain their temperature
without thermostat or switch. It's what Lovelock calls "the
wisdom of the body."

The Earth could not possibly work like a body, W. F.
Doolittle pounces, because Gaia would need a mind and the
ability to make conscious decisions. How else does the human
body cool and warm itself to maintain a normal temperature of
98.6° F?

According to Thomas, consciousness has precious little to
do with the kind of wisdom that Lovelock ascribes to Gaia.

> This is not a deadly criticism in a world where we
> do not actually understand, in anything like real de-
> tail, how even Dr. Doolittle manages the stability and
> control of his own internal environment, including his
> body temperature. One thing is certain: none of us can
> instruct our body's systems to make the needed correc-
> tions beyond a very limited number of rather trivial
> tricks made possible through biofeedback techniques.
> If something goes wrong with my liver or kidneys, I
> have no advice to offer out of my cortex. I rely on the
> system to fix itself, which it usually does with no help
> from me beyond my crossing my fingers.[1]

Most of the systems and mechanisms that keep our bodies alive
and healthy operate with little or no help from the conscious
mind.

All cybernetic systems, bodily and otherwise, automatically
operate on the principle of feedback, of which there are two
basic types: negative and positive. Negative feedback systems
modulate, balance, and contain, generally working to oppose
trends to any extreme. Margulis's example of a person in a
warming room is a perfect example of progressive negative
feedback. First the person sweats, then takes off a layer of
clothes, then opens a window, and so on—all to counteract the

rise in temperature. A positive feedback response, quite unlikely in this case, would be one where the person felt the temperature rise and wrapped himself in a blanket, making his body temperature soar.

One of the greatest and most complex negative feedback systems operating in the world today is the American system of checks and balances, as set up in the U.S. Constitution. This brilliant plan to balance the executive, legislative, and judiciary branches of the federal government (itself balanced against local and state authorities) has survived untold schemes and indignities for the past two hundred years. NASA biologist Penelope Boston calls negative feedback systems "the essence of Gaia"; both life and democracy, it seems, require systematic protection from the extremes.

Positive feedback is a process whereby an impulse builds upon itself. For example, when someone does something that miffs you a bit, you become annoyed at having been irritated, angry even. In fact, now that you think of it, you are absolutely vexed. You become so furious that you could *explode*! In theory positive feedback systems would spiral to the infinite, but in practice the amount of energy available to fuel any buildup is limited. So eventually you tire of your wrath and settle back down. Stereo amplifiers work on the positive feedback principle, taking the signals they receive and building them up and up and up, until restricted by governors built into their design and, of course, by the total amount of power available to them. Most of the Earth's positive feedback cycles are similarly self-limiting, but some key systems, such as the processes that create deserts out of fertile land, appear to have devastating runaway potential. Think what would happen if the amplifier boosted the signal high enough to blow the speakers into shattered silence. Or if the person getting angrier and angrier were the president of the United States, and checks and balances be damned, he pushed the nuclear war button before calming down.

Instead of a central control panel or flashing red button,

the Gaian cybernetic system may have a trillion trillion tiny switches. Constructive skeptic Boston describes the possibilities:

> Microorganisms form a critical link between the Earth's biosphere and atmosphere, and one of the goals of Gaian research must be to sensitize researchers to that fact. As with all life, the primary activity of microorganisms is the transfer of energy from one form to another, and they therefore have the ability to transform mass and transfer momentum as well. Microbes can make ice, change the optical properties of clouds and alter various mechanical properties of their environments, such as surface tension and viscosity. By producing gases microbes modify the chemistry of their environment and control its redox [reduction-oxidation, or electrical charge] state. They also affect directly the solar reflectivity, infrared emissivity and other radiative transfer properties of their surroundings.
>
> Microbes are opportunistic, diverse, their sheer mass is overwhelming, and they reproduce exponentially. The higher biota have really enriched the world for them. They have the stuff to make a global impact.[2]

Not surprisingly, Margulis concurs with Boston. In "Desiccation Resistance and Contamination as Mechanisms of Gaia," Stuart Brown, Margulis, and their colleagues examine the tendency of dormant microbes to come out of their spore states and remove gas from the atmosphere when conditions are right, as though they were built-in safety mechanisms for correcting environmental imbalances. They conclude that metabolic diversity, capacity for exponential growth and the resiliency of microbes are all properties that "contribute to the fundamental mechanism of environmental regulation by the biota."[3]

Traditional atmospheric science views the overall climatic system as much less biological and responsive; it regards temper-

115

atures and other conditions more as a function of automatic geological forces determined mostly by our planet's fortunate position with regard to the sun. Sometimes called the Goldilocks theory, traditional earth science sees our planet as the one heated just right, situated in between the too-hot Venus and the too-cold Mars, and with not much more capacity to regulate its temperature than a little girl's bowl of porridge. This chapter explores how the Earth's climate has remained within vital, narrow tolerances and which of the subsystems and cycles that have evolved are most important for keeping the world habitable today. Gaians insist that life's soothing, steadying influence is the key, but the weight of the evidence thus far shows that, like Goldilocks stumbling upon a hot cooked meal in the middle of the forest, Earth's system runs the way it does essentially because of geological dumb luck.

THE PROBLEM OF METAPHOR

"God does not play dice with the world!" retorted Einstein to the designless, dumb-luck universe implied by the quantum theory of probability he had helped to found. Perhaps less an expression of religious faith than the frustration of a genius's discovery that reality has no basis in sense or order, Einstein resorted to the above metaphor to vent his lonely outrage. Robert Berner and other critics have charged that Gaia is just such an analgesic analogy, a sop for those who find the spare reality of a dumb-luck global system too painful to bear. Lovelock calls this charge a failure of the imagination and intellect on the part of those who cling to traditional cause-and-effect reasoning rather than braving what he calls the "circular, recursive logic" necessary to understand cybernetic systems.

Marvin Minsky, one of the true pioneers of artificial intelligence (AI), a cybernetic offshoot that seeks to impart intellectual independence to machines, has long struggled to explain the cybernetic difference. During his keynote address at the

1983 International Conference on Artificial Intelligence, Minsky berated researchers who limit themselves to the traditional if-then-else reasoning of Aristotle when trying to understand (and re-create) the fundamentals of human language, associative thinking, and imagination. But later that afternoon Minsky looked kind of low. "I no longer believe that logic is a valid description system for reality," he confessed sadly. We have all had days like that, when things make so little sense that you wonder if there is any sense in the world to be made. "It's not that logic doesn't fit any more," I volunteered. "Just that it has to be bent a little. Like classical geometry. Non-Euclidean geometry doesn't invalidate it; it just takes those rigid planes and shapes them around the reality of a curved, spherical Earth." Minsky puzzled for a moment and then nodded. "That's an apt metaphor for my dilemma," he said, brightening perceptibly.

The search for metaphors that can be bent comfortably around the globe was once mostly the province of poets. Recently it has seen taken up by scientists. The global environmental crisis has seen human bodies, greenhouses, membranes, even beehives all hauled into descriptive service by otherwise literal-minded men and women, like ascetic monks and nuns faced with a crisis of faith so desperate that they would even try dressing up in costume, if it please the Lord.

Most scientists come honestly by their aversion to figures of speech. Science is not, as one popular New Age sentiment has it, "just another metaphor." The job of science is to determine the literal, physical truth. Figures of speech may be used quite effectively toward this end, but they are neither the goal nor usually the end product of scientific inquiry. $E = mc^2$ is not a metaphor. It is a precise symbolic representation of the relationship between energy and matter. "Hotter than boiling glass," to borrow a bit of hell from Dante, is a metaphor that describes how hot one might feel during the few milliseconds left after fooling with the mechanics of this literal, terrible truth.

Metaphors are like myths, often certifiably false yet purportedly chock-full of veracity and wisdom. These enigmatic figures

117

of speech are said to store truths in compressed fashion, yet the only way these truths can be extracted is by showers of words. Even Lovelock, a man with a weakness for a well-turned phrase, seriously considered removing the poetic word *Gaia* from the title of his second book on the subject, fearful of the simile's slippery slope.

GREENHOUSE V. MEMBRANE

The greenhouse metaphor for global climatic regulation is so common that the figure of speech soon may become fixed in the popular imagination as the literal truth. In some ways it captures superbly the finite and insulating effects of our atmosphere that can so easily be overlooked in an upward glance at the seemingly transparent and endless sky.

The greenhouse metaphor's visceral encapsulation of the way that certain gases trap heat in the atmosphere provides an excellent shorthand grasp of the process. When the sun's rays hit the planet's surface, they are either absorbed or reflected. Whatever a ray's wavelength as it comes in from the sun, once it reaches the Earth and reflects, the rebounding ray has a longer wavelength and lower frequency. Consider a Frisbee that soars freely through the air, then wobbles as if punch-drunk after bouncing off the ground. The radiation that whirred untouched to the surface in a tight spiral is now wobbly and more inclined to bang into greenhouse gas molecules.

Any gas that absorbs solar radiation with wavelengths in a particular range (8 to 15 microns) contributes to the greenhouse effect. Carbon dioxide, the most important greenhouse gas, accounts for roughly 50 percent of the global effect. Most current accounts identify human industry as the primary source of carbon dioxide, but as is explored a bit further on in this chapter, we are less the producers of CO_2 than merely the latest medium through which its cycle is being regulated.

Similarly, methane, which accounts for about 20 percent

of the greenhouse effect, is currently cycled through microbes, agriculture, and natural wells; nitrous oxide, through fertilizers and microbes, contributes 10 percent; and ozone, naturally occurring in the stratosphere but often the result of man-made pollution in the troposphere, accounts for 5 percent. Only chlorofluorocarbons (CFC's) and, to a lesser extent, bromofluorocarbons (BFC's), which absorb with unique proficiency at the low end of the infrared wavelength scale, can truly be called man-made. Not surprisingly, Lovelock believes that these CFC gases he discovered accumulating in the atmosphere may present their greatest threat not as ozone depleters but, since they account for the remaining 15 percent of infrared absorption, for their greenhouse properties. And since they are man-made— ironically, in large part for the purposes of cooling and refrigeration—CFC and BFC emissions may ultimately be the easiest for humans to control.

Yet, like a black-and-white stick figure of an Impressionist painting, the greenhouse metaphor is flawed in many ways. The worst fault of this operational analogy between the atmosphere and a man-made structure is that greenhouses are almost transparent to sunlight. This is not at all the case with our atmosphere. In fact, one of the most important factors determining the temperature of the Earth is its reflectivity, or albedo ("whiteness"). The color of the land and ocean surfaces and, most important, the extent and density of the atmospheric cloud cover determine how much sunlight the planet absorbs and how much bounces back into space. According to Lovelock, the planet's surface has a relatively neutral color, is about half covered with clouds, and reflects about 45 percent of incoming sunlight overall.

Thomas suggests that the "membrane" provides a better metaphor for the role of our atmosphere than does the term *greenhouse*.

When the Earth came alive it constructed the atmosphere for the general purpose of editing the Sun.

119

. . . It [the atmosphere] breathes for us, and it does another thing for our pleasure. Each day, millions of meteorites fall against the outer limits of the membrane and are burned to nothing by the friction. Without this shelter, our surface would have long since become the rounded powder of the moon.[4]

The Earth's atmosphere works much like the semipermeable membranes that surround all living cells, exercising vital control over what passes in—solar radiation from infrared to ultraviolet, assorted space debris (which actually supplies an interesting array of metallic oxides powdered on impact), and the occasional entry vehicle. It also controls what goes out—reflected solar radiation, hydrogen atoms too light to be held by the planet's gravitational field, and the occasional spacecraft.

Much as your skin absorbs excess ultraviolet rays within melanin pigment, the deep blue gas of the stratospheric layer of ozone also acts as a membrane, filtering out an even wider band of ultraviolet radiation. Also like bodily membranes, the Earth's atmosphere is extremely slender. From the planet's surface up to the very topmost layer, the exosphere, a region with air so thin that it is almost beyond definition as part of the Earth, is about 300 miles. The distance from the surface to the stratosphere—for all practical purposes the upper limit—is only about 50 miles. Compared to the 4,000-mile radius of the Earth, then, the atmosphere is not much thicker than the skin of an apple.

The membrane's selective translucence is certainly closer to the vital facts of atmospheric reflectivity than is the indiscriminate transparency of the greenhouse's glass roof and walls. Until recently, global reflectivity has been largely ignored by environmentalists because it seemed impossible to influence the planet's color or gloss, one way or the other. Yet Lovelock argues that cloud cover may be the tropical rainforests' single most important contribution to the global system.

By a process known as evapotranspiration, columns of moisture tower over tropical ecosystems like invisible mountains. When air masses from the ocean move onshore, they collide

120

with the rain forests' moisture mountains, causing clouds to form and rain to fall. And as Boston might remind us, microbes are catalytic to the whole process, providing the gases and particles necessary for clouds to condense. The cooling effects of rainfall have, of course, long been known, but now it seems that the simple transformation from an invisible air mass to one dense enough to reflect sunlight may be of equal or greater importance in climate control. Destroy the rain forest barrier and the reflectivity process could well be damaged or slowed.

The need for suppler, more versatile climate metaphors and models has driven many climatologists to develop mammoth supercomputer representations of the global system. Schneider notes that several teams have embarked on massive, three-dimensional models starting from the stratosphere and working all the way down to the bottoms of the oceans. Lovelock, the old contrarian, has taken quite the opposite tack, toward extreme simplicity.

The British maverick claims that it came to him accidentally one Christmas. Besieged by Darwinists who argued that nothing so magnificent as a global body could ever evolve by the laws of natural selection, that there was no way that all of those organisms would ever cooperate and there was no such thing as a giant species of one, *and* overwhelmed by the immensity of the modeling tasks that Schneider describes, Lovelock and his close colleague Andrew Watson came up with a model, a computerized metaphor to help them develop their intuitions about how the Earth's climate might run automatically under biological control. Known as Daisyworld, it is so astonishingly simple that it is hard to determine whether the model is a visionary breakthrough or just another sugarplum dancing in Lovelock's head.

DAISYWORLD AND THE FAINT YOUNG SUN

The daisy, by the shadow it casts, 121
Protects the lingering dewdrop from the sun
　　　　　　　　—William Wordsworth

One of the great advantages of computer models over conventional metaphors is that they typically are constructed to show how a particular figure or analogy might hold up over time (although Wordsworth's images seem to have held up quite well without mechanical aids). Daisyworld is a computer model constructed to show that all living things tend to regulate their environment and that they have done so automatically since life on Earth began. In "Biological homeostasis of the global environment: the parable of Daisyworld" Watson and Lovelock deliberately avoid choosing species like termites or forest trees known for their strong environmental impact, instead opting for a simple, comparatively passive and benign life form—the daisy—to illustrate that environmental regulation is an inherent property of all life. The mechanics of the Daisyworld model are best described in relation to the most intriguing real-world problem it attempts to solve—the paradox of the faint young sun.

One of the foundations of the Gaian argument for a homeostatically controlled climate system starts with the generally accepted fact that the sun has warmed some 30 percent over the 4.5 aeons of the planet's existence. The paradox is that the Earth's mean surface temperature has stayed much closer to constant than the general thermodynamics of standard physics and chemistry would predict. Every 1-percent change in solar output should increase the Earth's surface temperature approximately 3° or 4° F (2° C), according to the general consensus, which is echoed by Schneider. While opinions do vary over how much change in temperature has taken place, no one contends that the Earth's mean surface temperature has risen anywhere near the 100° to 120° F (50° to 60° C) that the sun's warming would imply. In fact, M. I. Hoffert, a geologist at New York University, states the consensus, which is that the Earth has cooled:

      The geologic record shows the Earth has maintained a habitable environment for evolving biological species over most of its 4.6 Gyr [giga-year] history. During this time, the sun brightened, continents formed, bolides impacted, and geological and volcanic activity oscillated about a long-term decreasing trend as the planet cooled.[5]

Lovelock cites the work of three atmospheric scientists: T. Owen, R. D. Cess, and V. Ramanathan, who in 1979 calculated the mean surface temperature of the Earth at the time life began—that is, about one billion years after the planet's creation and with the sun about 25 percent weaker than now—to be about 73° F (23° C). This balmy temperature compares to the current global average of about 55° F (13° C).

Few scientists challenge what has come to be known as the "faint young sun paradox" of a strengthening sun and stable or declining temperatures, since stars of Sol's type have long been known by astronomers to grow hotter as they grow older. Schneider leaves the backdoor open, saying of the belief that the sun is stronger now than when the Earth began that "there's a 10-percent probability it's not true." More serious exception is taken to the assertion that temperatures have remained "constant," or within a narrow range. Again, Schneider plays the useful foil; he attacks the simplistic notion that temperatures have not changed in 4.5 billion years without disputing the fundamental observation of climate modulation. He points out that temperatures frequently vary 15° F locally and 25° to 40° F globally on any given day. The temperature difference between the northern and southern hemispheres is approximately 25° to 30° F, much larger even than the 10° F variations between ice ages and interglacial periods like the one we are in now. True, the Earth's temperature is hardly constant, but it is markedly more stable than the unmitigated warming effects that the strengthening sun would imply.

Carl Sagan originally suggested the mechanism usually invoked for resolving the faint young sun paradox, essentially that the carbon dioxide blanket around the Earth has depleted gradually as the sun has grown warmer. The question is how that blanket happened to unravel so steadily. A number of traditional geochemists maintain that geochemical processes alone are sufficient for the process, the balance maintained basically by the Earth's fortunate position with regard to the sun. Gaian theorists accept Sagan's blanket supposition but question the implicit contention that the blind forces of physics and chemistry could produce such a delicately measured system of response without significant modulation from biological sources. Why would carbon dioxide levels diminish at all? Why wouldn't the proportion of that elsewhere ubiquitous and highly stable gas remain constant, as on Venus for example, while the Earth heated up?

HOW DAISIES KEEP US COOL

Imagine a planet that has daisies as its only life forms and circles a strengthening star like our own. At first, few daisies of any color grow because the sun is weak, but eventually, little clumps of daisies sprout up. (The model works assuming that the daisies are a full range of colors and shades, but for the purposes of this simple summary, there are two varieties, white and black.) In the cool, weakly sunlit environment, black daisies will outproduce their white counterparts because the dark flowers absorb the heat. Therefore, the clumps of black daisies that come to dominate Daisyworld's landscape heat up their environment, not through any intentions or consipiracies, as the Darwinist critics so often charge to be the case with Gaia, but simply as the result of the way they live. Eventually all this heat absorption by the black daisies raises local and global temperatures considerably, to the point where, supplemented by the ever-strengthening radiation from the sun, it gets too hot in some areas for black daisies, and white daisies begin to grow.

The albedo of the white daisies has the cooling effect that one would expect, and they spread. Like any system run by a thermostat, Daisyworld's climate corrections have a tendency to overshoot; in certain areas, the cooling trend is sufficient for black daisies to start growing again. Given the long-term trend toward a strengthening sun, however, the overall movement in the daisy population is from black to white: as the planet warms, more "cooling" white daisies emerge. The flowers act as a thermostat, or a switchless cybernetic system, keeping the planet habitable until the sun grows so strong that it kills off all life.

Few critics have addressed Daisyworld directly, a problem that most scientists face with their beloved models. Most everyone is more interested in presenting their own metaphorical creations than working to unravel the assumptions and pitfalls of someone else's. But Daisyworld seems so simple that friends and critics alike are a bit wary. The complexity that might usually deter them is instead daunting by its absence. At the AGU conference Lovelock and Watson tried to earn respect for their Daisyworld model, but their critics first demanded proof that carbon dioxide, one of the most important climate regulators known on Earthworld, and by consensus the most important greenhouse gas from the faint sun's birth right on through today, was biologically controlled. Then they would talk daisies.

VII

GAIAN MECHANISMS OF CLIMATE CONTROL

DARLING, DEMON CO$_2$

For such an important and well-known gas, there is comparatively little carbon dioxide in our air. While the early Earth is thought to have had something between 5 and 30 percent, the proportion of CO$_2$ once dwindled to the point where, before the Industrial Revolution, the gas accounted for no more than 0.028 percent, or 280 parts per million (ppm). The trend has not been strictly straight line; carbon dioxide levels fell during the periods of glaciation, or ice ages, and rose when the planet warmed back up. Over the past century and a half, CO$_2$ has risen slowly, to about 0.034 percent, or 340 ppm CO$_2$, and is expected to continue to rise 1 or 2 ppm per year for at least the next few decades. But over the long term, the trend has been steadily and inevitably down.

The fact that carbon dioxide has continued to dwindle over the Earth's history seems to get lost in much of the popular media's coverage of the greenhouse effect; it is difficult to demonize a substance on the wane. Even *Time* magazine, in its 1989 "Planet of the Year" issue, gets carried astray: "The conclusion: CO$_2$ levels and global temperatures have risen and fallen together, over tens of thousands of years. And there is evidence from space: Mars, which has little CO_2 in its atmosphere, has a surface temperature that reaches -24 degrees at best, while Venus, with lots of CO_2, is a hellish 850 degrees F."[1] As noted earlier, the atmospheres of both Venus and Mars have in excess of 95 percent carbon dioxide, and their relative surface temperatures have much more to do with the very plain facts of their distance from the sun.

Gaian theory asserts that carbon dioxide is regulated primarily by all manner of "daisies"—plants, trees, and marine organisms—and that it has been depleted and buried gradually as the sun has warmed, mitigating any tendency for surface temperatures to rise. In fact, algae process approximately half of the Earth's supply of carbon, making the microscopic plants, from the Gaian point of view, absolutely indispensable to climate control. Traditional geochemists cleave to their time-honored contention that the fundamental controls on carbon dioxide are physical rather than biological, arguing that CO_2 is emitted primarily by volcanoes and absorbed by calcium silicate rocks, in cycles sensitive to climate and temperature. The daisies are only bystanders in processes beyond their control.

Here is an example of the potentially misleading "rooting interest" of the living Earth theory. It is certainly more comforting to imagine the world's plants collectively working "like a giant pump," as Lovelock puts it, in the eminently understandable cause of photosynthesis, than it is to envision the silent adsorption of gas by stone. With rocks and volcanoes one can understand only that they have no motivation—that there is no reason why. As *New Scientist* observes of the debate over carbon dioxide regulation, "This argument is one of the central battlegrounds in the Gaia hypothesis."[2]

SEASHELLS START WITH TREES

As we have all been taught from an early age, plants breathe in carbon dioxide (CO_2) and release oxygen (O_2). Where does the C go? Most of it goes into the cellular structure of the plants, eventually returning to the atmosphere as the plants die and decay, or right back into the photosynthesis-respiration cycle, which works in reverse at night. (The reason flowers are removed from hospital rooms at night is that they exhale carbon dioxide and compete with the patient for the available oxygen.) But approximately one-tenth of one percent of the carbon falls out of this cycle, in a very gradual process whereby over the eons the warming sun has stripped away Gaia's thick carbon dioxide robe, leaving her with but a breezy veil.

When plants die, their roots decay into the soil, and the organic carbon reacts with the rocks in a process known as weathering. (Weathering also occurs while the plants are alive, since some of the carbon dioxide they absorb is not used but is conducted and deposited deep into the soil, initiating the same chain of chemical reactions.) In a process catalyzed and hastened by bacteria, the carbon and oxygen of the plant materials react with the calcium silicate (calcium, silicon, and oxygen), the substance of rock particles, releasing the oxygen into the atmosphere and forming calcium carbonate, or limestone (calcium, carbon, and oxygen) and gelatinous silicic acid (silicon and oxygen). Unlike their rock-solid silicate predecessors, limestone and silicic acid dissolve readily into the groundwater and are transported to local streams and rivers, which empty into the sea.

Marine organisms filter the limestone from the water to form their shells, essentially reconstituting the land stones for use as their shelter. When these creatures die, their shells and skeletons sink to the bottom, in what amounts to a continuous precipitation of calcium carbonate in virtually every body of saltwater on Earth. Particularly important in this process are diatoms, single-celled microorganisms that thrive in the shallow waters around the continental margins, and the tiny silicon dioxide "skeletons" or "shells" they leave behind. "Tiny ocean protists . . . extruded so much calcium into the water over such long periods of time that they made that famous piece of English real estate, the White Cliffs of Dover, a towering deposit of limestone and chalk,"[3] write Margulis and Sagan.

Those legendary white cliffs, and many others of similar composition, were once below sea level. They now stand essentially as burial grounds for the carbon dioxide that dominated the atmosphere of early Earth. (Margulis prefers to think of it as a great mass of organic carbon preserved in a sort of biospheric storage until life collectively finds ways of recycling the reserves.) Most of the mass of seashells simply fall to the ocean floor, where they are subducted (sucked under) by plate tectonics. The floor of the ocean acts as a conveyor, removing the carbon from atmospheric interplay for millions of years. Eventually it is all coughed up again by earthquakes, volcanoes, and other heavings from the Earth's crust. This process of return is at times spectacular, like the eruption of Mount Saint Helens, or the 1986 incident at Lake Nyos in the Cameroon, when the waters belched up a toxic cloud of carbon dioxide that asphyxiated seventeen hundred people.

As levels of carbon dioxide rise, so does air temperature, causing plants and trees to proliferate. The plants cool the atmosphere by pumping down more carbon dioxide, converting it to carbonates, which dissolve in groundwater that runs off into the oceans and seas. Seashells, therefore, are formed without any climatic intentions on the part of the various organisms involved but nonetheless with the result of cooling the atmosphere. Gaia will respond to our current high-CO_2 greenhouse warming by increasing the precipitation of carboniferous shells and skeletons, but that process probably will take many hundreds of years before things cool down.

The next time you pick up a seashell that has washed up on shore, you will be holding a rock that was dissolved by the roots of a plant or a tree somewhere on a nearby stretch of land. And the more CO_2 in the atmosphere, the higher the air temperatures and the more seashells in the ocean. This is a wonderful thing to tell a child the next time you are at the beach. Which is where you are more and more likely to find yourself, the kids and a whole lot of other folks trying to keep cool in the torrid summers expected for the next century.

BEFORE LIFE WAS, ROCKS AM

Few earth scientists differ with this basic biological scenario for the removal of carbon from the atmosphere. The critics simply contend that Gaians cannot see the forests for their fascination with the trees. James C. G. Walker of the University of Michigan forcefully defends the geochemical orthodoxy that with or without living organisms, the burial of atmospheric carbon dioxide through its reaction with the calcium silicate of the rocks would occur anyway; the biota just happen to be the medium through which the inevitable process transpires. With a deep monotone stilted slightly by a German accent, Walker reminds one of a younger Henry Kissinger. The scientist is so authoritatively quantitative and technical that there seems no difference between his spoken and written words:

> On different time scales there are different processes that dominate the biogeochemical cycles of carbon. On the time scale of decades the exchanges of carbon dioxide between ocean and atmosphere and between atmosphere and biota are important. On time scales of thousands of years the deep circulation of the ocean and the dissolution and precipitation of biogenic carbonate minerals play a role. On geological time scales of millions of years, the dominant processes involve metamorphic [shifting rock masses] and volcanic release of carbon dioxide from the solid phase and the weathering reactions that dissolve silicate minerals.[4]

130   By this argument Walker has Gaia coming and going. Plants, trees, and marine life specify the details of the process, but in

the very long run "there is an abiotic mechanism waiting to take over."[5]

Gaian theory finds Walker's explanations insufficient.

> James Walker and his colleagues tried to explain the low carbon dioxide of the Earth by a simple geochemical argument. . . . Unfortunately, this imaginative and plausible model could not explain the facts. The carbon dioxide it predicted for the present was about 100 times more than it is observed to be. James Walker's model can be brought to life by including within it living organisms.[6]

Gaian scientists do not accept the contention that living organisms are just another medium for carbon chemistry, arguing that the CO_2 content of the soil of any well-vegetated area on Earth is ten to forty times higher than that of the atmosphere. Living organisms do not just let it happen, nor do they help it happen. They make it happen, affirms Lovelock. Life draws down carbon dioxide and keeps things cool in response to the strengthening sun.

Raymond Siever, a Harvard geologist, takes almost as strong a stand as Walker. "On land, the efficiency of rock weathering presumably increased after evolution of bacteria, algae and fungi but seems to have been little affected by the appearance of vascular plants [trees and other plants with xylem and phloem, the equivalents of veins and arteries]." In other words, Lovelock's argument about the concentration of carbon dioxide around the roots of the trees is irrelevant, since they just happen to be the means of conveyance. Bacteria, Siever agrees, catalyze reactions that would proceed more slowly without them, but they do it with no greater efficiency now than before the evolution of trees.

How and at what rate rock weathering would proceed without bacteria is a very difficult speculation, since those microbes have been at it for some 3.5 billion of the 4.5 billion years of Earth's history. Very little is known about the geochemistry of the first billion years of Earth's history, the Hadean eon. As for Earth history since, carbon-fixation from air to soil has been carried on by an evolutionary progression of organisms, from the great microbial mats floating in the coastal seas to a variety of land organisms, some of the latest of which are the vascular plants to which Siever refers.

Contrary to the Harvard geologist's summary dismissal of the importance of vascular plants, Andrew Knoll and W. C. James, also from Harvard, have demonstrated that different ecosystems cause weathering of soil minerals at different rates. In an article published in *Geology* in 1987 they show that far from being inconsequential, all vascular plant ecosystems affect weathering rates and therefore, through the removal of carbon dioxide, global temperature. In fact, one type of vascular plant ecosystem, angiosperm-deciduous plants (those that have covered or enclosed seeds, including most flowers, and trees that shed and renew their leaves seasonally), weathers the minerals in the rocks and soil below at a rate of three to four times faster than ecosystems comprised primarily of conifers, which expose their seeds, and evergreens, which keep their needles year-round.

Building on their work, Tyler Volk, a young, painstaking geochemist from New York University, has concluded that angiosperm-deciduous ecosystems have been responsible for up to 20°F of global cooling and "could have contributed to the evolution during the last 100 million years of a cooler Earth, and thus were a factor in producing conditions that enhanced their global proliferation."[8] Quite counter to Siever's studied indifference, Volk concludes not only that vascular plants are integral to global cooling but also that by so doing they maintain and enhance climatic conditions conducive to their own growth.

> It is possible that the evolution of angiosperms and deciduousness operated as part of a positive feedback loop. If the evolution of ecosystems with high weathering rates cooled the Earth, they may have helped to

create the conditions—i.e., strong seasonality—that enhanced their success in competition with the conifer-evergreen systems. . . . A system that used deciduousness . . . to mobilize nutrients would gradually alter the climate to produce the climatic regime that possibly gave it advantage over the evergreen systems, particularly in certain latitude belts on Earth.[9]

In sum, deciduous forests may cool the Earth by perpetuating themselves.

TREES ARE BEING REPLACED BY GRASS

From the Gaian perspective, trees are vital to the removal of carbon dioxide, but that does not necessarily mean that their evolutionary appearance should have sped the process—not unless the sun or some other environmental variable hastens the warming of the planet. Although the appearance of trees may not have altered the overall *rate* of carbon dioxide deposition, they have increased the *efficiency* of the process. As the vital gas has grown scarcer, more efficient methods have been needed to soak it out of the air. Trees have acted as funnels for the steadily dwindling supply of carbon dioxide. In a coevolutionary context they are one of the latest CO_2-gathering tools.

Just as trees and other vascular plants represent an advance over their predecessors, many biologists believe that this entire category, known as C3 plants, shorthand for their mode of gathering carbon dioxide, are slowly being replaced by grasses and other plants without broad leaves, a group categorized as C4. This latter group of plants arose some one hundred million years ago, toward the end of the Cretaceous period of the Mesozoic era, the time when dinosaurs, marine and flying reptiles, fishes, and evergreen trees dominated. An evolutionary step up from the deciduous angiosperms, they are believed to have proliferated ten million years ago, during the current

133

Cenozoic Miocene era, a period of intense glaciation when atmospheric carbon dioxide is believed to have been as low as 180 ppm, not much more than half of what it is now. These slender-leaved photosynthesizers can fare better in low-CO_2 environments because they are even better funnels than are the vascular plants.

Three biochemists from Duke University, P. B. Heifetz, R. W. Schweikart, and A. V. Quinlan, have learned that a plant's ability to survive in the relatively low CO_2 concentrations of the modern world depends on its ability to deliver the gas to its supply of an enzyme known as ribulose diphosphate carboxylase, or RuDPC. They point out that although the current atmospheric CO_2 level is far below optimum for trees and other vascular plants, these C3's have compensated by overproducing RuDPC. However, the C4 grassy plants ultimately have the evolutionary advantage, because they funnel CO_2 more precisely to their RuDPC targets and therefore do not need to expend the extra energy to manufacture increasing amounts of the carbon-fixing enzyme that the scattershot C3 method requires. Trees are majestic beings, the biological and aesthetic climax of ecosystems from the great northern forests to the humid tropics. But as Lovelock observes, "Eventually, and probably suddenly, these new [C4] plants will take over and run an even lower carbon dioxide atmosphere to compensate for the increasing solar heat."[10] And one day (Lovelock guesses in about a hundred million years) the sun will heat to the point where carbon dioxide no longer can be tolerated and the darling, demon gas will disappear from the air altogether.

OXYGEN: THE BIG BLIP

For every carbon atom buried at sea in the breakdown of CO_2 in the weathering process, one oxygen molecule (O_2) is released into the air, a process generally believed to have run continuously since the oxygen crisis of two and a half eons ago.

Yet quite in contrast to the steadily dwindling supply of carbon dioxide, the level of oxygen appears once again to have remained roughly constant—about 21 percent of the atmosphere over most or all of those 2.5 billion years—quite fortunately as far as life is concerned.

What evidence is there that oxygen has held so steady? The Gaians argue that atmospheric O_2 could not have dropped much below the current level for at least the last 600 million years, or the larger animals and flying creatures could not have lived. And the fossil record probably would reflect the extinctions or physiognomic differences that an atmosphere 5 or more percent lower in oxygen would create. Neither could oxygen have risen too far above the current level of 21 percent, argues Andrew Watson.

Watson conducted a series of experiments to show that atmospheric oxygen never can have been more than 4 percent greater than it is now, and probably not even 1-percent greater, because of the increased likelihood of conflagration (the same principle that precludes one from safely smoking in an oxygen tent). Watson demonstrated that a simple 1-percent jump in oxygen increased the likelihood of forest fires by 60 percent; at 25 percent oxygen, even the soggy material rotting on the rain forest floor would ignite and the Earth's vegetation would be burned from the surface. Perhaps the fires that Watson envisions would use up enough of the oxygen available locally to burn themselves out in a typical negative feedback reaction, but that would mean the fundamental control mechanisms for oxygen were biological in origin. Otherwise, whatever else was pouring in the O_2 would start those fires right back up. As Lovelock sums it up, "Our present oxygen level of 21% is a nice balance between risk and benefit; fires do take place, but not so often as to offset the advantages that a high potential energy gives."[11]

Few geologists seem to take serious, substantive exception to the suggestion that atmospheric oxygen has stayed within the 15 to 25 percent range for at least the past several hundred million years, since the advent of large animals, beyond the

135

occasional tart reminder that circumstance and a few experiments do not constitute solid proof. The Gaian assertion that these levels are actively maintained by the biota, however, is what ignites the smoldering debate.

In "Gaian and Non-Gaian Explanations for the Contemporary Level of Atmospheric Oxygen," G. R. Williams of the University of Toronto points out that the debate is far from simply Gaia versus the geologists when it comes to explaining how oxygen is regulated in the atmosphere. There are at least four schools of thought, with no one having anything near an undisputed claim. According to Williams, geochemists traditionally hold that the percentage of oxygen in the atmosphere is a function of the composition of the Earth's mantle and crust, as per a theory advanced by the late Robert Garrels. Garrels, who died at his home in Florida while the AGU conference was underway, has long been hailed by Lovelock as one of the greatest geochemists of his generation. Heinrich Holland, who certainly seems to have emerged as one of the new leaders, essentially concurs with Garrels that the impact of the biota on the planet's atmospheric system is relatively trivial compared to the state of the planet's crust: "The most important process of oxygen depletion is its reaction with surface rocks," says Holland.

Robert Berner and Antonio Lasaga of Yale University deepen the geochemists' crustal notions. Their wider geophysical explanation is that the most important process in determining atmospheric composition is plate tectonics, since that process underlies and controls volcanism, sea level, uplift, and the development of sedimentary basins. Still, there nags the question of how the percentage of oxygen is maintained with such apparent precision by the all-encompassing tectonic process. When Aristotle was asked why the sun rises, he responded that it is the sun's nature to do so. Perhaps sensing the inability of their semitautological big-picture explanation to account for the maintenance of oxygen within narrow tolerances, Berner and Lasaga claim that the tolerances are not so narrow, that "significant fluctuations of O_2 and CO_2 over Phanerozoic time (the past 600 million years) have occurred, and that biological processes generally have played a secondary role to geological processes."[12] They do not, however, address the question of how higher plants, animals, and flying birds and insects might have survived those substantial, if unspecified, oxygen fluctuations.

A simpler geophysical explanation is currently propounded by W. S. Broecker, an enigmatic, brilliant oceanographer who refused to attend the Gaia conference on the grounds that the theory is too mystical and unscientific (he is said to have expressed unofficial regrets later on) but who nonetheless has sponsored some of Andrew Watson's work. Broecker contends that the amount of atmospheric oxygen is determined primarily by the volume of the oceans; since processes like seashell formation are integral to carbon dioxide regulation, the same also goes for oxygen, since it is a byproduct of those reactions. The biogeochemical explanation, advanced by Alfred Redfield, is that contemporary percentages of oxygen are determined jointly by the nutritional requirements of the marine phytoplankton that form carbonate shells, as well as the purely chemical factor of the solubility of calcium phosphate, part of the shell-creation process, in seawater. Known as the Redfield ratio, this solubility factor essentially determines how much organic matter can be buried how fast.

THE METHANE-OXYGEN BALANCE

The Gaian explanation is that oxygen has been steadied by the regulatory effects of the biota. But how does the process work?

The argument goes as follows: We have an abundance of oxygen, 21% of the atmosphere, and a trace of methane, at 1.5 parts per million (0.0000015%). We know from chemistry that methane and oxygen will react when illuminated by sunlight, and we also know the rate of this reaction. From this we can confidently conclude that the coexistence of the two reactive gases methane and oxygen at a steady level requires a flux of methane of 1,000 megatons a year. This is the amount needed to replace the losses by oxidation. Furthermore, there must also be a flux of oxygen of 4,000 megatons a year, for this much is used up in oxidizing the methane. There are no reactions known to chemistry which would make these vast quantities of methane and oxygen starting from the available raw materials, water and carbon dioxide, and using solar energy. Therefore, there must be some process at the Earth's surface which can assemble the sequence of unstable and reactive intermediates in a programmed manner to achieve this end. Most probably that process is life.[13]

Methane, also known as swamp gas and firedamp (because of its combustibility) is a colorless, odorless gas about half as dense as air. It is produced mostly by bacteria, confirming Penelope Boston's bold declarations on the power of microbes to produce gases "that modify the chemistry of their environment and control its redox [reduction/oxidation] state."[14] Methanogenic microbes live mostly in airless places, such as rice paddies and swamps, as well as in the guts of cattle, termites, and human beings, from whom methane is emitted by flatulence. While it is certainly easy to discount the atmospheric significance of random farts, they do add up. For example, the collective flatulence of the world's billion head of cattle, buffalo, and camels, with each animal emitting as much gas on average as three hundred human beings, accounts for something on the order of 25 to 50 megatons of methane per year, up to 5 percent of the total annual production. And termites are believed to contribute a much greater share.

A recent *Technology Review* article points out that while methane is not exactly a man-made pollutant, recent studies indicate that methane concentration has been growing for the past two hundred years, paralleling the rise of industrialization and the growth of the human population. "The increase of rice paddies and cattle herds may be one factor," the article explains. "A population explosion of termites on deforested land in the tropics also may have boosted global methane production."[15]

Whatever the vehicle, methane as oxygen governor and also as greenhouse gas pollutant is on the rise. Shouldn't the proportion of free oxygen in the atmosphere drop commensurately, since there is more methane to neutralize it? Or hasn't the increase in methane become large enough yet to make a noticeable impact? A more appropriate explanation seems to lie with the cycle of CO_2. Just as the production of methane has risen over the past two centuries, so too have human emissions of carbon dioxide increased, mostly by the geologically premature reintroduction of CO_2 buried in fossil fuels. Some of that extra CO_2 has remained ambient and, like methane, heated up the air. The remainder appears to have gone to the increased rock weathering and photosynthesis that has resulted from milder temperatures; plants respond well to warmer temperatures and more carbon dioxide to feast on, pumping more of it down and slowing the warming trend in a classical negative feedback loop. The overall increase in atmospheric carbon dioxide is not equal simply to the increase in human output, it is equal to the difference between the increase in human emissions and the capacity of the environment, biological and geological, to absorb new infusions. What is not absorbed by photosynthesis or other means remains as a greenhouse factor; what is photosynthesized yields, as its major product, more O_2. Whether by chance, design, or automatic Gaian self-control, the growing supply of methane seems to be balancing off an increase in oxygen. Or is it all, as Berner and Lasaga insist, just a function of groaning plates and heaving crusts?

"How could oxygen be biologically controlled? If plants are to make oxygen for the good of the biosphere, imagine a mutant plant which saved itself the costs of oxygen manufacture," Richard Dawkins responds without hesitation, referring to an argument against Gaia in his book *Extended Phenotype*. "It would

139

outreproduce its more public-spirited colleagues, and genes for public-spiritedness would disappear." Doolittle concurs: "There's no way that natural selection could possibly produce a system like the one Lovelock's talking about on a global scale. You just can't stop the cheaters, like Dawkins's oxygen-selfish plant. The theory is totally radical and heretical."[16]

Yet nowhere does Lovelock claim any altruism, sacrifice, or public-spiritedness on the part of oxygen or methane producers. In fact, it would muck up his calculations. He simply observes that the net effect of their normal, rational functioning is to maintain the precious, vital balance necessary for survival.

Stephen Jay Gould might appreciate the cyclical irony of Lovelock's contention: today's oxygen-loving organisms are kept alive only by the vital and constant methane contributions from creatures subordinated aeons ago. The farts from microbes thriving in the guts of termites, cattle, and even schoolchildren are ultimately what keep our air breathable today. In *Phenomenology of Mind* Hegel argues that the slave is superior to the master because the master depends on the slave for his existence. (Little consolation, one would suppose, to those forced to serve.) Hegel's notion has its parallel in Gaian theory: Lovelock once declared that oxygen, by its reactive power and versatility, has emerged as the "leader of the evolutionary orchestra." But by Gaia or by accident, we never would have made a note of music without those methane-producing throwbacks and their lowly little toots. And if one day the final depletion of carbon dioxide from the atmosphere means that methane will eventually overtake and neuter a stabilized supply of free oxygen, Gaia's evolutionary orchestra may have to relearn some very, very old liberation hymns.

LOW-SALT OCEANS AND THE GREAT LAGOON DEBATE

Oceans are the largest component of the biosphere and also the one component about which we know the least. Trying to understand the global climate, including pressing issues like the greenhouse effect, without including the oceans' role would be like trying to understand why your bathroom is steamy without considering the tub full of hot water. In fact, imagine adding box after box of bubble bath or skin conditioner to that tub yet finding that the water always stayed the same clarity, composition, and consistency. You might guess that your bathwater had reached its saturation point, but upon further investigation you would realize that some special drain had opened and flushed away only the chemicals you were adding, leaving the water level unchanged.

For eons the world's rivers and streams have poured more than half a billion tons of sodium chloride and other salts into the oceans annually. During that time, the oceans have remained approximately the same size. The salinity of their water does not appear to have increased, however. "Analysis of sedimentary rocks has provided geologic evidence that the composition as well as the total salinity of the oceans has not appreciably changed for at least 500 million years,"[17] writes Gregory Hinkle, citing the work of Garrels and others. Today the world's oceans average 3.4 percent inorganic salts by weight, of which about 90 percent is sodium chloride. (Human blood, by comparison, is about 0.8 percent salt by weight.) The saline saturation point for water is much higher, on the order of 25 percent salt by weight or more, depending on temperature and other conditions! No living cells known to man can survive in a medium greater than 6 percent saline, because the osmotic pressure of the water crushes the cell walls. How fortunate for the oceans' residents that some process has steadily removed all of this excess salt, perhaps through that special drain.

Not surprisingly, Margulis's protégé Hinkle sees this as more than just coincidence: "Models based solely on physical and chemical equilibria do not adequately explain marine chemistry or why the oceans are 90 percent undersaturated with respect to NaCl. . . . Although the mechanisms are not yet clear, biologic modulation of geologic phenomena most likely controls ocean salinity."[18] At which point Hinkle and his Gaian confederates toss their hats into the great lagoon debate, a subject that has both entertained and obsessed oceanophiles for at least a century.

Lagoons, shallow ponds or sounds near or communicating with larger bodies of water, have the look of being engineered or added on to islands or coves, like a porch built onto a house. Of particular interest to Gaian scientists are evaporite lagoons, found in many places along the continental margins, which are essentially vast salt-storage warehouses. Ocean water is trapped in these lagoons and slowly evaporated into the atmosphere, later falling elsewhere as pure rain. Most of the salt is left behind in chemically and physically stable crystalline layers along the shore.

Chamisso, an eighteenth-century French geologist, proposed that lagoons were the tops of underwater volcanoes, but the lid was blown off that theory when no volcanoes were found. Darwin believed that lagoons were formed when islands developed barrier reefs and these reefs gradually submerged. This explanation satisfies a number of cases but still does not explain how the reefs were formed in the first place. The English oceanographer Alden Murray believed that reefs are accumulated by the precipitation of the spiny shells of the carbon burial cycle, and the Gaians carry on in his tradition: "the evidence that lagoon formation and maintenance depends on the specific behavior of marine microorganisms is strong," writes Lovelock, recounting an expedition with Margulis to her beloved microbial mats in Baja.

Here I was able to see at first hand the subtle economy of the bacterial mats that covered the lagoon. The red and green communities of microbes at the surface acted as a raincoat, preventing the salt from being dissolved in the rain and washing back into the ocean. . . . Salt crystals at, or near, the surface, are also coated with their own specific varnish, and protected against easy solution in rain water. . . . Is all this a grand, unplanned civil engineering enterprise by Gaia?[19]

The versatile Britisher goes on to point out that unusually gentle ocean wave patterns spotted in the vicinity of these reefs in satellite photographs were subsequently found to be caused, at least in part, by an oily substance secreted by coral microorganisms that lowered the water's surface tension. "It is engaging to speculate about the geophysiological development of this remarkable action in microorganisms, and to wonder when it developed and whether it is a mechanism for protecting the reefs from wave damage,"[20] says Lovelock.

"Engaging speculation" is about all anyone, including Gaian proponents, will credit to this oceanic salinity hypothesis of "unplanned civil engineering" by communities of microbes. The burden of proof lies with the new generation of Gaian scientists, like Hinkle. Even Andrew Watson, who has developed chemical markers used to trace the flow of ocean currents, cautions that of all the Gaian arguments, the one concerning oceanic salinity is by far the most speculative. Too speculative, apparently, for W. S. Broecker, the oceanographer who worked with Watson but refused to attend the Gaia conference.

Michael Whitfield, a colleague of Lovelock and Watson at the Marine Biological Association of the United Kingdom, is an encouraging skeptic. Pointing out that since life has evolved in the oceans for four billion years, "one might expect the oceans to provide good examples of Gaian regulation. . . . If active biological regulation does exist in the oceans, the composition of sea water should reflect an intricate interweaving of the physically and chemically possible and the biologically useful."[21] That blend would be pretty thin on life, however, since these vast bodies of water have less than 1 percent of the biomass of total land plants. Except at the continental margins, life in the oceans is spread very thin. Lovelock might respond that the percentage of living matter in a redwood tree is similarly sparse,

143

but as of now, the mystery of oceanic salinity and the regulatory role of life remains unsolved.

DMS: THE MISSING SWITCH?

Martin Hoffert observes that even though the biomass of the oceans is but a tiny fraction of that on land, oceanic biota contribute almost as much in the way of total chemical production as do land organisms. Pound for pound, the organisms of the ocean are as much as one thousand times as productive as those on land. In fact, sulfur, an element vital to the global system, is produced almost entirely in the oceans. This led Lovelock to wonder if somewhere in the cycle of sulfur production and absorption there might be some clues as to how the oceans, atmosphere, and land masses function together cybernetically. Once again his imagination was triggered by his sense of smell.

Conventional wisdom had it that large quantities of hydrogen sulfide were emitted from the ocean to make up for losses of land sulfur, due to the runoff of rivers. Without some return of sulfur, land organisms would have been starved of it. (Essentially, sulfur is in short supply on land and nitrogen is in short supply in the sea, so the atmosphere is the medium of exchange.) However, hydrogen sulfide stinks like rotten eggs. Fish straight from the sea do not stink like this, Lovelock noted quite sensibly; instead they have the rather pleasant fragrance of dimethyl sulfide (DMS). Fresh water fish do not have this smell. Knowing from the work of earlier scientists, particularly Frederick Challenger, that many marine organisms emit DMS, Lovelock decided to find out if that compound served as the carrier of sulfur from ocean to land. He took what has now become his historic voyage on the research ship *Shackelton* and then published his findings in *Nature*.

144 Microscopic marine algae called phytoplankton produce DMS to protect against high salt concentrations of the seawater

outside. The substance is gradually excreted, or released into the water when the plankton die. DMS accumulates in the seawater and gradually diffuses up to the atmosphere, where winds carry the sulfur-bearing product to the land, once again to the good fortune of most terrestrial beings.

Dimethyl sulfide would not have been sought as a candidate chemical transporter had it not been for the stimulus of Gaia theory that required the presence of geophysiological mechanisms for such transfers. But what on earth, you may ask, could be the mechanism? Why should marine algae out in the open ocean care a fig for the health and well-being of trees, giraffes, and humans on the land surfaces? How could such an amazing altruism evolve through natural selection?[22]

asks Lovelock coyly, for he knows that no altruism is involved.

This phenomenon was no more than a curiosity until Bob Charlson, an atmospheric scientist from the University of Washington at Seattle, wondered how clouds formed over the open ocean. Clouds need not just moisture, but also particles around which the moisture can condense. Charlson wondered where those particles came from. Lovelock and Charlson discovered that when DMS rises through the atmosphere, it is transformed by a series of reactions into condensation nuclei. The more nuclei in a given cloud, the denser it is, and the greater its reflective properties. So the natural metabolic product of these tiny ocean phytoplankton appeared to influence the creation and reflectivity of the clouds, as Boston noted at the start of the AGU conference.

M. O. Andreae of the Max Planck Institute in West Germany soon demonstrated that the output of oceanic DMS was crucial. "We now suspect that the compound accounts for 80 to 90 percent of the particles necessary for cloud formation over the open seas. If the phytoplankton didn't produce DMS, the Earth would be a lot warmer."[23] Andreae then mounted an

145

oceanic research expedition to see if he could "close the loop," to show that a warm climate stimulates phytoplankton to produce DMS, which forms clouds and therefore cools the environment, which would in turn mitigate the production of more DMS, slowing the cooling and keeping the local climate balanced. The problem, as any sailor ever rocked by an ocean breeze might have guessed, was that the winds and waves of the ocean churned havoc with the neat little loops of the scientists' diagrams. The DMS rising into the atmosphere would blow far from the original sites of emission; warming and cooling currents would confuse the temperature chemistry and disperse the DMS gathered in the seawater. Nothing resembling a negative feedback loop ever has been identified.

The failure to find the DMS "switch" is perhaps the biggest single disappointment in the brief history of Gaian scientific research, and some of Gaia's critics have pounced. In a recent *Nature* article Stephen Schwartz, a chemist from the Brookhaven National Laboratory, claims not only that the DMS-producing phytoplankton have little or no role in controlling global temperature, but that sulfur in general has no significant influence. He goes so far as to suggest that the sulfurous gas actually adds to the global greenhouse effect. Schwartz concedes that DMS certainly makes clouds whiter, driving temperatures lower, but he asserts that this is at best a local, not global, impact. Here the pro and con devolves into conjecture, for to determine the net global impact of DMS one would have to model a world without the controversial gas and factor in the clouds that never were. Like the question of oceanic salinity, the ocean-atmosphere mechanisms of DMS and temperature control are just beginning to be understood.

LIFE IS THE MAGIC INGREDIENT

One might assume that the gap between the Gaians and the geochemists is really quite bridgeable, that carbon dioxide, oxygen, and oceanic chemistry are all regulated by a complex of geological and biological feedbacks. But ask the question of what would happen if all the living organisms were to die and disappear, and then the cat's fur flies. The Gaians maintain that living organisms uniquely regulate themselves and their environment and that destruction of life would mean destruction of the Earth's thermostat. James Walker and Jim Kasting respond that life is not crucial. They allow that if, for example, all marine life were to die out, there would be a massive accumulation of carbon dioxide in the air because there would be no organisms left to form shells and draw down the carbon. Temperatures might rise, they guess, by up to 10° C. (No minor inconvenience, since by most accounts the year 1988 was the hottest on record, about 1° C above the century's average.) Eventually, however, a nonbiological carbon burial cycle would correct this temperature phenomenon and the Earth's climate would return to normal.

Rather than disputing numerical hypotheticals with the learned establishment, Lovelock prefers chatting with the Three Bears. If the Earth is about 40 million kilometers (25 million miles) from too-hot Venus and almost double the distance, 80 million kilometers (50 million miles), from too-cold Mars, what temperature should be just right? Venus, twice as close and almost exactly the same size, has an infernal average surface temperature of about 477° C (890° F). Earth, at 13° C (55° F), is seven times closer in temperature to its more distant neighbor, Mars, which averages about −53° C (−63° F). Both flanking planets' atmospheres are filled with carbon dioxide, so any greenhouse explanation is unlikely. Lovelock calculates that, based on the facts of planetary positioning, Earth's average surface temperature should range between 240° and 340° C (464° to 644° F). Plenty hot enough to boil away the seas and insure that there would be no porridge or Goldilocks in the first place. Lovelock's estimate for the lifeless Earth's temperature is, of course, open to debate, but the fundamental observation that we are much closer in distance to boiling Venus and in tempera-

147

ture to frozen Mars does seem a good candidate for further explanation.

Andrew Watson also encourages us to take the long view to resolve the mystery of how our planet has cybernetically kept its cool. The global climate appears to run in cycles of about 115,000 years, of which about 100,000 years are glacial periods, or ice ages, and 15,000 years are interglacials like the one we find ourselves in now. Some climatologists break down the peaks and valleys of temperature into shorter intervals, declaring ice ages to come and go every 10,000 years or so, while others see cycles of up to 700,000 years. No one knows for sure what triggers glaciations, although the great Yugoslavian mathematician Milutin Milankovich has found that wobbles in the Earth's orbit every 26,000 years correspond with known glacial downturns in which carbon dioxide levels and temperatures spin lower in a vicious causal circle for a thousand years or more. No matter the time frame, the basic principle holds that it takes much longer for the great ice sheets and glaciers to build and brighten up the planet's reflective albedo in a positive feedback of cold and colder than it does for them to melt away. There always will be disputes about how long glacial periods last, but more important is that by most accounts, glaciation is a continuing cycle, the great ice sheets contracting and expanding in an endless ebb and flow.

Compress geological deep time into something more manageable, and suddenly the climatic system seems the excellent thermostat that Gaians claim. Watson suggests looking at Earth history as though it were compressed into a single day. Examined from this perspective, the global climate runs in cycles of about 2.5 seconds (115,000 years). About 2.2 seconds (100,000 years) during each of those periods have been in a glacial period. Interglacials, including the current one, pass in the blink of an eye. And when Earth history is cast on the scale of an average human lifespan, the climate seems like winter in Norway—a procession of cold days, each interrupted by a few hours of light and warmth. Whatever the time frame one chooses, the cycles come quickly enough to suggest thermostatic regulation on a very long term basis—once again, to life's very good fortune.

Gaia soothes and steadies the Earth's climate, Lovelock muses, by eating the chaos of the sun:

> Noise and chaos are near the equilibrium state. The way I look at it, if you just blow in a tube, you get a hiss, which is noise, but if you blow into a flute you get a gorgeous musical note because the chaos generated by your blowing has been tamed and used by the solid structure and been turned into the coherent sound of a flute. This is what life is doing all the time; it's taking the chaotic flow of energy coming in from the sun and turning it into coherence . . . it's not just that order comes out of chaos, the great thing about Gaia is that it accepts chaos and uses is.[24]

A poster presented by J. Lancaster of the Scripps Institute of Oceanography at the AGU conference cleverly substantiates Lovelock's rather cosmic claim. In his Biospheric Energy Storage (BES) hypothesis, Lancaster points out that the biosphere essentially tames the chaotic stream of solar energy into chemical potential or physical structure, and has done so ever since it began to evolve some 3.5 billion years ago. "Increasing structure and complexity within the biospheric system, however, require that the total energy of the biosphere increase."[25] As life evolves to higher and higher forms, more energy is needed to create these structures, so the surplus of solar energy flowing to the Earth is creatively absorbed and locked in as potential energy, or structure. The BES hypothesis also may help to explain the biophysics of the K-T and other catastrophes, illustrating the awesome power that would be released into the global environment were the biosphere forced by mass extinctions to release the energy it has stored. From Lancaster's innovative perspective, Gaia not only eats chaos, but evolving toward ever-greater complexity, she always is hungry for more. Biospheric energy

149

storage is one of the few positive feedback systems identified as helping to allay the warming sun's tendency to overheat the planet.

On balance, the geochemical hardline is no more satisfying than extreme Gaian claims of biotic mastery. Life is more than just another medium for gas to pass through; regulatory behavior seems inherent in uniquely self-organizing and self-maintaining properties of protoplasm. Walker's argument about the vastness of geological time scales is well-taken, yet it must be remembered that life has been there to modulate carbon dioxide uptake for most of Earth's history. There may always be an abiotic mechanism ready to take over, as he says, but that inanimate understudy has been waiting around for 3.5 billion years.

The middle ground in this debate seems to have been staked by the Earth Systems Group at New York University. As Tyler Volk observes, the terrestrial biosphere has the "capacity to moderate, but not perfectly regulate, climatic changes." Hoffert, head of the NYU unit, elaborates: "Chemically, a planetary atmosphere is not a thermodynamically isolated system, but one in a near-steady state pumped by solar radiation. It is more reasonable to assume chloroplasts and blue-green algae act as catalysts to speed up the reactions forming both carbohydrates and oxygen."

Hoffert implies that the climatological status of life be upgraded from incidental to catalytic, an astute compromise. A catalyst is a substance, usually present in small amounts (as the biota are in comparison to the whole of the planet), that modifies, especially increases, the rate of a chemical reaction without being consumed in the process. Enzymes are catalysts produced by living organisms to facilitate their own internal chemical reactions. The biota rarely dominates or overpowers but regularly accounts for the kind of critical difference that catalysts and enzymes naturally provide. Life is the magic ingredient.

SO WHY WORRY?

So why worry about threats to the environment? If biological mechanisms are as important as even moderate Gaian theorists argue, one might conclude that all the fuss about the carbon dioxide greenhouse, to take one example, is really much ado about nothing, since the biota will adjust or at least buffer the climatic impact. And in the meantime, the warming trend might warm up our winters and even forestall the replacement of our beloved trees by C4 plants and grasses. As those Duke University biochemists conclude, "Such a largescale feedback system should serve to regulate atmospheric CO_2, thus preventing a catastrophic rise in global carbon dioxide and temperature levels."[26]

Depending on which model you believe, the next fifty to seventy-five years could see CO_2 levels double or more. As the Duke University scientists maintain, in the long run this is likely to stimulate the growth of more C3 and C4 plants to pump down the gas, but the short-term scenario may be quite different. Greenhouse warming in the northern latitudes is now believed to be a threat to some species, particularly birch trees, in the temperature forests. One calculation by the Oak Ridge National Laboratory in Tennessee finds that it would take an area the size of Australia planted completely with sycamore trees, which are especially good at CO_2 absorption, to halt the current greenhouse trend—even more, one would surmise, if northern forests are dying. To ignore biological feedback on the global environment, such as the impact of trees on carbon dioxide, would of course be foolish, possibly fatal to many. Yet to count on the biota collectively to restore comfortable conditions is at least as foolhardy. Gaia, to the extent she exists, runs on her own sweet time, and her adjustments could take hundreds or thousands of years. A blink of the eye for Gaia is an eternity for us.

Science is to environmentalism as philosophy is to politics. Basic research is always sliced, diced, distorted, and matured into economic and legislative reality. Like any other new theory,

151

Gaia has had to go through a shakedown phase before it can be properly fitted to real-world applications; nothing is more valuable than those early errors, since one never can be confident that all has been foreseen. Very fortunately, Lovelock's expedition into the ozone issue has provided more mistakes than could ever have been hoped for when it comes to knowing how, and how not, to apply Gaian insights to heal and manage the environment. It really was a blessing.

VIII

THE GREAT OZONE WAR

A PARABLE OF ERROR

The story of Lovelock, CFC's, and the stratospheric ozone layer is fascinating because ultimately it has proved to be the story of a great compound error, a parable of vanity and desire. James Lovelock's greatest mistake undermined his most famous discovery, that aerosol CFC's have been accumulating in the Earth's atmosphere. In the late 1960s the British scientist designed and carried out the first experiments to show that CFC's did not degrade biologically, as had always been assumed, but instead were so chemically stable that once released into the air, they amassed indefinitely. These data, published in a 1973 *Nature* magazine article, have launched fifteen years of subsequent research on CFC's and their chemical cousins, BFC's (bromofluorocarbons). Today scientific consensus holds that these aerosols have been largely responsible for the dangerous depletion of the stratospheric ozone layer, including the infamous ozone "hole" over Antarctica.

Chlorofluorocarbon pollution could have had no more effective opponent than the scientist who first ferreted it out. But it was not until 1988, almost twenty years of bitter debate after his first CFC experiment, that the maverick researcher grudgingly acknowledged the full malevolence of the atmospheric poisons he had discovered. For two decades Lovelock had confounded the worldwide public of scientists, environmentalists, and grant-givers who have built on his work, stubbornly refusing to ascribe much ecological significance to the relationship between CFC's and the ozone. The scientist denied the significance of his own findings and scorned the entreaties of an international environmentalist movement ready to honor his pioneering work, all because he was blinded by faith in Gaia's capacity to adjust to almost any situation that arose—in this case, to the depletion of atmospheric ozone by CFC's or any other man-made pollutant. Gaia, the theory he had created, the goddess he adored, would take care of the aerosol-ozone problem.

When Lovelock first discovered the CFC's, they were present in almost infinitesimal concentrations, no more than 100 parts per trillion in the air. So when first reporting his findings in *Nature* he wrote, "The presence of these compounds [CFC's] constitutes no conceivable hazard."[1] He has since called that sentence "one of my greatest blunders. Of course I should have said, '*At their present level* these compounds constitute no conceivable hazard' " (italics added).[2] Lovelock claims that at first he was worried that some enthusiast would use his CFC data as the basis of a doom story, because "as soon as numbers are attached to the presence of a substance, these numbers seem to confer a spurious significance."[3] Tell someone the dose, and it will sound too high. As a prospective planetary physician, Lovelock set out to ward off the hypochondriacs. But as every physician who pays malpractice insurance knows, there is always the possibility that this time the complaints will prove too true.

Lovelock is fond of saying that he much prefers a fruitful error to a sterile truth, but this particular apple must have had a very bitter taste. For, like a schoolboy who has had his mouth washed out with soap, he now repeats the proper motto "Poison is the dose" over and over again, in what has become his continuous homage to Paracelsus. The great Swiss physiologist spoke of the health of people, but Lovelock, the geophysiologist, expands that wisdom to the global system. If there is too little oxygen, most everything alive on the Earth will suffocate. But if there is too much, we will all burn to a crisp. Too much salt, and everyone will shrivel. Too little, and no membranes would cohere to begin life in the first place. Too hot or too cold, too much or too little carbon dioxide, dimethyl sulfide, methyl iodide, water, CFC's, damn near anything—and eventually there will be problems beyond Gaia's capacity to recover.

Lovelock now realizes all too well that this is what happened with CFC's. At concentrations in parts per trillion in the air, they were no threat. But since his discovery of them they have soared 500 percent or more in intensity, and the dose is now potent enough to make Gaia sick. But it was not until 1988 that he publicly conceded the fact: "It may turn out that I was wrong to have opposed those who sought instant legislation to stop the emission of CFC's. . . . The first symptoms of poisoning are now felt. I now join with those who would regulate the emissions of the CFC's and other carriers of chlorine to the stratosphere."[4] Yet even that concession remains conditional. While Lovelock finally acknowledges that he may have underestimated the impact of these aerosols on the ozone layer—the hole over Antarctica is hard to argue with—to him it is all a minor matter compared to other environmental issues, such as tropical rain forest depletion and greenhouse gas accumulation, two issues that he sees as a single global system coupled in a dangerously vicious cycle of escalating temperature and climatic chaos. In fact, Lovelock still contends firmly that the greenhouse heat absorption properties of CFC's ultimately will prove far more deadly than their effects on ozone chemistry.

DADDY NEVER GOES ON VACATION

When the wind blew from the Atlantic it was sparkling. But when it blew from Europe, a thick, acrid haze settled over

155

his family's country vacation cottage in western Ireland, obscuring their view of the bay. Lovelock was upset, and he refused to believe, as the meteorologists and air pollution experts back home contended, that smog could not travel that far and that the haze was actually some strange concatenation of the Irish bogs. So, much to the dismay of his wife Helen and the children, the indefatigable researcher brought along his gas chromatograph and electron capture detector on their 1968 summer holiday, intent on finding the presence of some unequivocally man-made substance, such as chlorofluorocarbon gases, in the hazy air. The little lighthouse a mile into the bay would still be besmogged, but at least Father would have the satisfaction of shaking his fist at the decadent despoilers to the east.

Lovelock proved his point and then some. He found that the concentration of chlorofluorocarbons was three times greater in the air blown from Europe than from the open sea. He now had proof concerning the nature of the smog, including the unsettling news that it could travel a lot farther than everyone would prefer. Though prompting a flurry of environmental studies and initiatives, many of whose projects would employ those who had discouraged him in the first place, Lovelock was far more intrigued by the fact that the wind coming from the open ocean also contained significant, if smaller, concentrations of the CFC gases.

> Could it be that we were breathing polluted air
> blown right the way across the Atlantic from America?
> Or were they [CFC's] accumulating in the world at
> large because they were so stable? The way to find out
> would be to make a journey aboard a ship or an aircraft
> and take samples in the northern and southern hemi-
> sphere, to examine their global distribution.[5]

Lovelock pursued this line of inquiry for almost four years before he found a way to fund the research. He and a colleague, Peter Fellgett of Reading University, the same man who had invented the multiplex interferometer spectroscope used by Lovelock's team to analyze the Martian atmosphere, submitted grant proposals to every likely prospect in the United Kingdom and the United States. They were always turned down, sometimes quite haughtily. Lovelock takes perverse relish in citing the comments of one referee:

> Every schoolboy knows that the chlorofluorocarbons are among the most stable of chemical substances. It would be very difficult to measure them in the atmosphere at parts per million on account of their lack of chemical reactivity. The proposer suggests that he can measure them at parts per trillion, the application is clearly bogus and the time of this committee should not be wasted with such frivolous proposals.[6]

That was the last time Lovelock ever formally applied for a research grant.

Stubborn is the man who drags along unwieldy scientific apparatuses on his family's holiday over their united objections (although Helen seems incapable of anything angrier than tart amusement at her husband's impetuous curiosity), and stubborn is he who endures the slings and arrows of self-righteous overseers just to satisfy his need to know. As an independent scientist without a steady salary, such perseverance is quite expensive in income lost and more practical opportunities missed. Nonetheless, in 1971 Lovelock took advantage of some other discussions he was having with Britain's Environment Research Council to ask if he would be allowed to travel and take measurements on one of their research ships, the R. V. Shackleton, on its regular journey to Antarctica and back. They kindly agreed, and also offered to pay fare for him and for a graduate student to join the ship in Montevideo, so that measurements could be taken on outbound and return voyages, which Lovelock eventually completed in 1972.

Using his electron capture detector, the only instrument

157

sensitive and versatile enough to measure substances present at
the level of several parts per trillion parts of air (the equivalent
to sniffing out an average week's pay floating around somewhere
in the hundred trillion–dollar global economy), the renegade
researcher found just what he had predicted. CFC's were building
up throughout the atmosphere. The heaviest concentrations,
approximately 50 to 70 parts per trillion, were in the northern
hemisphere, where most of these gases are produced and emitted
from aerosol sprays and from leaking or discarded air-conditioning and refrigeration units. Significant concentrations, in the
range of 40 parts per trillion, also were found in the southern
hemisphere, demonstrating that CFC circulation was global and
that the north was polluting the south.

Like very little found in nature or made by man, CFC's are
so stable that they will not disappear. In essence, these gases
have half-lives lasting for thousands of years, far more durable
than the radiation that lingers from such disasters as the explosion of the nuclear power complex at Chernobyl and every bit as
stubborn as the toxins that would fall out from the "dirtiest"
atomic bombs. Once Lovelock published findings on CFC's in
Nature it became imperative to know more about the environmental impact of these eternal compounds. In 1973 Ralph
Cicerone and his colleague Richard Stolarski of the NCAR drew
the scientific world's attention to how chlorine catalyzes the
destruction of the ozone, showing how one slippery and promis-
cuous chloride ion can slide in and out of hundreds of thousands
of unstable ozone molecules, lingering just long enough to shred
their bonds. In 1974 Sherry Rowland and Mario Molina demonstrated that CFC's, as carriers of chlorine to the stratosphere,
were therefore a grievous threat to the ozone layer, delineating
the complex reaction sequence of the destruction mechanism.
Lovelock writes, "This paper stands like a beacon, a natural
successor to Rachel Carson's book, *Silent Spring*. It heralded the
start of the ozone war."[7]

A BIT OF EDWARD VIII

Lovelock was in the perfect position for glory. Fit and in his mid-fifties, he had just helped to found the second of two of the most important environmental movements of the century, by experiments he had designed, conducted with instruments he had invented. Why on earth did he instead downplay the importance of his own pioneering results? The man had battled poverty, insult, and the funding powers that be, to sail halfway around the world and confirm a suspicion that authorities and colleagues had dismissed with sneers. Now research inspired by his work indicated that CFC's were the vehicles for the destruction of the ozone shield. No one expected Lovelock to have known this; the value of his basic research on the presence of CFC's far outweighed his incidental opinion underestimating their importance. Why not join the crusade that preached his data and become one of our "ozone saviors," to the world's everlasting gratitude? Even though the bandwagon had already begun to roll, Lovelock would have been pulled up and onto the seat of honor by a thousand welcoming arms.

Such everlasting gratitude does not pay the rent, the mortgage on that dream vacation home in the Cote d'Azur, or buy one of those hot new Cray superminicomputers with which Lovelock could work out every last Gaian detail. His NASA space consultantships had petered out in 1966, at which time he accepted a retainer project from Shell Research to examine the global consequences of air pollution from the combustion of gasoline and other fossil fuels. Did the lone wolf researcher stalk this megabuck connection and pounce on his chance to cash in? Did Lovelock sell out to the aerosol industry on the CFC issue? What more valuable defense could the chemical manufacturers have than testimony by the atmospheric explorer that the gases he had discovered were probably not harmful to the ozone layer and that even downward fluctuations in atmospheric ozone were not necessarily bad?

159

"In the 1970s Lovelock had two cults following him: the polluters and the eco-freaks. He did not sell out to either group," says Steve Schneider firmly. "He took the position that he did because he was trying to protect friends in the chemical aerosol industry who were losing jobs because of his research." When he first met Lovelock at a 1975 conference organized by Margaret Mead, Schneider suspected that Gaia was no more than an elaborate excuse to pollute. The youthful veteran of sixties idealism had considered Lovelock a scientific shill hired by industry to thwart legislation restricting pollution, starting with the CFC aerosols. While the two men clearly have come a long way since, Schneider, ever the ardent environmentalist, still grits his teeth: "I'm not out to force Lovelock into recantation. He's already done a very good job of that himself."

Lovelock nettles at any suggestion of a sell-out.

It no more follows that research work supported by Shell or any other multinational corporation must be suspect than it does that similar work coming from a communist country would also be tainted. The real winners were the academics, the poppinjays! They got between $10 and $100 million in grants. The real losers were organized labor, who lost a lot of jobs permanently. Industry broke even. It always does.

Nowhere in the research conducted for this book did I come across any written or spoken opinion that Lovelock acted in any way but honorably on the CFC issue. And it is interesting to note that since his work for Shell, Lovelock has consistently campaigned against pollution from automobiles as one of the greatest environmental hazards facing the planet. Still, Schneider's contention that Lovelock diminished his own career to help his aerosol chemists friends seemed only a partial explanation at best—a bit too noble, and too unlike a scientist.

"He was protecting friends, though that was just a part of

160

it," says James Lodge, an NCAR alumnus who is now a consulting chemist in Boulder and editor of *Atmospheric Environment*. Lodge was a friend of Lovelock's before the ozone wars, saw him through the battles, and has stayed in touch ever since. He offered a very personal observation about Lovelock and the ozone controversy: "Jim has a deep physical aversion to having too many people around, and he always longs to retreat to the countryside. He had a taste of aerosol-ozone celebrity and it had little appeal for him, since it meant conferences, dinners, symposia—crowds." Lovelock does indeed spend ten months of the year in rustic seclusion in his Cornish Brigadoon. And there is beyond doubt a panicky nervous cringe to the man, perhaps indicative of much deeper discomfort, when he finds himself at the center of a crush. Quite possibly this was an important motivation to stay out of the limelight. Yet he also manages to receive press and visitors from all over and to tour the world to give speeches and attend conferences, banquets, and so forth, and he usually seems quite at ease.

No one knows more about a person's physical likes and aversions than a compatible spouse, so I decided to ask his wife, Helen. A daughter of the English countryside, even less inclined to the madding crowd than her husband is, she found Lodge's explanation, if anything, understated: "The reporters somehow got hold of our number and would call at all hours. Others were bold enough to drive right up to the house. We had to ask them to leave the property at once." A shy, pretty woman with the liveliest blue eyes in the south of England, Helen Lovelock has been confined to a wheelchair for quite some time and cares not a jot for those who take it upon themselves to invade her family's privacy. When welcoming an invited guest, however, lighthearted good spirits bubble out of her quite musically; this infirm woman well into her sixties is still an English country girl who loves a bit of fun. To her, "cashing in" on the CFC discovery, if it meant throwing oneself to those dreadful people, would have been downright silly.

Protecting friends and ducking crowds are good enough

161

reasons for Lovelock to have refrained from capitalizing on his discovery of CFC's but insufficient to explain his fifteen-year campaign against the importance of his own work. Why else do men make foolish, potentially self-destructive mistakes like that? When pressed, Lodge confided that "with Gaia on his mind, Jim was not about to overestimate the destabilizing influence of any single system, including ozone. The theory was new and exciting, and perhaps Jim was a bit infatuated with the whole idea." Lovelock was so in love with his own theory that he was blind to any facts—even important ones that he had discovered—that contradicted Gaia.

Few of us can fully appreciate what it must be like to fall in love with one's own theory. The fact that there is no possibility of physical communion might incline one to discount such a romance as simply metaphorical and thus of no real consequence. Must an affair be consummative to be genuine, or can an imaginary love be as powerful, exciting, and disruptive as the real, sexual thing? I have spent dozens of hours with Lovelock and hundreds with his writings, and I can faithfully report that never once have I known him to confuse Gaian theory with the deity after which it is named; I never heard him refer to Gaia as a female, a goddess, or any other manner of convivial creature in anything but a lighthearted, figurative way. A less-disciplined imagination might lapse across the anthropomorphic boundary on occasion, but Lovelock has got it straight. But what about those early, poetic days of Gaia? Did the young man have a secret fling with the earthy Greek goddess he had spied from Mars?

UNSAFE AT ANY LEVEL?

Plato mused that poets should be banned from the republic because of their potential for inciting insurrection. While the idea of banning something or someone may be very satisfying intellectually, it is mostly a plan of action to clear the mind.

Available as an alternative only to philosopher kings, rarely does eradication turn out in real life to be practical, desirable, or just.

Ban CFC's once and for all! that was the decree that issued from a 1976 conclave of scientists, lawyers, legislators, and journalists held in Logan, Utah, to ponder the aerosol-ozone problem. Rather than setting limits and scheduling goals, the crusaders were determined to rid the world of this carcinogenic menace that they, thank God, had discovered.

For Lovelock it was like reliving a nightmare.

When Rachel Carson made us aware of the dangers arising from the mass application of toxic chemicals, she presented her arguments in the manner of an advocate rather than that of a scientist. In other words, she selected the evidence to prove her case. The chemical industry, seeing its livelihood threatened by her action, responded with an equally selective set of arguments chosen in defence. This . . . seems to have established a pattern. Since then, a great deal of scientific argument and evidence concerning the environment is presented as if in a court-room or at a public inquiry. It cannot be said too often that, although this may be good for the democratic process of public participation in matters of general concern, it is not the best way to discover scientific truth. Truth is said to be the first casualty of war. It is also weakened by being used selectively in evidence to prove a case in law.[8]

For the second time in his life, Lovelock saw his pioneering work used in a polemical way that he abhorred, and he found it all so absurd that he lost his own perspective as well. Rather than realize that exorbitant claims and accusations almost always accompany the birth of a reform movement, particularly in the free-for-all of American politics, and that hysterical polemics

163

are what usually seem to be needed to overcome the terrible moment of inertia imposed by the mere presence of such offending establishments as the multibillion-dollar chemical industry, Lovelock overreacted to the weaknesses and excesses of environmentalist zeal and fled to his lover's pliant embrace. "Anyone who was not for the immediate banning of the CFC's was clearly a traitor to the cause. . . . At Logan they tried to form legal judgments on plausible but untested scientific hypotheses. It is not so surprising that the result was of little credit to any of the participants."[9] Instead of staking the middle ground, Lovelock struck out for the opposite extreme and sacrificed his greatest discovery to the theory-goddess he adored. No need to ban CFC's. Gaia would adjust.

Far too shrewd to count on goddesses for anything but the spectacularly unexpected, Plato would have caught the problem right away. The sage's aversion to poets in the republic came not from his low estimation of their worth or from his annoyance with their tendency toward wild claims, but from his profound respect for their power. His fabled instruction never to attack the weaknesses of an opponent's argument and always to challenge the strengths may seem a bit idealistic, but ultimately it is great practical advice. Although you may not win as many verbal battles, you are certain always to get to the core of the issue. And doing justice to the best of the opposition sure cuts down on the risk that you can end up being very, very wrong.

Whether or not Lovelock has finally been proven wrong on the issue or was just heavily outvoted, current policy initiatives to curb CFC and BFC emissions and reduce human exposure to ultraviolet radiation concur mostly with the evidence presented at the Logan conclave, if not with the off-with-their-heads spirit that seems to have prevailed. This policy is based on three assumptions: (1) that CFC's and BFC's are depleting the stratospheric ozone layer, which is by now well proven; (2) that a decrease in the ozone layer leads to an increase in ultraviolet radiation, which is virtually beyond dispute; and (3) that ultraviolet radiation is harmful to humans, which certainly is true in some cases, but just as often it is healthy. The question is how much and for whom.

All of these points become moot, and policies unnecessary, if it turns out that the depletion of the stratospheric ozone layer is temporary and that through Gaian or other mechanisms our protective shield is coming back. This is where Lovelock starts his counterattack.

THE SUNSPOT FACTOR

"When sunspot activity ebbs, as it had during the mid-1970s, the ozone layer diminishes significantly. It is the same eleven-year solar cycle that has gone on forever, and throughout which human beings have survived quite well," points out James Lodge, who has followed this whole issue closely in his journal *Atmospheric Environment.* Every eleven years or so, the sun reverses and rebuilds its magnetic field by redirecting the flow of the hot gases on its surface. Sunspots—dark patches that erupt on the surface—are the magnetic nodal points that block and reverse the sun's molten surface flow. As though the sun were condemned to go through a form of electromagnetic puberty every decade, sunspot blemishes are most plentiful at the time of transition and tend to cluster in several active regions on the sun's face. In one of the more curious paradoxes of contemporary astronomy, the average sunspot, taken singly, has been reliably measured to decrease solar luminosity, as one might expect from a dark, photo-absorbent area. Over time, however, an overall increase in sunspot activity results in the brightening of the sun, about 0.1 percent greater at the peak ends of the cycle than at the ebbs. Like a tree that has been pruned loses some short-term green in the cause of longer-term leafiness, the sun appears to be revitalized by these intermittent, localized diminishments. In fact, northern Europe's "Little Ice Age" from 1645 to 1715, with record low temperatures, is now believed to have been caused, at least in part, by the virtual absence of sunspots during that period.

Lovelock and Lodge contend that atmospheric ozone levels vary with sunspot activity much in the same way that the sun's strength does. Sunspots act a bit like rocks in a stream, at times causing the molten surface gases to splash up into violent sunstorms, or solar flares. When sunspot and associated sunstorm activity are at the peak of their cycles, vast outpourings of plasma, an electrically balanced gas so highly ionized that it is sometimes referred to as the fourth state of matter, stream throughout the solar system. This can have a dramatic impact on the Earth. Peak plasma flows can disrupt and increase the brilliance of auroral northern lights displays. And, as Lovelock and Lodge remind us, the plasma also ionizes oxygen (O_2) molecules, ripping apart their bonds to form ozone (O_3), the deep blue poisonous, explosive gas that protects the planet's surface from undue exposure to ultraviolet radiation. Ironically, it is a new flood of energy from the sun, the source of all of that troublesome ultraviolet radiation, that Lovelock counts on to help Gaia adjust her protective ozone layer.

As of this writing, the eleven-year sunspot cycle is just emerging from its ebb; a return to peak conditions is expected sometime in 1990. Little is made of this fact in the vast amounts of coverage that the ozone hole has received. One suspects that this sunspot-ozone connection has deliberately been underplayed by the scientific establishment in what is essentially an honest effort to focus public and legislative attention on the destructive effects of CFC's without complicating and undermining the issue. Is it possible that some Gaian compensatory mechanism will take advantage of the increased solar plasma flow, just as other living organisms exploit new energy sources in their environment, and restore the ozone to its former levels, despite the CFC's? Lovelock does not go so far as to predict this, but if it were to happen, it would do his heart proud.

THAT DEADLY UV

Far from being an unmitigated hazard, as many ozone alarmists would have it, ultraviolet radiation is at worst a mixed blessing. So those who clamor for a policy of zero UV radiation—and Lovelock contends that there were many in the early years of the ozone debate—are benighted.

Intense ultraviolet bombardment may give you a bad burn, wrinkles, or even skin cancer, depending largely on the level of your skin pigmentation. No matter what your color, deprived of sufficient UV radiation, and therefore of the vitamin D the body produces from it, you will likely suffer from any or all of a variety of bone disorders. Such deficiencies are almost unknown in Western societies, where lighter skins are more UV porous and diets are supplemented with vitamin D. In these countries, skin cancer is far greater a threat. Yet in a number of populous Third World nations with deep pigmentation but poor diets, rickets, which stunts and perverts bone growth in children, remains a common crippler. In those regions, Lovelock notes, an increase in ultraviolet radiation may actually lead to a net improvement in public health. Quite a fair-skinned fellow, the Englishman wonders if racism has had anything to do with the skin cancer argument managing a rather greater share of global policy voice than has the rickets argument thus far.

Rather than pure black or white, the ultraviolet issue comes mostly in subtle shades of gray. Lovelock observes that while visible light varies 160 percent between the Arctic and the tropics, ultraviolet varies some 700 percent in intensity. It is well known that immigrants from high to low latitudes suffer from the increased UV levels of their new surroundings, but the reverse—migrants from the tropics to temperate regions suffering from decreased UV exposure—also holds true. And there are indications that low ultraviolet concentrations may be contributory to osteomalacia, a bone disorder afflicting adults, as well as to multiple sclerosis.

167

Lovelock has a long history of involvement with this particular issue and takes pride in citing experiments he conducted in
the early 1940s at the NIMR in London, assisting Robert
Bourdillon and Owen Lidwell. They wanted to find a way to stop
infections from spreading in hospital wards and operating rooms,
so they tried to kill bacteria by exposing them to unfiltered
ultraviolet radiation. This proved comparatively easy when the
bacteria's normal coatings were washed away, but as Lovelock is
quick to point out, bacteria "do not live naked any more than
we do." The thin coatings of mucous and dirt that microbes
normally acquire from their environment—analogous to a light
layer of summer clothes—proved quite adequate to block out
intense doses of UV radiation.

Lovelock contends that a distorted view of ultraviolet radiation and its effects is endemic to scientific thinking.

I found it to be common among the scientists
who sought life on Mars. I could not help wondering
how they could think that there was life on the
intensely irradiated surface of Mars and at the same
time believe that the land beneath the thick and
murky Archaean [pre-oxygen and ozone] atmosphere
of Earth was sterile. How could they fit into their
minds such contrary ideas?[10]

In fact, life arose and flourished for at least a billion years
without any absorbent ozone shield at all. Lynn Margulis has
done numerous experiments illustrating this, showing that photosynthetic algae survive exposure to ultraviolet radiation equivalent in intensity to pure sunlight unfiltered by the atmosphere.
And as Lovelock notes, while sevenfold variations in rainfall,
temperature, salinity, and a variety of other factors can make all
the difference, nowhere on earth can there be found deserts
created by too much or too little ultraviolet.

MAYBE JUST A LUCKY GUESS

Despite Lovelock's rejoinders, the campaign against CFC's has marched on; the aerosols are now banned in the United States, Canada, Norway, Sweden, and Denmark, with voluntary restrictions in West Germany, Australia, Switzerland, and Japan. The United Nations Environmental Program (UNEP) helped launch the movement by responding to pressure from nongovernmental organizations, such as Friends of the Earth, and in 1980 requested member governments to reduce CFC manufacture and use. By 1985 the Vienna Convention for Protection of the Ozone Layer was adopted by the European Economic Community and twenty-one other states, although this agreement appears to have been much loftier in principle than in practice. In 1986 DuPont, the world's largest producer of CFC's, announced that it would develop alternative carrier propellants by 1991. And in 1987 a comprehensive treaty was forged in Montreal between the world's major CFC-producing and consuming nations. The Montreal Treaty froze CFC manufacture at 1986 levels and specified cuts of 20 percent by 1994 and an additional 30 percent by the year 2000. Production will be cut by no more than a third, however, since many developing countries are exempted from the treaty's restrictions for ten years. And states that currently consume low volumes of CFC's can actually raise their usage up to 0.3 kg per capita per year.

Many environmental advocates now maintain that these restrictions on CFC production and usage are too little, too late. Pressure for the total worldwide ban that was first called for at the 1976 Logan, Utah, conclave has mounted as reports of ozone depletion at both poles, particularly the hole in the ozone layer over the South Pole, have worsened. But the demands of developing countries, particularly those in the humid tropics, where air-conditioning units are sorely welcome, and chemical manufacturers, who feel that the Montreal Treaty is already quite an attack on their bottom line, make it seem unlikely that any further steps to reduce global CFC's will be taken in the near

169

future. Enforcement of the Montreal Treaty is the next step of the campaign.

Very few share Lovelock's faith that Gaia ultimately will compensate for CFC depletion of the ozone layer, either by taking advantage of plasma from sunstorms or seizing upon some other regulatory mechanism. Yet it is possible that Gaia may be in the process of doing just that. As of this writing, atmospheric scientists around the world are puzzling over an apparent partial recovery: according to *Science News*, the amount of Antarctic ozone depletion is only about half of the drop that had been expected. Researchers confidently predicted that 1988's annual summer thinning would bring a loss of 25 to 30 percent below winter ozone levels, but data from the Total Ozone Mapping Spectrometer (TOMS) aboard the *Nimbus-7* satellite, showed that the maximum loss of ozone was in the 10- to 15-percent range. Winter ozone losses in 1987 hit 50 percent, the worst on record. Moreover, rather than the sharply defined "hole" of recent years, centered directly over the South Pole, this year's gap has much less structural integrity, wobbling erratically around the Antarctic skies.

Scientists are at a loss to explain the apparent recovery. Unusually dynamic weather patterns appear to have shaken CFC's and other pollutants out of the air of the stratosphere, diluting the chlorine chemistry of ozone depletion. Meteorologist Jerry Mahlman, director of the Geophysical Fluid Dynamics Laboratory at Princeton University, was quoted in *Science News* as saying that "dynamics can essentially fight back, making it harder for chemistry [the chlorine chemistry of ozone depletion] to operate."[11] Great gusts of wind blowing troublesome pollutants away . . . did Gaia sneeze?

One season's encouraging news can hardly be cited as proof of recovery, and subsequent data on stratospheric ozone levels are not encouraging. But even if that deep blue ozone blanket were to be eaten completely threadbare, there is every indication that life, particularly at the microbial level, and therefore probably at the level of the complex microbial communities that we now think of as higher organisms, would continue to grow and evolve. Gaian theory predicts that the global system will adjust whenever possible to maintain the conditions necessary for life to continue on this planet, but not necessarily human life. There are no favored species. If the current replenishment of Antarctic ozone does prove to be a compensatory adjustment, it was a quick response—two decades of CFC ozone depletion, extrapolated to a human lifescale, works out to be about six seconds between irritation and sneeze. If human CFC pollution did sicken the living Earth, guilt feelings are less appropriate than mortal fear. Though it is easy and comfortable to feel that Gaia exists to take care of us, the living Earth is like any other organism—she exists to take care of herself. And she will do her best to get rid of whatever is making her ill.

IX

THE BODY OF THE EARTH

GEOPHYSIOLOGY AND THE ART OF PLANETARY MEDICINE

The greater the scientist, goes the grim maxim, the longer his reputation will discourage progress in his field. By this measure, the greatest medical scholar in history was Galen, the second-century Greek physician to the Roman court whose virtually undisputed authority hampered medical research for most of the next fifteen hundred years. The core of the problem was that the man who had proved that arteries carry blood, not air, and who had authored approximately five hundred masterful medical treatises on the brain, spinal cord, pulse, and nerves, never was allowed to study a human cadaver. He derived all of his anatomical conclusions from animal dissections. But rather than qualifying these observations as more analogous than exact, Galen decreed them from Imperial Rome. His favorite research animal was the pig.

If the Earth functions like a body, as Gaian theory holds, it must have vital organs. But what are they? How do they work? The answers to these questions may be centuries away, for just as

Galen could only guess at the inside of the human body, contemporary scientists of planetary medicine are constrained from dissecting the globe and must rely on analogous knowledge from the bodies of animals and plants. Nonetheless, Lovelock believes that the principles of physiology and medicine (the field in which he earned his doctorate) must be applied in order to understand how the global body works and how it may be healed. His favorite research animal is the human.

Geophysiology, the name Lovelock has coined for this new discipline of global medicine, examines the roles of major regional ecosystems, such as tropical rain forests, coastal seas, grasslands, and so forth, in the overall modulation of the planet's climate. In contrast to traditional ecology, which normally considers ecosystems individually, examining how each biological region obtains and conserves water, heat, and essential nutrients, geophysiology examines the exchange processes between ecosystems—those adjacent as well as those communicating across disparate parts of the globe. Lovelock likens the difference between ecology and geophysiology to the difference between the medical study of a single organ to that of the whole body.

> Geophysiology reminds us that all eco-systems are interconnected. By analogy, in an animal the liver has some capacity for the regulation of its internal environment, and its liver cells can be grown in the isolation of a tissue culture. But neither the animal nor its liver can live alone; they depend on their interconnection.

For now, the practical difference between geophysiology and mainstream ecology is in the emphasis on systems. Gaians ask themselves how the global climate might compensate for a perturbation like greenhouse warming: the system could restore itself, like a fundamentally healthy body recovering from a fever, or it could suffer a sudden and rapid deterioration, like a patient plunging from serious to critical condition. But this systemic approach can unduly minimize the consequences of global warming for specific regions and species, since the state of the whole system—the whole patient—is the geophysiologist's overriding concern. Mainstream ecologists tend to concentrate more on the practical problems of individual ecosystems than on their relationship to the whole system. In the Gaian framework, geophysiologists are the general practitioners of planetary medicine and traditional ecologists are the specialists.

Ultimately, geophysiologists face even deeper problems than those that misled the legendary Roman physician, since there is nothing genuinely analogous to the body of the Earth to dissect and compare. Discerning the internal workings of the planet by the seismic and geomagnetic means now available is like learning about the human body through muffled stethoscopes and blurry X rays. This is one reason why Lynn Margulis much prefers that the Gaia theory be limited to discussions of the surface of the earth, since there is really no way of testing whether the planet's organismic behavior is limited to the surface or if the biosphere is just the skin of a global creature, alive from its molten heart that goes glub, glub, glub, on out.

DISCOVERING THE BODY

Lovelock dreams of blazing the trail for geophysiology, much as William Harvey, the great seventeenth-century English physician, challenged Galen's orthodoxy and pioneered modern anatomy. With his discovery of how the heart works and the way blood circulates through the human body, Harvey accomplished what Lovelock has yet to learn about the planetary body. That the Earth has vital organs is an article of Gaian faith, but what they are and how they work is still a matter of conjecture.

Perhaps the rivers that transfer nutrients and wastes from the continents to the oceans are in fact analogous to the arteries and veins that circulate blood. One of the best-understood

174

geophysiological processes is the one (detailed in chapter 5), by which carbon is drawn from the atmospheric CO_2 by tropical forests, combined with the calcium of the rocks and soil, carried by groundwater, streams, and rivers to the coastal seas, where it is reformed as seashells by marine organisms and eventually buried as waste beneath the ocean floor. But there is no way at present of telling whether this cycle is as thoroughly envisioned as Harvey's diagrams of the circulatory system or if it is as seriously incomplete as Galen's sketch, which, among other shortcomings, left out the heart.

While few mainstream earth scientists and physicians (Lewis Thomas is chief among the exceptions) have joined in Lovelock's anatomical expedition thus far, a growing cadre of holistic healers have embraced the Earth-as-body concept. Quick to point out that similar beliefs have long been held by a variety of indigenous cultures, including a number of native American societies, many alternativists feel that the principles of wellness are as applicable as traditional medicine to the science of planetary physiology. Or even more so, since the non-invasive modes of diagnosis and massage therapy common to holistic healing are more compatible with the physical constraints of earth science.

One fascinating hypothesis is that the Oriental system of acupuncture points in the human body has its counterpart in the planetary body. There is something intuitively amenable about this proposition; indeed, the term *meridian* has been adapted from cartography to the acupuncturist's body map. And it certainly is true that there are points around the planet of greater geomagnetic intensity, as is the case with the distribution of any magnetic field. Moreover, the idea of planetary nodal points is in keeping with folkloric traditions of sacred or "energized" places on the Earth; from the druidical origins of the site of the cathedral at Chartres to the ruins at Angkor Wat, disparate cultures have held that certain key locations on Earth are endowed with a special vibrancy.

The Colorado Plateau, a 150,000-square-mile region in the southwestern United States, covering parts of Utah, Colorado,

New Mexico, and Arizona, and including the Grand Canyon, may be a geophysiologically vital part of the globe. The plateau pulses with every conceivable form of natural energy. Drenched from above with one of the highest daily averages of sunshine in North America and from below with great underground rivers and springs, this vast semiarid expanse also harbors approximately one-third of all of the continent's uranium plus huge deposits of coal, molybdenum, copper, and other minerals. In the most highly energized areas of the plateau the air is said to be as lively and ionized as a morning shower.

Most curious are at least seven native American "sacred breathing mountains," peaks that have a filigree of blowholes around their base. According to Doyne Sartor of NCAR, air flows in and out of these caverns with almost respiratory regularity—in for about 6 hours at the rate of about 30 miles per hour, then out for 6 hours, in a continuous cycle. Sartor, who estimates that there are about 7 billion cubic feet of underground waterways and caverns in the area, once deposited fluorescent particles in one blowhole and collected them from another one 24 miles away.

While the ecological significance of all of this energetic activity is far from understood, the plateau's general effects on human health do seem salutary. As Joan Price writes in the article "The Earth Is Alive and Running Out of Breath,"

> A significant percentage of contemporary diseases and deaths has been correlated to anxiety and stress; the Colorado Plateau has the nation's lowest death rate per thousand inhabitants. Stress has also been shown to significantly increase the difficulty in giving birth; the Colorado Plateau leads the nation in live birth rates per thousand inhabitants. [1]

Acupuncture also lends itself to the study of geophysiology, because of the Oriental discipline's counterintuitive insistence that certain points on, say, the foot or the elbow are crucial to the health of organs elsewhere in the body. This is precisely the kind of interdependence that geophysiologists aim to prove for their planetary organism. Warning of the danger of development to the Colorado Plateau, Price concludes that "a blocking of energy leads to imbalance and disease such as droughts, floods, extremes in climate, and attendant human struggles to adjust."[2]

The body metaphor personalizes the abstraction of planetary ecology. How much easier to think of pressure points on a global body than geomagnetic anomalies in a biogeochemical system! But most earth scientists still contend that this intellectual convenience has been obtained at the price of too much distortion. Perhaps, like Galen's intellectual shorthand of understanding the human body as though it were the same as a pig's, geophysiology's working assumption that the planet is an animal body will remain fruitful as long as the purpose of the comparison is to identify not only similarities but vital differences as well.

FEVER, AND CHILLS?

Not blood or energy, but four bodily humors, Hippocrates believed, were what coursed through the human system. Each vital fluid was deemed a glandular secretion, and none had anything to do with the heart. Imbalances resulted in disease, so the goal of medical treatment was to restore harmony to the humors. All in all, the father of medicine really did not know much about human physiology; still, odds were pretty good that with his standard prescription of rest, better diet, and better hygiene, he could bring a fever down.

Most contemporary environmentalists, regardless of scientific ideology, find themselves in a similar position: the mechanics and time cycles of the greenhouse warming of the earth (to take what seems the predominant environmental problem) are still far from understood, particularly in the way that disparate parts of the globe influence one another. But at least one aspect

177

of the solution—to reduce carbon dioxide, methane, and CFC emissions—is eminently clear.

In fact, Hippocrates's program of recovery is not far in spirit from the consensus ecological prescription: a general slowdown and cleanup of industry, development, and agriculture and the toxins they produce would go a long way toward cooling and cleansing the overheated Earth. And though the Greek apostle of medical moderation resorted to drastic therapy only when absolutely necessary, it is a safe bet that the founding physician was not above the occasional dire threat to get a stubborn patient to calm down and take the cure. Could it be that all of those doomsday warnings from today's environmental community, particularly the fashionable sentiment bandied about that we only have a decade left before the damage to the planet becomes irreversible, are also in the great tradition of preventive hyperbole?

Lovelock, who prides himself on being neither alarmist nor extremist, believes that the environmental threat of greenhouse warming has, if anything, been seriously *understated*. He is on record as certain that the Earth has begun a major climatic transition, a change that eventually could prove anywhere from two to six times as drastic as that from the last ice age, some thirty thousand years ago, to the interglacial period today. Reminding us that glaciers had reached as far down as St. Louis and London, and that the sea levels in the cooler climate were some 400 feet lower, probably exposing an area as large as Africa above water and covered with vegetation, Lovelock asks us to imagine a change just as dramatic, but to a heat age instead: "The temperature and the sea level will climb decade by decade, until eventually the world becomes torrid, ice-free, and all but unrecognizable."[3] This time, instead of being covered by glaciers, London and Boston as well as a number of other cities, including Venice and Miami, might disappear beneath the sea. Deserts will accelerate their inimical expansion, with the Sahara quite possibly extending above the equator, like eczema desiccating smooth and healthy skin.

Eventually is a long time ahead, it might never happen, and need not worry us now; what we do have to prepare for are the events of the transition itself, events that are just about to begin. These are likely to be surprises in the way of extremes, like storms of great ferocity, and unexpected atmospheric events like the ozone hole over Antarctica."[4]

The only short-term certainty over the next several decades is greater chaos as the global system wobbles like a plucked string.

This general scenario of an overheating Earth is shared by any number of mainstream environmentalists. The Gaians are glad for the orthodoxy, because eyebrows start jumping when Lovelock goes on to opine that a period of glaciation may result from all of this furious global warming: "But what of Gaia? Will she not respond and keep the status quo? Before we expect Gaia to act, we should realize that the present interglacial warm period could be regarded as fever for Gaia and that left to herself she would be relaxing into her normal, comfortable for her, ice age."[5]

In Gaian theory, the oscillation between glacial and inter-glacial periods is understood as a continuing thermostatic process. The fact that the planet has been in a relatively warm interglacial period for the past thirty milennia or so indicates, therefore, that the global climate should gradually settle back into yet another cooling cycle. Though warmed "momentarily" by the century and a half of greenhouse gas injection, the planet's 3.5 billion–year pattern of climate correction ought not, to the Gaian way of thinking, be permanently disrupted. In fact, a brief glaciation could even be precipitated prematurely, like the chills that sometimes convulse the frame of one with a high fever. "If you have an unstable system it doesn't matter which way you kick it. We're kicking it one way, but it will bounce back,"[6] declares the arbiter of Gaian dogma.

But what if the global system does not bounce back? 179
Lovelock has worried of late that Gaia may find it difficult to

relax, "because we have been busy removing her skin and using it as farmland, especially the trees and the forests of the humid tropics, which otherwise are among the means for her recovery."[7] Compounding the problem by adding a thick blanket of greenhouse gases to an already feverish and debilitated patient, the vicious cycle of heat and suffocation is bound to cause grievous injury. Unable to divine the outcome, Lovelock concludes simply that the global system probably will be spurred into "a new stable state fit for a different, more amenable biota. It would be much hotter or much colder, but whatever it is, no longer the comfortable world we know."[8]

THE VITALITY OF THE MIDSECTION

Since much of the northern hemisphere is buried periodically by glaciers, this region, from a geophysiological point of view, is far less important to the health of the Earth than are the warm regions close to the equator that are perpetually biologically active. Geophysiologists may have only the faintest inkling of what the Earth's vital organs are, but that's where some of the most important ones have got to be. This bias toward tropical regions underpins the Gaian environmental agenda.

Second-class status does not, however, cater to the First World's proud self-image. Though Lovelock does not exactly delight in minimizing issues of importance to our precious domain, he is a bit quick, for some people's tastes, to reduce them to context.

Geophysiologists do not ignore the depletion of the ozone layer in the stratosphere with its concomitant risk of increased irradiation with short-wave ultraviolet, or the problem of acid rain. These are seen as real and potentially serious hazards but mainly to the people and ecosystems of the First World—from a Gaian perspective, a region that is clearly expendable.

It was buried beneath glaciers, or was icy tundra, only 10,000 years ago.[9]

Ironically, it is a developmental policy financed and administered by the "expendable" nations that is destroying the region that no one can afford to lose. Over the past decade the World Bank, the largest institution to finance Third World development (to the tune of $15 billion to $20 billion in First World loans annually), worked with the West's largest lenders to assemble a multibillion-dollar aid package for the Amazon rain forest. The massive project included constructing fifty hydroelectric dams that would flood out huge portions of the Amazon basin and setting the largest forest fires in history to deforest much of the land that was not to be flooded. The primary goal was to develop the land for agriculture, mostly grazing land for what is oxymoronically known as rain forest beef.

Of course, it is now widely believed that the carbon dioxide and methane spewing from those mammoth infernos have choked and parched the globe in a burgeoning greenhouse effect. The vibrant mat of greenery that would have photosynthesized some of the excess CO_2, embodying carbon as plant structure and returning oxygen to the air, lies as scorched fallow instead. Perhaps it is poetic revenge that as the rain forest land barrier has been cut away, moisture-laden ocean winds can no longer form clouds to dump their rains or deflect the sun's heat. The region's rainfall already has begun to diminish, lowering the water levels of the Panama Canal to the point where that vital waterway soon may become impassable, strangling the trade that the woefully misguided deforestation project was supposed to create.

It is interesting to note that while all of this information has been publicly available for the better part of a decade, only in late 1989 did the prominent news magazine *Time* choose to feature rain forest issues on its cover. To be fair, recently the World Bank did a dramatic turnaround under new leadership, canceling plans for most of the destruction that it has not already

181

incited or caused, including many of the Amazon dams it had planned to build. But as the Natural Resources Defense Council, an environmental advocacy group, still maintained in late 1989, World Bank policies still give "shockingly short shrift" to the role of forests in global climate change. Is it any wonder that the governments of tropical nations balk with anger when the same First World institutions—the World Bank among many others— that had sponsored the defoliation of their jungles in order to reap the profits of cheap fast-food beef now apply righteous pressure to "do the right thing" and save the rain forests?

Fed up with what they see as foreign meddling in their sovereignty—particularly from northern nations like the United States that cleared their own wildernesses for development earlier this century and that continue to overcut their remaining timberlands today—many of the people of tropical nations see themselves as victims of heavy-handed hypocrisy meant to keep poor countries poor. It comes as no surprise that a number of Latin American leaders have succumbed to a sort of nationalistic machismo, often rejecting innovative solutions such as debt-for-rain-forest swaps, in which the staggering national debts of Brazil and other less-developed nations are forgiven or favorably refinanced in exchange for placing tracts of rain forest in trust against destruction. Too much external influence over their land is usually the rationale for vetoing such arrangements, despite successful pilot programs in Bolivia and, particularly, Costa Rica. (Yet another in a long list of reasons to admire the tiny Central American nation that abolished its armed forces after World War II and now has the best-educated, healthiest, and longest-lived populace in Latin America.)

Even mixed-use agroforestry programs, in which the rain forest is harvested for such natural resources as latex rubber sap, herbs, and medicaments, with selected portions logged or cleared for cultivation—programs that are proving to be at least as profitable in the long term as slash, burn, and graze—have remained largely experimental. Sadly, the most recent debt-reduction package negotiated between northern banks and the Mexican government, an agreement widely expected to be the model for other Latin American debtors, seems implicitly to *encourage* economic development, with plans for wilderness preservation lying as fallow as burned-out fields.

Lovelock warns that the consequences of what he calls the geocidal acts of rain forest clearance and greenhouse gas suffocation soon will dominate the world news, scooping even politics and war for the headlines.

> Soon and suddenly, in the regions that are now the humid tropical forests, there could be a billion or more humans enduring drought and floods, perhaps with mean temperatures of 120 degrees F. They would be without support, in a vast, arid region around the earth. All this could happen at a time when we in the North, who might otherwise come to their rescue, are facing rising sea levels and major changes in our own climate, and the most amazing surprises.[10]

Lest we be inclined to dismiss all of this as an old man's parting melodrama, Lovelock adds, "These predictions of events are near certain and not the fashionable fiction of doom scenarios."[11]

THE EVILS OF AGRICULTURE

The most important practical difference between Gaia and mainstream environmental policy is in its emphasis on the evils of agriculture over those of industry, since deforestation for the purpose of food cultivation is what most immediately threatens the tropical rain forests and the warm coastal seas that surround them. Modern agriculture, whatever the region, results in the massive destruction of forests and other wildlands, the flattening of shelter and windbreaks, the erosion of topsoil, and the pollution of the watershed. Yet the Gaian bias flies in the face of

183

the popular imagination; the wholesome images of family farms and manly cowboys hardly seem as evil as the black-smokestack spewers of industrial waste that have incurred righteous wrath from Dickens's days. After all, didn't all of the pollution start when we left the farms for the cities?

In Dante's Renaissance cosmology, betrayal was considered the deadliest sin; Judas Iscariot, at the bottom of the inferno, was stuck eternally upside down in ice so black that not even the heat of Hades could melt it. In the sooty visions of Dickens's Industrial Revolution, exploitation of the labor of men, women, and, especially, children, for profit was sordid to the extreme. And in Lovelock's environmental ethics, ravaging a tropical rain forest to graze cheap beef is in fact to betray millions, sin enough to be mulched into the pitch manure of ecological Hell.

Of what the British scientist calls the three deadly C's— cars, cattle, and the chainsaws used to clear forestland—the last two are the stock and trade of agribusiness, particularly in the Third World. "Getting rid of cattle is one of the most important Gaian steps of all. The amount of land one man requires for producing food through cattle is twenty times as much as if he were eating the grain directly,"[12] says Lovelock, who is opposed on all counts to the proliferation of these wasteful creatures, especially in the humid tropics. Grazing cattle herds also stamp and compact the earth beneath them, causing rainwater that might otherwise have been absorbed to run off, carrying away loose topsoil and hastening the desertification process.

If the champion of Mother Earth could wave his wand once, it just might be to remove red meat from the world's diet, easing the economic incentive to mutilate vital parts of her body. So intent is this scientist (whose own diet runs vegetarian, with some chicken and fish) that at the 1988 AGU Gaia conference the diehard iconoclast "confided" to several startled listeners that one project they might consider would be the development of a virus to wipe out the world's cattle population.

Dr. Intensli Eeger, a character Lovelock invented to illustrate that even the best-intentioned biotech quick fixes can end

184

up paving the road to ecological hell, might go for the cattle virus scheme, but fortunately his creator seems satisfied that the plan works best as a rhetorical ploy. To most of us, cows seem placid, pleasant creatures, albeit dim-witted and treacherous to the footing, but hardly evil or malign. That these animals, along with other red-meat livestock, might collectively represent a dangerous environmental threat is a jolt to our usual assumptions—a service that the British maverick is more than happy to provide.

Lovelock becomes aggravated every time another patch of wilderness in his beloved southern England is despoiled by the perverse subsidy-and-surplus economics of the world food trade. Sometimes his grudge reaches comic proportions, and the lifelong industrial scientist can be goaded into antiagricultural hyperbole. "One project that ought to be funded *big*, like Star Wars, is the purely synthetic production of food from crude chemicals,"[13] he says. Arguing that chemists would prove to be even more efficient in nutrient creation than they have been in grain cultivation, the inveterate inventor has nonplussed more than a few listeners with his industrial approach to solving world hunger. "Look at margarine. It has an absolutely acceptable taste. Let the food chemists have at it. They can make foods that are absolutely palatable."[14]

The Gaian case against inefficient agriculture means practical support for measures to increase yield while controlling the degradation of farmland. High on the agenda for Third World development are innovative plans such as the agricultural conservation and recycling program conducted by the Chinese government in the semiarid Loess Plateau. Topsoil dams, terraces, and water catchments have enabled local farmers to increase total food output by 17 percent, even while cutting total planted acreage in half. The next step is to reclaim and reforest the liberated land that remains. Much less exotic than high-biotech plots, but a lot more useful.

First World tariffs and import restrictions on rain forest beef might have some impact, but without extensive international

185

cooperation the ecological benefits probably would not be worth the political and economic costs. Far more powerful would be a domestic red-meat tax, a federal levy imposed to discourage the consumption of beef, lamb, and pork. These commodities lend themselves to regulation, because the bulk and weight of red meat makes it relatively difficult to smuggle. With environmental benefits analogous to those intended from the excise tax on gasoline, and medical benefits similar to those derived by the federal tax on cigarettes, such a law could contribute significantly to the public health. Except, of course, to the health of any politicians who might advocate it. In meat-and-potatoes America, you might just as well try to tax apple pie.

GAIA AND THE CASE FOR BIODIVERSITY

An axiom of Gaian geophysiology is that biological diversity begets ecological stability—the wider the array of plant and animal species that normally inhabit an ecosystem, the more dynamic and resilient it will be. The assumption that diversity is not only desirable but essential to the survival of a region can be a telling argument in the fight to save plant and animal species from extinction. And as environmental advocates are well aware, until tough legal and economic measures are taken, the weight of expert argument is frequently all that stands between millions of square miles of tropical rain forests (the most diverse ecosystems in the world) and destruction.

Critics who believe that Lovelock has gathered up a lot of unoriginal concepts and packaged it all as Gaia have been inclined to regard the diversity-equals-stability tenet as yet another opportunistic embrace of a useful truism. Yet the scientific basis for preserving the wondrous variety of nature, and by extension, the richness and breadth of human experience, is by no means confirmed. In fact, the sharpest attacks on the supposed survival value of biodiversity come from the prevailing school of ecological theory, which ostensibly underpins environ-

186

mentalist research and policy. In his book *Theoretical Ecology,* Robert May, one of the founders of the field, holds that the treasured quality of diversity has little survival value in the natural world.

> As a mathematical generality, increasing complexity makes for dynamical fragility rather than robustness. . . . This inverts the naive, if well intentioned, view that complexity begets stability and its accompanying moral that we should preserve, or even create, complex systems as buffers against man's importunities.[15]

By this logic, cattle pastures may be hardier than the rain forests that they replace.

John Harte, a theoretical ecologist from the Energy and Resources Group of the University of California at Berkeley, sums up the current scientific conundrum:

> Many ecologists are disillusioned by the new results discrediting the traditional notion correlating the biotic diversity and the stability of an ecosystem. Yet no current model of which I am aware demonstrates such a correlation; complexity does not promote stability. Complex ecosystems do resist invasions more effectively than simpler systems, since invaders must attack a greater range of organisms, but diverse systems are also given to greater fluctuations, since their stability is dependent upon a much longer chain of interactions, disruptable at many more junctures.

Harte, an aggressive critic of Lovelock, concludes that the brute simplicity of a monocultural wheat field makes it as potentially sturdy a survivor as a complex and resilient tropical forest or fertile coastal sea. This poses a clear challenge to Gaian theory, which holds that the biota have collectively stabilized the Earth's ecosystem for the past 3.5 billion years. If there is no special difference at the local level between complex and simple ecosystems in terms of how well or how long they endure, how could the net effect of the global biosphere be so powerfully controlling?

Lovelock disagrees with this analysis so violently that when discussing it, he finds it hard to remain civil.

> In spite of years of effort and computer time, the ecologists have made no real progress towards modeling a complex natural ecosystem such as a tropical rain forest or the three-dimensional ecosystem of the ocean. No models drawn from theoretical ecology can account in mathematical terms for the manifest stability of these vast natural systems . . . the impression remains that diversity is, in general, a disadvantage and that Nature, by disregarding the elegant mathematics of theoretical biology, has somehow cheated.[16]

The Gaian difference comes from the conviction that intrinsic to the survival of an ecosystem is its ability to regulate the local environment. Biodiversity provides vital redundancy, essentially backup regulatory systems that are there to take over if a primary system is perturbed. And Lovelock takes pains to point out that he and his colleague Andrew Watson have demonstrated precisely what Harte claims has not been modeled—in their Daisyworld computer model, the greater the diversity of species, the more stable the global environment.

In the Gaian microcosm, species diversity and interdependence are part of life's definition. "Many types of microbes persisting or growing well in mixed cultures do not grow at all in pure culture. They depend on the alteration of the environment by other organisms in order to grow," writes Margulis.

188   The resiliency of microbial communities and their enviromental modulation stems from fundamental

properties of the biota, some of which we have observed here: rapid exponential growth, which alters the environment and high species diversity. . . . Our results most likely can be generalized to communities over the entire planet, indeed to the entire planet and its biota.[17]

Much more appealing than the analyses of May and Harte, though often less rigorous, is the philosophy of deep ecology. Virtually the polar opposite of its theoretical counterpart, deep ecology is a holistic concept in which no organism is seen as discrete or separate; all, including humans, are members of a globally interdependent biotic community. Ethicist Anthony Weston finds this approach to be profoundly compatible with Gaia.

Deep ecology thus sounds very close to some of Lovelock's formulations. Though I have stressed those points where Lovelock suggests that humans can or do play a special role in Gaian processes, the Gaia hypothesis itself essentially contextualizes humans within the vast movement and self-adjustment of life on Earth; it offers precisely Naess's "total field" conception. We can only understand ourselves as part of larger and older life processes, just as deep ecology insists.[18]

Taken to its logical extreme, deep ecology accords to all species an equal right to survive. The issue of biodiversity switches from utility to ethics—if all species have a right to exist, then the question of whether or not they can become extinct without harming the overall ecology becomes moot, since no species, including humans, has the right ro make the life-or-death decision. Yet the practical value of deep ecology lies less in any doctrine of species equality than in the reminder that not all decisions on environmental policy ought be made on a human-interest basis. Whooping cranes have a right to live—not only because we say so, but because they have a right all their own.

Gaia's scientific evidence that biodiversity has practical survival value gives the theory far more influence than simple moral suasion. Arguments for preserving the flora and fauna of an ecologically endangered region need rely no longer on pleas for beauty and variety or on the trenchant but often rhetorically ineffective litanies of the valuable pharmaceuticals and other organic products that have come from exotic ecosystems. (Too many people seem to think that drugs come from chemicals and that chemicals come from laboratories.) Instead Gaia demonstrates that the ecological and climatic integrity of an entire region may be threatened, with potentially disastrous costs in life and property, if key plant and animal species are extinguished.

THE POWER TO POLLUTE

"We are like a modern version of the Gadarene swine, driving our polluting cars heedlessly down the slope into a sea that is rising to drown us,"[19] writes Lovelock.

Ever since his days in the mid-1960s as a researcher for Shell, Lovelock has inveighed against the third deadly C, convinced that people's love affairs with their cars would eventually cause untold misery to them and to the countryside paved to accommodate their lovely Sunday drives. From this point of view, the fewer the automobiles the better, and even with all of the astonishing advances made in fuel efficiency and emissions control, one suspects that Lovelock's private opinion might run to a more sweeping disenfranchisement of the right to drive. Especially, as is particularly the American custom, of one or two individuals cruising in big, powerful cars over to fast-food restaurants for a few double-beef burgers to go. (A pity, because with a thick strawberry shake, fries, maybe some extra special sauce, and the car stereo booming, this New Age mortal sin is also one of life's cheapest splurges.)

One easily could add a fourth C, coal, to the Gaian list of critical hazards. Few environmentalists would disagree that the combustion of coal, oil, and other fossil fuels is largely responsible for greenhouse warming, acid rain, and general tropospheric pollution. Yet even fewer mainstream activists would go as far as Lovelock in their opposition to the burning of these carbonaceous fuels. Perhaps the most important policy difference between traditional ecology and geophysiology is the adamant Gaian opposition to power generation by coal or oil, even if this means accepting nuclear power as a substitute. Declares Lovelock, who probably would fight his damnedest to keep any power stations whatsoever out of his bucolic paradise:

> You see if they said they were going to build a one thousand megawatt power station here in Launceston, and you gave me the choice of coal, oil or nuclear, I would rate them nuclear first, oil-burner second and coal-burner last. . . . [In terms of immediate pollution and personal discomfort,] the coal-burner would ruin life here totally. It would be down-wind of us and we'd just be wiped out. An oil-burner wouldn't be very nice, because it would still be polluting. But the nuclear thing, you wouldn't know it was there. And if it blew up? Well, I mean it's a good way to go; but it wouldn't blow up, because even Chernobyl, which is probably the worst conceivable accident possible, was not all that bad. And that was almost unbelievable. It was almost equivalent to the flight engineer of a 747 switching off all four engines in mid-Atlantic to see if the safety system would work.[20]

The latest analyses of the accident at Chernobyl suggest that the power plant in question actually did blow up like a nuclear bomb, according to the consensus of scientific opinion

191

as reported in the July 1989 issue of Technology Review. And in September 1989, more than three years after the catastrophe, another hundred thousand people had to be evacuated from their homes nearby because radiation levels were judged to be still too dangerous. Fortunately, those same Western scientists concur that the chances of such an explosion happening in one of their reactors are "vanishingly small." One hopes that these nuclear luminaries are not suffering from the same "expert overconfidence" to which so many scientists seem to succumb. For according to Baruch Fischoff, a Carnegie-Mellon psychologist, nuclear engineers are among the most likely to suffer from this form of self-delusion, often overestimating their own accuracy by factors of 1,000 percent or more.

"Gaia would not care a fourpenny damn" about radiation from an all-out nuclear war or a chain of nuclear power plant accidents, retorts Lovelock, at times seeming to forget that Gaia's human inhabitants might pay dearly. But nuclear power proponents maintain that the costs in life and property of fossil fuel–burning plants, particularly those that use coal, have been just as seriously overlooked. That diseases caused or aggravated by air pollution from carbonaceous combustion, damage from acid rain, acceleration of greenhouse warming, and so on simply do not seem to inspire the outrage and emotional protests that (potentially explosive) nuclear plants almost always draw. And perplexing though the problem of storing nuclear wastes may be, the ravages of strip mining, oil spills, and the like are prices just as ecologically dear.

Lovelock regards the now-famous story of the natural nuclear reactors at Oklo, a French uranium mine in Gabon, Africa, as a parable for the sound management of radioactive wastes. When the first ore shipments were readied for processing, they were found to have been stripped of the fissionable isotope U235. Terrorists or fanatics were suspected, and government officials braced for nuclear extortion or worse. But they soon relaxed when it was revealed that the theft had taken place some two billion years earlier, when oxygen first permeated the African atmosphere. It seems that the hitherto insoluble uranium ore was oxidized, dissolved into the ground water, and ran into the streams. There bacteria collected and processed it, eventually accumulating enough U235 that a "critical mass" was reached and a chain reaction was started and sustained. The reactor appears to have run at the kilowatt level for millions of years, distributing the wastes harmlessly as stable fission products throughout the environment.

Of course, solar, wind, and tidal power generation produce much less waste, but as yet they are unable to deliver the big power payloads of their fission and combustion counterparts. Hydroelectric power generation is too expensive, except in regions that have powerful water flows, although that may change as superconducting transmission technology extends electricity distribution grids. Natural gas combustion, the World Bank's current pet candidate for power generation, has distinct environmental advantages, but at least in the United States there is one distinct disadvantage: more and more municipalities refuse to permit liquid natural gas tankers to pass within city limits. Does this mean that the environmental virtues of nuclear power, unsung for so long, will now be . . . hummed?

THE POLLUTION OF POWER

The prospect of cold fusion certainly put a lilt in a lot of hearts, including, one might suspect, Lovelock's. Incredibly, the whole world, it seemed in those heady, early days of 1989, was rooting for the development of a form of nuclear power. (Perhaps there will be some carry-over calming of the reflexive opposition that always seems to greet any proposals concerning nuclear fission.) Whatever the final outcome, those two renegade chemists, Stanley Pons and Maurice Fleischmann, will long be remembered for their exhilarating contention that the same process that gives life to the sun can be cooked quietly in a jar.

Though Lovelock could not have helped but identify with

193

the two researchers' homegrown attempts to stick it in the ear of the scientific establishment, their vision of unlimited clean nuclear power was, to him, a catastrophe narrowly averted. Wrote Lovelock almost two years before cold fusion's near discovery:

> I often have a nightmare vision of a simple, lightweight nuclear fusion power source. It would be a small box, about the size of a telephone directory, with four ordinary electricity outlets embedded in its surface. The box would breathe in air and extract, from its content of moisture, hydrogen that would fuel a miniature nuclear fusion power source rated to supply a maximum of 100 kilowatts. It would be cheap, reliable, manufactured in Japan, and available everywhere. It would be the perfect, clean, safe power source; no nuclear waste nor radiation would escape from it, and it could never fail dangerously.[11]

Forever warm in the winter and cool in the summer, with no greenhouse, acid rain, or waste disposal problems. Pollution-free transport around the block, or the solar system. This is Lovelock's idea of an ecological nightmare?

> That is how it might be sold, but the reality almost certainly is ominously expressed by Lord Acton's famous dictum, "Power tends to corrupt, and absolute power corrupts absolutely." He was thinking of political power, but it could be just as true of electricity. Already we are displacing the habitats of our partners with agricultural monocultures powered by cheap fossil fuel. We do it faster than we can think about the consequences. Just imagine what could happen with unlimited free power.[22]

194

For the geophysiologist, the health of the world's ecosystems takes precedence over humanity's convenience. Just as the world's population growth has been spurred by the bounty of the Industrial Revolution, Homo sapiens sapiens (sic) would proliferate even more wildly if given the omnipotence of limitless electrical power. In Lovelock's contrarian vision, the indiscriminate mass extinctions of plant and animal species resulting from the agricultural frenzy to feed the burgeoning populace would sabotage vital ecosystems and throw the global climate into chaos. We would eat our world to death.

Ironically, the cumbersome and capital-intensive process of building power plants, especially nuclear plants, is to Lovelock something of a saving grace. Or an "effective negative feedback" to counterbalance humankind's destructive dominion. This lesson is drawn from the conquest of the Earth some 2.5 billion years ago by cyanobacteria, which, as noted earlier, rapidly covered the globe with a thick, blue-green scum. More than half of all species were extinguished and the world was plunged into a holocaust of oxygen pollution for millions of years. No species, not even our own, can gain that much power without wreaking havoc on all the rest.

CANCER OR HEALERS? THE ROLE OF HUMANS IN GAIA

One wonders at the hubris of creatures that inflict so much damage on the Earth and then declare themselves its stewards or healers. Might not the first prescription be to reduce the number of human beings, or eliminate them altogether, if improvement of the general ecological health of the planet is the goal? What is the role of humanity in the great Gaian scheme? Are we the culmination, the cancer, the central nervous system, or, as Lynn Margulis maintains, are we the mammalian weed?

From time to time Lovelock indulges himself in speculation that our species may in some way represent a collective brain or

195

nervous system of Gaia, but aware of the thicket of contradictions that come with trying to define the specific role of any species (especially the one species about which no human being can be objective) the man asserts only that "the Gaia hypothesis implies that the stable state of our planet includes man as a part of, or partner in, a very democratic entity."[23]

A similar trans-species notion of democracy is embedded in the burgeoning animal rights movement, where the underlying value is that cruelty, no matter against what type of creature, is an unforgiveable sin. Chickens cooped in cages so small and foul that they become hysterical and peck their beaks off; veal calves cramped and slaughtered before they ever get a chance to run around; laboratory animals subjected to all manners of intrusive torture only to test out yet another overpriced cosmetic—the outrage is not only at the killing of animals but also at the brutal treatment inflicted on their brief, miserable lives.

Sometimes an antihuman bias creeps into the anticruelty ideology: human beings are uniquely able to defend themselves, so cruelty against them is less of an outrage than is cruelty against more defenseless creatures. But much like the antiabortionists' crusade on behalf of the defenseless unborn, there is a greater nobility to this rhetoric than to some of the motivations behind it. By relegating the problems of human beings to some secondary status, a philosophical back door is opened to excuse a lack of concern, or even disdain, for people who suffer.

At its most humane, animal rights legislation has assumed a hierarchy of sentience—of the ability to feel the pain that must be prevented—with human beings at the top of the chain. (Without any species delineations, the ban on cruelty, taken to its logical extreme, would condemn insecticides and antibiotics as instruments of torture and genocide to bugs and microbes. The counterargument might be made that the anticruelty doctrine still holds, though, since these pests thereby are being prevented from the cruelty they would impose on us.) The Swedish government recently passed the world's most comprehensive animal rights law, mandating that all chickens have limited free range, calves have room enough to move around, and so forth. In that nation it is particularly fitting, since Sweden is second to none in its regard for the rights of people at home and abroad.

Still, human chauvinists can become quickly incensed at the Gaian implication that we are just another species, ultimately of no greater importance than any other breed. And even if it is the case, ecologically, is not our first duty still to our own kind? Their umbrage is hardly surprising, since human beings constitute the most powerful self-interest group in the world.

What does take one aback is the almost perverse pleasure that other people gain from group self-deprecation. "White liberal guilt," the soul-satisfying mea culpa of the American upper middle class in the 1960s as it accepted responsibility for the subjugation of the nation's blacks, seems to have an emerging counterpart in the breast-beating sentiment that not only are people no better than any other creatures, but we are a plague on the Earth.

Ralph Metzner, one of the enduring impresarios of the American counterculture, makes the case for humans as a global cancer:

> It is also ecologically unhealthy, unwholesome we might say, for cells of one kind to proliferate wildly and spread all over the body with reckless disregard for the delicately balanced interrelationship of the whole system. In the individual body, we call such cellular behavior tumors. And the analogy of mankind as a cancer upon the Earth has occurred to quite a few observers.[24]

Lovelock waves this one away as misguided self-hate and yet another projection of the irrational fear that the disease cancer usually seems to inspire. One certainly can argue that similar analogies would be drawn between, say, tuberculosis and humanity if the latter ailment were currently the most dread disease.

But the comparison with cancer's wildly disruptive proliferation, almost a parody of healthy reproduction, does seem a bit too close to dismiss easily.

Others reverse the metaphor and see the scourge of AIDS as Earth's punishment for humankind's existential sins. In fact, a flurry of letters to the editors of New Scientist debated whether that terrible disease were not in some sense a Gaian regulatory response to the "rogue species" threatening the Earth's stability and survival. However, the AIDS-as-ultimate-negative-feedback argument falls quickly to the simpler explanation that, like the terrible plagues of earlier centuries, microorganisms causing the disease have arisen through the normal Darwinian process of mutation and natural selection and have spread because conditions were suitable.

Comparisons of humanity to disease are invidious but unavoidable when considering the planet as an integrated organism. But when speculation turns to which groups of people might deserve to be blighted, such as Africans suffering from AIDS or southeast Asians from famine, ecological rhetoric can be used to mask some very ugly beliefs. Between understanding that population growth has outstripped a region's natural resources, and concluding therefore that all of the suffering is somehow nature's justice, is a fine line all too often scuffed away by the clodhopper mentality of bigots. In a global economic system so internationalized that crop planting decisions are regularly financed by consumer demand half a world away, the blame is roundly apportioned.

Geophysiology may prove to be the art and science of healing the planetary body, but that does not mean that the Earth needs five billion doctors administering their cures. In order for our species to assume the healing role that idealists envision, our first job is to act as a healthy influence. Until a blueprint is developed for this noble evolutionary leap, the following set of guidelines, developed some four thousand years ago and presented by classicist J. Donald Hughes, will serve:

198

These, then are the major ideas of the ancients about the Earth.

First, the Earth is the oldest goddess, supporter and nurturer of her children, human and non-human, and therefore entitled to respect and worship. Environmental problems are seen as a result of the failure of human beings to worship the Earth and her unwritten laws.

Second, the Earth is a living being of whom humans are only part. Right relationship with the Earth means that the total organism is in good health; so environmental problems are seen as illness, as a failure of one part of the organism to interact supportively with the others.

Third, Earth is seen as responsive to human care or the lack of it, giving rich returns to those who treat her well and punishing those who are lazy or who weary her by trying to wrest from her what she is not ready to give. Environmental problems are seen as the revenge of Earth on those who fail either through ignorance or greed, to practice well the art of the attentive tender of the land.[25]

X

THE WORLD ACCORDING
TO GAIA

SAVE THE EARTH!

Nikola Tesla, the brilliant pioneer of wireless energy transmission, had the annoying habit of setting off miniature earthquakes. It all started one day in 1898 when he decided to test out a pocket-size oscillator and attached it to an iron pillar that ran down the center of his loft building in New York City's Lower East Side. The tiny whirligig began to pulse, and one after another the objects in his workshop started to dance. The wooden desk chair tapped a four-toed jig until Tesla stepped up the oscillator's frequency, whereupon the wastepaper basket shimmied until it tossed out some of its trash.

But as Margaret Cheney recounts in her delightful biography *Tesla: Man Out of Time*, unbeknownst to the mesmerized miscreant, the oscillator's vibrations also were traveling down the iron pillar and into the building's foundation. And with the same escalating force that makes earthquakes more devastating at a distance from their epicenter, Tesla's little vibrator shook the substructure of Manhattan.

"Buildings began to shake, windows shattered, and citizens

poured onto the streets in the nearby Italian and Chinese neighborhoods," writes Cheney.

> At Police Headquarters on Mulberry Street, where Tesla was already regarded with suspicion, it soon became apparent that no other part of the city was having an earthquake. Two officers were dispatched posthaste to check on the mad inventor. The latter, unaware of the shambles occurring all around his building, had just begun to sense an ominous vibration in the floor and walls. Knowing that he must quickly put a stop to it, he seized a sledgehammer and smashed the oscillator with a single blow.[1]

Ever the showman, Tesla told policemen and reporters that he could destroy the Brooklyn Bridge in a matter of minutes with just such a palm-sized device. The following week, the Croatian-American inventor confirmed his boast when he attached the same type of oscillator to the steel frame of a ten-story building that, had he let the structure shake just a few minutes longer, would have been brought down in a heap simply by "a fusillade of taps, no one of which would have harmed a baby." The Empire State Building, Tesla later addded, could just as easily be reduced to a twisted wreck.[2]

Tesla, the man who never got the credit he deserved for developing the radio (despite his 1943 U.S. Supreme Court victory over Italian Nobel laureate Guglielmo Marconi and the Marconi Wireless Telegraph Company of America in their patent dispute), was, very fortunately, vindictive only in his wizard's imagination. Reasoning that the earth, like everything else, constantly expands and contracts, Tesla calculated that a sound wave would travel round-trip through the planet in one hour and forty nine minutes (a figure that in the late 1970s was found by computer scientists to be uncannily accurate). By setting an oscillator to vibrate sympathetically, he announced that he could split the Earth "as a boy would split an apple—and forever end the career of man."[3] While the practicalities of handing the planet a fate worse than asteroids are open to serious question, the basic principle has remained unchallenged. And the potential for smaller-scale telegeodynamic communication or destruction, say from one point on the earth to its diametric opposite, perhaps New York to Melbourne, is yet to be fully explored.

Save the Earth! Even just a few decades ago the notion might have seemed as comically grandiose as Tesla's showmanship, bravado almost as hollow as a public offer to rescue God Almighty himself. But as Sir Fred Hoyle brilliantly foresaw in 1948, "Once a photograph of the Earth, taken from the outside is available . . . a new idea as powerful as any other in history will be let loose."[4] Ironically, the scientific maverick best known for successfully challenging Big Bang theorists to come up with the evidence to disprove his nonevolutionary "steady-state" theory—which holds that the universe has no beginning or end and is infinitely old and infinitely large—understood that the blue-green image of our planet floating in space would explode in the popular imagination.

The world itself soon became an object of reverence and beauty, made all the more magical by a touch of Narcissus as we fell in love with our very own pond: "Aloft, floating free beneath the moist gleaming membrane of bright blue sky, is the rising earth, the only exuberant thing in this part of the cosmos. . . . It has the organized, self-contained look of a live creature, full of information, marvelously skilled in handling the sun,"[5] writes the inimitable Lewis Thomas of humanity's first glimpse of home.

This shift to a global perspective is what Fritjof Capra and a number of other New Age philosophers like to call the new paradigm. Though in many ways inspiring, the bird's-eye view also has had its unsettling aspects. Now that the spell of infinitude has been broken, our planet finally has had to obey Copernicus; the Earth has been demoted from unencompassable immensity to no bigger, say, than the moon or the sun. No telling what manner of mischief might befall the orb.

Carl Sagan frequently observes that "many of the leaders of the ecological movement in the United States were originally stimulated to action by photographs of Earth taken from space, pictures revealing a tiny, delicate and fragile world, exquisitely sensitive to the depradations of man—a meadow in the middle of the sky."[6] A sobering experience, like when a grown child first realizes that it is now time to take care of an aging parent—except that in this planetary case the parent must remain healthy, or the whole family dies.

SAVE THE EARTH?

Save the Earth! Who could possibly disagree? And why on earth undermine a notion that stirs men and women to righteous, ecologically correct action? That moves us to care for our planet the way we care for our homes? Possibly because the reasoning that underlies this sacred canard is about as sensible as the sun is small. Earthly life has 3.5 billion years of evolutionary momentum behind it, and it is not about to be stopped dead by the latest dominant species.

> The environmentalist who likes to believe that life is fragile and delicate and in danger from mankind does not like what he sees when he looks at the world through Gaia [theory]. The damsel in distress he expected to rescue appears as a buxom and robust man-eating mother. . . . We are bound to be eaten, for it is Gaia's custom to eat her children.[7]

Our planet is chemically compelled to beget life from death. As explored earlier in this book, holocausts from meteor impact to oxygen poisoning, each on average more catastrophic than if many times our entire arsenal were to be exploded at once, have been absorbed with ease. Judging from the progression of the fossil record and confirmed by the extraordinary diversity of

203

natural development today, anywhere from 10 to 50 percent of the visible biota survives and eventually thrives from even the worst cataclysms. The global ecosystem invariably regenerates quickly and to a higher level of complexity, usually in less than a hundred thousand years. Though this may seem an eternity in terms of human civilization, to a life form thirty-five-hundred-million years old, one hundred milennia is, at most, a long afternoon.

Microorganisms fare the best. Even if humanity were to multiply its destructive power a billionfold, unleash it all, and exterminate all higher plants and animals, there are numerous microbial species that would process the energy from nuclear fallout, prosper, and evolve.

Strip away all of the ozone and, as Lovelock and Margulis have shown, most microorganisms still frolic in the sun. Suck away the oxygen, and the anerobes reclaim their dominion, a destiny that may be inevitable once the last bits of carbon dioxide are pumped out of the air. Plunge the world into heat or cold, and thousands of species find refuge or go dormant until temperatures balance out. And ineluctably these microscopic creatures would compete and cooperate their way into the diverse higher organisms of a rich natural world.

Humankind is already responsible for the cruelest mass extinction of plant and animal species in history, a fathomless moral and aesthetic atrocity that deepens every day. Yet the fact that we cannot annihilate every living thing on the planet, that total and final extermination is beyond our capability, is hard for some people to accept. It bruises the human ego, which suckles on the ability to kill. Of course annihilating five billion or more humans along with the rest of the natural world is quite out of the question, but let us sic a few supercomputers on the subject anyway. There has got to be some way, hypothetically of course, to wipe out every last microbe for good.

"The idea that we're wrecking the Earth is wrong; but wrecking ourselves is another story,"[8] says Margulis. The surest way, possibly the only way, to sustain human civilization is to restore and preserve the natural environment that gives it rise. So why continue to cultivate a delusion? A noble crusade to rescue Mother Nature may be sentimentally appealing, but in the long run the basic rule of evolution and common sense is that people, plants, and animals all work a lot harder when they work for their own good. Save the Earth? Sure, because that is the way to save ourselves. But not to worry. As Admiral Hyman Rickover once wryly observed, even if human civilization is entirely wiped out, a new and wiser species will evolve.

GAIA AND ME

When in the late 1960s Lovelock and his partner Dian Hitchcock first beheld the Earth floating in space from their imaginary observatory on Mars, their impulse was not so much to save our planet as to pity all of the others. So struck were they by the planet's unique vitality that they seemed to forget that whatever lives must, by definition, eventually die. So when Lovelock spread the good news of Gaia in the early 1970s he tended to overemphasize the mammoth creature's power and strength, much as the first person to discover that dinosaurs once roamed the earth might have been so overawed by their size and power that he overlooked the fragilities that led to their rapid extinction.

Steve Schneider and a number of others feared that the gospel of the living Earth was yet another guilt-free, gusto-grab manifesto of the 1970s "me-decade" in ecological disguise. Books such as Robert Ringer's *Looking Out for Number 1* and *Winning Through Intimidation* and Dr. Wayne Dyer's *Your Erroneous Zones* were the core of an expanding new liturgy of selfishness that had spurred the baby-boom generation into the economic and sexual free-for-all of young adulthood. Guilt was dismissed as a sense-less, useless emotion that paralyzes the will and cripples the soul with despair. Ethics and humility were systems gone disco, just series of excuses to make cowards and losers feel good. If Gaia

205

will clean up after you, why feel guilty about polluting? Of course Mother Earth wants you to get ahead.

Lovelock has been dogged by this pro-pollution tag ever since the ozone controversy and certainly has not helped matters by making such declarations as: "The very concept of pollution is anthropocentric and it may even be irrelevant in the Gaian context."[9] Yet even the earliest formulations of the Gaia theory were not justifications for environmental abuse but simply arguments that "we have been led to look for trouble in the wrong places."[10]

The same sentiment—not that guilt was always wrong but that people had been made to feel guilty about the wrong things—was at the heart of the best of those seventies-self-help guides. Women who had been raised to feel ashamed for besting a man's wit, for acting aggressively in business, and for taking the romantic initiative were justly counseled to feel proud in asserting their rights and encouraged to dismiss the guilt pangs that stubbornly remained. Men who had been raised in the postwar boom with the assumption of traditional gender roles found themselves vying with members of both sexes in an era of OPEC-induced economic scarcity. Good old boy gentility gave way to indiscriminate competition tooth and claw, and books that formerly might have been disdained as Baedekers to bad manners became handy survival guides.

Unlike the alternative environmental prescriptions of Gaia, most me-decade philosophers left unspecified the question of what the new ethical boundaries might be. Who wanted to read the sequels about the new sets of qualms they were supposed to take on? But as the baby boomers have paired into families and communities, the *me* gradually has been stood on its head to a *we* orientation instead. The giddy, guiltless ethos of those predatory seventies grows faint in the memory; most spouses can come up with more than a few things, right off the tops of their heads, that ought to prick a mate's conscience but good. The odes to selfishness that once dominated popular culture have since fallen from the bestseller lists, and they seem likely to stay off until this new "echo-boom" generation of children grows up and starts buying self-help books of their own.

Gaia also has progressed, from a theory of feckless humans picked up after by an indulgent mother to a point where individual liberty, human and otherwise, is seen as far less important than the organic whole.

> The consortial quality of the individual preempts the notion of independence. For example, what appears to be a single wood-eating termite is comprised of billions of microbes, a few kinds of which do the actual digesting of the cellulose of the wood. Gaia is the same sort of consortial entity but it is far more complex. Consortia, associations, partnerships, symbioses, and competitions in the interactions extend to the global scale. Living and nonliving matter, self and environment, are nicely interconnected. In this sense, a Gaian view is potentially far more powerful than the ideologies of selfishness.[11]

Where critics first attacked Gaia on the grounds of environmental selfishness, now their objections are much more often that the theory takes the principle of collectivity too far. In his essay "Forms of Gaian Ethics" Anthony Weston challenges on this very basis: "The Gaia hypothesis, however, seems to have no way of valuing *individuals*. What matters is the operation of Gaia herself, the homeostasis of planetary life, and her individuals are clearly irrelevant."[12]

The me-we pendulum is a perpetual dialectic, a philosophical perspective that swings back and forth as social circumstances, such as generational demographics or the unifying effects of war, dictate. Whether or not Lovelock and Margulis have been directly influenced by the social philosophies of their time, much as Darwin clung (some say for his wife's benefit) to the doctrines of the Church of England or as Freud rebelled against and yet was defined by Victorian mores, these Gaian

207

exponents of infinite interdependence are hardly immune from the individual-versus-group debate. What makes Gaia of special and enduring interest, however, is not its rhetorical position one way or the other but that, unlike most modern ideologies and doctrines, human beings, taken in groups or individually, are not at the center of Gaian belief. *We,* in the Gaian worldview, starts with the most primitive microbes and ends up with the great planetary organism and does manage to include human beings along the way.

FROM HYPOTHESIS TO WORLDVIEW

Broad philosophies frequently start out as a profound set of insights in a specific field. Freudian psychology, Marxist economics, and the physics of relativity each have expanded by application and analogy to well beyond their original disciplines. Now that Gaia has matured into a responsible scientific theory, growth into a more encompassing worldview seems almost inevitable, for it is, by definition, a way to look at the whole physical world.

What makes the Gaian philosophical perspective unique is that it offers a secular alternative to the doctrine of humanism. Currently, most views of the world fall into two broad categories: human-centered, or deity-centered. Battles over the last decade between the "accursed" secular humanists and the "lunatic" religious fundamentalists illustrates the depth of this philosophical divide. Gaian theory falls into neither camp. Lovelock rails at the "heresy of humanism" with just as much relish as he denies any religious mechanisms behind the workings of the living Earth; Gaia may be worthy of spiritual awe or devotion, but not because there is any mystical deity making it all work.

Neither is Gaia "cosmic," in the sense of the Big Bang or other theories of the universe. The theory's scope is the Earth and, hypothetically, other planets that bear life or have that potential. Nor is Gaian theory localized to the extent of other

nature-centered belief systems, such as the shamanism of indigenous cultures, that might hold that spirits reside in trees, that
particular mountains are sacred, and so on. As worldviews go,
Gaia is refreshingly mid-size.

Like Sigmund Freud's hardline contention that there is no
such thing as a mistake and there is no dream without an
encoded deeper meaning, the Gaian conviction that the Earth
is a living organism may well qualify as a necessary overstatement. In Kant's terms, both assumptions are regulative concepts,
guiding principles that remain valuable even though significant
exceptions may be found. For example, Freud's diligent suspicion
that the mind was up to more than we realized has led to an
appreciation of associative thinking—a mode of thought that
had been largely ignored or spurned as childish chaos but now is
regarded as integral to creativity. Gaia's philosophical proponents hold that by regarding the Earth as a living system, we
will discover more about how complex global subsystems—
biological, political, economic, or spiritual—organize and control themselves.

But not every slip is Freudian, nor every dream revelatory
or prophetic. The Viennese psychologist's relentless search for
significance ultimately led him to confuse the process of discovery with the process of recovery, eventually prompting a rebel-
lion in the field; behavioral psychologists virtually ignore the
causes and treat only the results of disorders, particularly com-
pulsions like gambling and intoxication. Likewise, Gaians may
find that they have placed undue emphasis on heady theories of
system and evolution and not enough on the more practical,
timely matters. And just as Freud seems to have attributed too
much consequence to root causes, particularly infantile traumas
and desires (he probably would maintain that Lovelock has an
Oedipal fixation on Mother Earth), geophysiologists run the risk
of concentrating too much on speculative histories of their
patient, from the time of the original "bacterial takeover" 3.5
billion years ago. Nuclear power is as new to humanity as humans

are to the Earth, but that does not negate the unprecedented and cataclysmic potential of either.

"Scientific hypotheses are all too often used as metaphors in arguments about the human condition. This misuse of Gaia is as inappropriate as was the use of Darwin's theory to justify the morality of laissez-faire capitalism. Gaia is an hypothesis within science and is therefore ethically neutral,"[13] writes Lovelock, but only, one suspects, to defend himself in advance against distortions made in Gaia's name. Darwinism, Marxism, and all other powerful belief systems have been taken too far at one time or another by ideologues eager to have a single set of answers to explain everything. Eventually most of these belief systems contract, usually back to their field of origin and a few surrounding suburbs; tomes on Marxist physics and Freudian economics have been written and largely forgotten.

Gaia is not immune from the same expansion-contraction cycle of any other view of the world, and much of what springs from this early, excited state of the new way of thinking may one day be reassigned to the circular file for intoxicated overstatements. And what today seems a dynamic new way to understand the life of the world may yet prove no more fruitful than trying to understand a peach by adding on another layer of fuzz.

FEARS OF THE FUZZY-MINDED

You know those ancient maps of the world, back when the world was flat? At each corner there was a fellow with great puffed cheeks, blowing an eternal gust of wind. Those guys did not retire upon the discovery that the world is round. They went into whole-Earth philosophy, some say for revenge.

The great bane of holistic philosophy is that whoever is talking is talking about the whole thing, whatever that whole happens to be. So in order to describe the whole Earth, universe, human body, or even compost heap, a heck of a lot of words are usually required. At its most aggravating, Gaia gives everyone an excuse to talk about everything; speakers offer sweeping solutions to the world's problems, proclaim how neat it is to be here, and praise the whole-Earth goddess to the heavens on high. Wholes may indeed be greater than the sums of their parts, but rarely so much as to merit the amount of verbiage it takes to explain the difference.

In fairness, few modern philosophical systems manage to conserve their words. Phenomenology, which strives for streamlining by excluding all abstract presuppositions and focusing solely on perceptible events, still cannot avoid the showers of context that replace the forbidden premises and rules. And its philosophical scion, existentialism, which takes the notion of freedom from the a priori a step further by emphasizing each individual's unique duty to make his or her own choices, has, like a nervous eater faced with crucial decisions, put on quite a few pounds of philosophical fretting over whether or not a body can do without all of the comfortable old rules and still get it right.

Take semiotics—please. The infatuation of haute academe for the past fifteen to twenty years, semiotics has been touted as a value-neutral, ahistorical (an approach that always appeals to the losers of the last war and thus currently is quite popular in Germany) mode of interpretation and analysis with limitless potential for application.

Translation: endless discourse, usually in French, the language that boasts the brilliant work of Roland Barthes and also Jacques Derrida. Linguistically epochal as Ferdinand de Saussure's delineation of (1) sign, (2) signifier, and (3) signified may have been in differentiating between (1) the word *table*, (2) one's mental image of a table, and (3) the physical object itself, and however flexible this semiotic system for decoding the complex constellations of (1) communication, (2) perception, and (3) existence that are asserted to constitute true knowledge in any field, for all but those with the hottest intellectual furnaces, semiotics can be like ice-nine, Kurt Vonnegut's infectious, frozen crystals, numbing the brain.

Among scientists and other hardheads, the tendency of Gaia to fuzz over everything with a world of words has come under incisive attack. At the AGU Gaia conference in San Diego, Tuesday night was philosophy night, and everyone was loaded for bear. After a marathon presentation by Gaian philosopher David Abram on whether or not we human beings are on, inside, or a part of the great superorganism, and what it all means, an aggrieved representative from the Midwest stood up and asked if there were not a danger that all of this Gaia stuff would lead to "woolly-mindedness." Abram, whose work is of such density and rigor that it reads far better than it plays to the ear, took ten minutes of extemporaneous paraphrases, analogies, and allusive musings to say *no*.

The correct answer is *yes*. There is a very real propensity for Gaian whole-earthism to lead to woolly-minded, touchie-feelie thinking, by what NASA microbiologist Penelope Boston derides as its "almost religious, chameleonic ability to be applied to conflicting explanations of natural phenomena." This tendency, however, does not invalidate Gaia any more than a worst-case extreme might disprove any other reasonable theory.

Relativity, for example, is too often reduced to the borderline nonsensical "after all, everything's relative," an aphorism that has been used to excuse lax logic and amoral nonchalance ever since Einstein kicked the last strut out of the ageless assumption that somewhere in the universe, something was unmoved, absolute. And the Darwinists' survival-of-the-fittest doctrine has been perverted even beyond the savage ideology of social Darwinism and on through even to the Nazi perfidy of eugenics. None of these vulgarizations undermines the immensely valuable scientific theories that give them rise, although such nutshell compressions are instructive as to the extremes to which each philosophy may lead. If Darwinism tends to be perverted into brutality, Gaia falls into circular befuddlement, somewhat akin to relativistic fuzziness, which, as far as downsides go, is not so bad.

PEACE, JUSTICE, AND THE GAIAN WAY

"Gaean economics embraces and participates in Gaea's aliveness and wisdom. A Gaean Economy has, as its foundations, the ecological principles of Gaea. . . . The seeds of a Gaean economy are being planted; some are sprouting like blades of grass pushing through a cement sidewalk."[14] Nosing around the Bound Together Anarchist Book Collective in Haight-Ashbury, I found Susan Meeker-Lowry's brief encomium to "an economics for the living earth" in the proceedings of the North American Bioregional Congress II, held August 1986. Right-brained economics, just as Norman Myers calls Gaia right-brained science. Maybe a touch fuzzy as well.

If a theory is best measured by the questions it prompts and the investigations it launches, then Gaia, if nothing else, has range. In the name of Mother Earth, everything from the economics of altruism to the jurisprudence of forgiveness has been predicated, hypothesized, and rhapsodized. As classicist J. Donald Hughes points out, there is deep historical precedent for a Gaian system of values, dating from ancient Greece, when justice was considered an attribute of Mother Earth: "It is because Earth has her own law, a natural law in the original sense of those words, deeper than human enactments and beyond repeal. It is not the justice of human morality: it is written in the nature of things."[15]

But in contrast to the fond New Age notions that proliferate as the philosophy of Gaia, Hughes points out that ancient mythology is full of stories in which the Earth exacts its own version of eye-for-an-eye justice. When Erysichthon ignored a tree spirit's protests and cut down the tree anyway, the dryad complained to Mother Earth, who afflicted the felon with insatiable hunger. And when Orion boasted that he would kill

213

all of the animals, Gaia sent a monstrous scorpion to sting the great hunter to death. Which is closer to true Gaia, mother nurturer or mother avenger?

Thomas Berry, president of the American Teilhard Association, is one of the most influential philosophers of ecology today. Definitely of the "nurturer" school, the deep ecologist believes that human society must emulate the natural world. "For the ecologist, the great model of all existence is the natural ecosystem, which is self-ruled as a community wherein each component has its unique and comprehensive influence,"[16] Berry writes. Berry and others of his romantic persuasion believe that nature provides humankind with its best model for peace and harmony, virtues that human civilization has frittered away, usually for material gain.

Of course, there are also those who maintain that humankind's imperative is to triumph over the savagery of nature. To draw on whatever makes humans higher and nobler than the animals is to quell the urge to kill. "But humans are the only species that murders not just from need but for pleasure," goes the timeless rebuttal in the argument that will probably remain unsettled until the last arguer sinks silently into mulch.

Johan Galtung, professor of peace studies at the University of Hawaii and founder of the International Peace Institute, dances nimbly on the fence:

> There is something ecological to peace. Nature's balance is rooted in diversity (of biota and abiota) and symbiosis between the components of an ecosystem. I would say that peace is also rooted in diversity and symbiosis, meaning the functional interdependence, not only of diverse "actors", like countries, but also of municipalities, international organizations, transnational corporations and so on, not to mention non-human life and non-living resources. However, there is a limit to the organic analogy. Nature is also a brutal place where the strong devour the weak.[17]

From Darwin's hard-line "nature red in tooth and claw" to the idyllic symbiosis of deep ecology, the fact is that contemporary environmentalism is not based on a coherent set of scientific precepts. There is no more general agreement on the principles of ecology than there is on what constitutes sound economic theory. Yet the burgeoning Green political movement is built on an environmentalist ideology. Does this mean that the movement is therefore also built on a set of logical contradictions?

GAIA AND THE GREENS

"We are neither left nor right; we are in front," trumpets the slogan of the political movement that has always had to battle just to keep from getting left out entirely. In their superb and sympathetic book *Green Politics: The Global Promise*, Charlene Spretnak and Fritjof Capra have followed the proliferation of the Green movement since the spring of March 1983, when twenty-seven newly elected representatives to the lower chamber of West Germany's national assembly paraded through the streets of Bonn bearing a huge rubber globe and the branch of a tree that was dying from acid rain pollution of the Black Forest.

"The emergence of Green politics is an ecological, holistic and feminist movement that transcends the old political framework of left versus right," declare the enthusiastic authors.

It emphasizes the interconnectedness and interdependence of all phenomena, as well as the embeddedness of individuals and societies in the cyclical processes of nature. It addresses the unjust and destructive dynamics of patriarchy. It calls for social responsibility and a sound, sustainable system, one that is ecological, decentralized, equitable and comprised of flexible institutions, one in which people have control over their lives. . . . Green politics, in short is the political

215

manifestation of the cultural shift to the new paradigm.[18]

Ecology, peace, and justice—who could disagree? The
Green movement has since spread as a political force to several
dozen other countries and, quite naturally, has diversified and
divided even further, like a fertilized egg that has found its supply
of nourishment. Since its members regard the planet as a unified
ecosystem, expansion of the philosophy beyond national borders
is as natural as the lay of the land and the movements of sea and
air. National boundaries are even less relevant to the Green
ideology than to the doctrine of world communism. The movement toward world organization that started after World War I
with the League of Nations and accelerated after World War II
with the United Nations has taken on an ecological dimension.
The Greens believe that the common threat uniting humankind
today is not just World War III but the monsters emerging from
our own waste.

"Pro-nature" has thus far proven more of a galvanizing
sentiment than a workable political framework. Battles between
the Realos (realists) and the Fundis (fundamentalists) have
splintered the Greens into what Spretnak and Capra now identify as three basic ideological groups: (1) visionary-holistic
Greens, the philosophers and moral guardians of the postpatriar-
chal society that will one day emerge; (2) eco-Greens, who
tackle environmental problems and promote ecologically responsible development; and (3) peace-movement Greens, who oppose nuclear weapons programs and support demilitarization and
closer relations with the Soviet bloc. Communists and left-wing
socialists, sometimes called Red Greens, have formed the rather
sinister-sounding Group Z within the Green party, to insure that
workers' rights are included among the ecological priorities (and,
some right-wingers insist, to obey the secret commands of their
Soviet masters).

216 Not unlike the frequent attempts to unify the Democratic
party in the United States with an inspirational political vision,

such as Kennedy's "New Frontier" and Johnson's "Great Society," many a political thinker today longs to find the right slogan or metaphor to guide the Greens back to pluralism from their current state of disarray. Gaian philosopher William Irwin Thompson, long sympathetic to Green ideals, maintains that ecology as a political organizing principle is a simple thought with sweeping ramifications:

> What physics was to engineering in industrial society,
> biology has become to ecology in our new society. As
> we move from economics to ecology as the governing
> science of our era of stewardship, our politics will have
> to help us realize, beyond all budgets and bottom lines,
> that what truly counts can't be counted. [19]

As the next step toward an ecological world order, the expatriate American proposes international sharing of satellite reconnaissance information for military and environmental defense purposes, to detect and deter anything from sneak attacks by armies to dumping by giant corporations. Managing this wealth of information would be the United Nations, which Thompson reconceives as "the third house of every nation's form of self government," [20] a cross between a global university and a governmental consulting firm, akin to the role that the Organization for Economic Cooperation and Development (OECD) plays for countries of the European Economic Community.

Thompson's agenda sounds "Green" enough, but until very recently the chances of any ideology named Gaia being embraced by that environmentalist movement were slim. Indeed, Gaia and the Greens are still a pretty prickly pair. The defenders of the Earth have been wary of Lovelock ever since the ozone controversy, with some of the more radical exponents still suspicious that Gaia is ultimately just a ruse to pollute. And Lovelock can become irritable at the memory of the radical ideologues, still sore from those ozone attacks and from other policy clashes, particularly on the issue of nuclear power.

In late 1989 Lovelock was invited to give the keynote address at the annual meeting of Friends of the Earth, a major international environmentalist organization of kindred spirit to the Greens. In part the group's overture was an indication that bygones were just that, and that Lovelock was now welcome to take his place as one of the heads of the family. But the invitation was just as much a bow to Gaian theory's burgeoning power as a political organizing principle. After all, under what other name had the likes of Gorbachev, Reagan, the pope, and the secretary general of the United Nations been publicly united?

GAIA AND GLASNOST

Writing in *The Gaia Peace Atlas* in 1988 Mikhail Gorbachev, president of the USSR and general secretary of the Soviet Communist party, stresses the relationship of peace to interdependence: "A notable feature of recent decades has been that for the first time in its history mankind as a whole, and not only individual representatives, has begun to feel that it is one entity, to see global relationships between man, society and nature, and to assess the consequences of material activities."[21] War is suicide even if you win, declares the master ambassador: "There would be no second Noah's Ark for a nuclear deluge,"[22] concludes the head of a state that until Gorbachev's leadership refused to officially recognize any ark at all.

By contrast, Ronald Reagan's brief submission on *The Gaia Peace Atlas*'s theme of global interdependence stands out as uniquely unilateral, including a pitch for the Strategic Defense Initiative and praise for the American way: "One of the greatest contributions the United States can make to the world is to promote freedom as the key to economic growth. . . . This movement in so many places toward economic freedom is indivisible from the worldwide movement toward political freedom and against totalitarian rule."[23]

In his foreword to the Gaia atlas, an extensive collection of essays from world political and religious leaders, such as South Africa's Archbishop Desmond Tutu and Norwegian Prime Minister Gro Harlem Brundtland, Secretary General of the United Nations Javier Perez de Cuellar argues that war is a double ecological threat: "The damage to the natural environment as a result of the arms race is also serious and, at times, irreparable. How utterly senseless it is that precious non-renewable resources should be used to build weapons that may destroy more of those resources if they are ever used."[24]

Pope John Paul II's contribution to the anthology assembled in the name of the pagan Greek goddess transcends ideology: "I am deeply convinced that to reflect together on the priceless treasure of peace is in a way to build it."[25]

Is Gaia providing the theoretical basis for a new, ecological era of understanding, or is it just the latest rubric under which superpower shibboleths are spouted? Lovelock and Margulis have dug up a bit of glasnost that has the potential to keep the Gaia-peace connection forged for quite awhile. Vladimir I. Vernadsky, the Russian researcher who founded the science of biogeochemistry (which is sort of halfway between traditional geochemistry and Gaia), was inspired by his uncle, a lyrical woodsman who taught that the Earth is really alive. Although Vernadsky considered the living Earth notion quaint and overstated, he felt strongly that his scientific colleagues had erred too far in the opposite direction. In his most-famous book, *La Biosphère*, he wrote:

The importance of life in the whole structure of the Earth's crust penetrated only slowly into the mind of scientists, and is not yet penetrated today in its full extent. It was as late as 1875 that E. Suess [the man who coined the term *biosphere*], professor at the University of Vienna, one of the most eminent geologists of the last century, introduced into science the notion of the biosphere as the idea of a particular envelope of the terrestrial crust, a layer permeated by life.[26]

Jacques Grinevald, a Swiss science historian who has exhaustively researched the history of the Gaia theory, reports that although Vernadsky had been considered brilliant, he was consigned to oblivion by Marxist ideologues who saw religion lurking in his holistic conceptions. (Not at all unlike what many scientists of the capitalist establishment have tried to do with Lovelock.) Now, in the era of glasnost, Vernadsky has been revived by Soviet academicians and even quoted by Gorbachev, a fact that may in part explain the Soviet premier's participation in *The Gaia Peace Atlas*. Gaian theory, which for almost two decades has been ignored or scoffed at by the Soviet scientific establishment, with special vehemence coming from the Moscow-establishment geochemist Gregor Budyko, is now considered so acceptable that several representatives from the Moscow Academy of Sciences participated in the 1988 AGU Gaia conference.

Lovelock and Margulis are of course delighted. "When Lynn Margulis and I introduced the Gaia Hypothesis in 1972 neither of us was aware of Vernadsky's work and none of our much learned colleagues drew our attention to the lapse. We retraced his steps and it was not until the 1980's that we discovered him to be our most illustrious predecessor,"[27] writes Lovelock in *New Scientist*, in his review of the English translation of *La Biosphère*, which was written in 1929 but did not appear in what is supposed to be the lingua franca of science until a few years ago. "The all-too-common deafness of English speakers to any other language kept from our common knowledge the everyday science of the Russian-speaking world,"[28] concludes Lovelock diplomatically, the possibility of a joint East-West Gaia conference not having escaped his, or the multilingual Margulis's, imagination.

SAVE MARS!

Neither has the planet Mars, on which the Soviet space program has been so intently focused, escaped Lovelock's atten-

220

tion. His suggestion in *The Greening of Mars* that the Martian atmosphere could be injected with CFC greenhouse gases and warmed up to life-sustaining levels may have been intended only as "faction"—speculative fiction based on scientific principles— but it has been taken seriously by planetary scientists in both the United States and the USSR. The novelists' off-the-cuff estimate that about 50,000 tons of CFC's would be required annually to heat up the red planet has been checked over by NASA's Chris McKay, a planetary geologist who concludes,

> We could have a warm Mars. There are detailed models for fluorocarbon windows on Earth, and I believe that in general principle they could apply to Mars. Four fluorocarbon gases, $CBrF_3$, C_2F_6, $CFCl$ and CF_2Cl_2, all stable, fully halogenated hydrocarbons, would together block out that infrared-window region completely. Anywhere from 78 thousand metric tons per year would need to be produced, well within the range of an automated factory.

McKay does not doubt that the atmosphere could be transformed but says that

> an earthlike Mars is another question entirely. There is certainly enough oxygen up there locked into carbon dioxide, and also silicon dioxide, which this warming process would likely free up. Many of us believe that there is still a lot of water on Mars, an average of 100 meters deep around the planet, although Lovelock fears that all Martian water has been outgassed already. For me the big question is nitrogen. Earth's atmosphere is almost 80 percent nitrogen, so that's crucial. Is there nitrogen buried on Mars, as nitrate deposits? To find out, we need a sample return mission. There's been lots of talk about the Soviets sending a manned space- craft to Mars early in the twenty-first century, and

some wishful noise about the U.S. sending one too. We could build the Rover. They could provide the return craft. That would really be a match made in the heavens.

And collaboration could save a megabundle for both countries—especially the United States, since we are so far behind.

Konstantin Skryabin of the Moscow Academy of Sciences has long expressed interest in Martian terraforming, or what his colleague, Robert Haynes of the University of Toronto, prefers to call "ecopoiesis," either way essentially the process of imparting a biosphere to a planet without one. In other words, the propagation of Gaia. In addition to Lovelock's gas-injection scheme, others have proposed the progressive dissemination of microbes suited to the chemical composition of the Martian surface and atmosphere. This would be more truly Gaian, since organisms would be given the task of creating and sustaining a habitable environment.

Unlike the Earth's moon, quickly abandoned after its conquest, and with much too thin an atmosphere for Gaian procreation, space travel to Mars could have a greater goal than just making the trip or even than colonization. What better way for the two deadliest enemies on Earth to bond than by exporting life to the heavens? And what a beautiful irony! That Lovelock, the scientist who first understood that there was no life on Mars, would ultimately bring the red planet to life.

XI

THE GODDESS AND HER RITUALS

> Gaia, mother of all, I sing, oldest
> of gods.
> Firm of foundation, who feeds all
> creatures living on earth.
> As many move on the radiant land
> and swim in the sea.
> And fly through the air—all these
> does she feed with her bounty.
> Mistress, from you come our fine
> children and bountiful harvest:
> Yours is the power to give mortals
> life and to take it away.
> —"Homeric Hymn to Earth, Mother of All"

GAIA BEFORE GOD

Gaia, the great pre-Olympian Earth goddess and first possessor of the oracle at Delphi, dates back to the beginning of written recorded history, from around 3000 B.C. But the Greek deity is actually a relatively recent incarnation of the great mother goddess first adored by the Aurignacian Cro-Magnon of the upper Paleolithic period of the Old Stone Age, some twenty-five thousand to thirty thousand years ago. Images of Mother Earth, the oldest religious images in human history, appear on canyon and cave walls from Spain to Siberia.

Gaia's closest cousin is Terra, the Roman Earth goddess; both are kin to Isis of the Egyptians, Kwan Yin of the Chinese, Lakshmi of the Hindus, Yemanja of many African peoples, Shekinah of the Jews from the days of the cabbalah, the Changing Woman of the Navajo, and many others, including Mother Nature, who at one time or another has appeared or occurred to almost everyone. All are sublime female Earth deities, givers of life, wisdom, pleasure, and death.

Christine Downing, author of *The Goddess*, warns that Gaia, daughter of Chaos, "is still rebellious, alive and eruptive. Gaia is earthquake and volcano, molten lava and shifting rock. She is earth as it is in itself, not earth subdued by humankind. She may be goddess of all that grows but she is never the goddess of agriculture. . . . Gaia reminds us all that cannot be brought under control."[1] The life of the Earth can never be tamed, even by Gaia herself.

After Gaia bore Uranus, the god of the heavens, she took her son as lover and bore him the Titans, the Cyclops, and the Hundred-handed Ones. But her ingrateful scion hated the monstrous appearance of their issue and thus hid the last two groups inside his mother-wife's body, causing her terrible pain. Gaia rebelled, made a sickle of flint, and begged her Titan sons to help her get even. Only Cronus would dare. When Uranus lay with Gaia that night, Cronus castrated his father with the sickle and threw the genitals onto his mother, Earth. From the drops of blood that fell on the land, Gaia bore the Giants, the Erinyes, and the Meliae, or ash-nymphs. The sky god's semen then gave the sea its foam. From her son and lover Pontus, god of the sea, Gaia begat Nereus, Thaumas, Phorcys, Ceto, and Eurybia. And Uranus retired to a part of the cosmos so remote that it would be thousands of years before contact was reestablished. Even today, as the *Voyager* spacecraft's recent flyby confirmed, the denatured deity remains frigid and abashed.

Mother Gaia had even less luck with her later offspring. Cronus turned out to be as nasty as his father Uranus, also forcing his mother to keep monstrous siblings buried inside as well as swallowing his own offspring for fear that one of them would overthrow him. But with Gaia's help, grandson Zeus survived Cronus's vengeful feast and overthrew his rapacious father. Old habits die hard, especially among the immortal, so when Zeus was warned that his first wife Oceanid Metis would bear him a rebellious son, he swallowed her whole. Enraged in the spirit of sisterhood, Mother Earth sought to avenge the death of her daughter-in-law and urged the Giants to storm Zeus on Mount Olympus. Gaia searched frantically for a drug to make her warriors immortal in battle but Zeus commanded the sun not to shine, and he found the drug himself.

GODDESS DAYS

Despite her failure to control Olympus, Gaia was worshipped in the Aegean cultures of pre-Hellenic Greece, particularly the Mycenaean civilization of the mainland and the Minoan civilization of Crete, roughly from 3000 to 1500 B.C., as the primal goddess, the mother of all things. She was most revered for her torrential fertility: "Many of Her temples were built near deep chasms where yearly the mortals offered sweet cakes into Her womb. From within the darkness of Her secrets, Gaia received these gifts,"[2] writes Spretnak in her charmingly poetic rendering of Gaia's birth and early worship in *Lost Goddesses of Early Greece.*

Spretnak, whose work on ancient Greek goddesses sets the lyrical and scholarly standard for the field, writes that the pre-Athenian Greeks perceived a correlation between the processes of the Earth and those of the female, and this connection was frequently expressed with sexual imagery. . . . So the conceptualizations of Gaia, even from the earliest expressions, were a celebration of the elemental power of the female. Our ancestors viewed all life as coming from the womb of the Earth Mother, into which all beings were received at the end of life.[3]

Writing of the same period, Downing captures the immanence of that earthy religion: "There is a with-in-ness to Gaia; souls live in her body. The Greeks understood that soul-making happens in earth, not in sky. Soul (unlike spirit) relates to the concrete imagination."[4]

The classic artistic representation of Gaia is as a woman emerging breast-high from the earth. The goddess arises but never leaves her planetary body. Visceral rites, including plant, animal, and (presumably ecstatic) human sacrifice as well as unabashed sexual ceremonies were held to adore the goddess's fecundity. Downing believes that reckless abandon was particularly appropriate because there was

> a different kind of identification between the worshipper and the goddess than we find in the worship of her Olympian offspring. Ecstatic, perhaps orgiastic, possession (as in the cult of Gaia's byforms, Rhea and Cybele) has no place in the worship of Athens or Hera. The Olympians may be seen as human writ large, in whom we can recognize ourselves; whereas to be taken over by Gaia is to be overwhelmed by a clearly extra-human force, to be taken out of ourselves.[5]

Spretnak exults in the peaceful, artful, Goddess-oriented culture of ancient Greece. Going to church was certainly more fun. But according to her gnashing re-creation, one day a massive wave of horsemen swarmed in, bringing a few women, a chieftain hierarchy, and primitive stamps to impress their two symbols, the sun and a pine tree. "They brought a sky god, a warrior cult, and a patriarchal social order," laments the vanguard feminist, nostalgic for the days some four thousand years gone by.

Yet sun worship really is quite perceptive, as the maverick Soviet scientist Vernadsky reminds us (perhaps because he was a privileged member of the patriarchy):

> The biosphere is as much, or even more, the creation of the Sun as it is a manifestation of Earth process. Ancient religious intuitions which regarded terrestrial creatures, especially human beings, as "children of the Sun" were much nearer the truth than those which looked upon them as a mere ephemeral creation, a blind and accidental product of matter and earth-forces. Terrestrial creatures are the fruit of a long and complicated cosmic process, and, subject to predetermined laws, form of necessity part of a harmonious cosmic mechanism in which chance does not exist.[6]

Religious history was to gravitate skyward: "They moved in waves first into southeastern Europe, later down into Greece, across all of Europe, also into the Middle and Near East, North Africa and India . . . *and that is where we live today*—in an Indo-European culture, albeit one that is very technologically advanced," concludes Spretnak, who nonetheless still seems to hope that this stubborn old warrior god might, like his Greek forbear Uranus, be similarly inconvenienced one day soon.

FROM CREATOR TO CLOCKMASTER TO THE GREAT DETONATOR

Margaret Mead once remarked that she never came across a people who lacked a creation story. Be it the eternal mythology

227

of Greece, the Babylonian love battle between Marduk and Tiamat, the cracking of the great cosmic egg, or two lovers and a snake in a garden, people seem to need some explanation of how they all came to be.

"People of the Book," as Moslems, Christians, and Jews are known in Islam, have for milennia derived their creation theology from the book of Genesis, the principal character of which is God. As New Age theologian Philip Novak writes, these biblical religions institutionalized the shift from an immanent deity like the Earth goddess Gaia to an external and superior "sky-god":

> The Hebrews were among the first to introduce a significant variation on this ancient outlook (in which the world's creatures and natural processes—the rain, the tides, the rotation of the starry vault—were understood as the multiform expression of divine life). They, and the Christians and the Muslims who branched from the same Abrahamic tree, framed the conception of a God who transcends the world he created.[7]

It is as though the gravity of reason has struggled ever since to bring God back down to Earth. For unlike many of Mead's primal peoples, we have also grown used to the evolution, and in many ways dilution, of our sustaining myth. From the Bible's God the Omnipotent to the Clockmaker God of Newton and the Enlightenment, and even on through quantum theory's God the Oddsmaker, Einstein's famous "God does not play dice with the world!" notwithstanding. With every century that passes, our deity has lost a little more control. Now, with the growing understanding that the universe is not static and eternal (as Einstein would later admit to have been his saddest mistake) but has a beginning, a middle, and an end, evolving according to natural laws just like everything else, our sacred story no longer has much need for any main character at all. Certainly not a creator light years away.

The Big Bang theory of the universe's evolution seems destined to gain acceptance as scientific creed. Even if it doesn't, Stephen Jay Gould's scrupulous distinction—between the fact of evolution and the sundry theories of how it all happens—holds just as well for the history of the universe as for the history of life on Earth. Maybe it was a whimper or a spin, not a bang. But unless there is a radical reversal in scientific thinking, possibly some masterful reconception of time à la Prigogyne, where our concepts of progress through time might be replaced with, say, more Joycean notions of simultaneity, the fundamental conviction that the universe evolves will stand, no matter the details of how. And if it began with a bang, as those Nobel laureates from Bell Labs who found background radiation left over from the creation explosion appear to have proved, God the Creator will have been diminished once again. This time, at best, to the one who set off the big boom.

Arguing that theologians should not be troubled by the facts of evolution, Gould likes to quote the words of the great nineteenth-century preacher, the Reverend Henry Ward Beecher: "Design by wholesale is grander than design by retail," meaning that "general laws rather than creation of each item by fiat will satisfy our notions of divinity,"[8] according to the scientist's conciliatory interpretation. But what role can a creator have in the general laws of the Big Bang? Not nearly so awesome as the creator of Genesis or even the clockmaker of the Enlightenment, who at least designed the whole apparatus and wound it up before walking away. What sort of worship is due an entity that set off a cosmic bomb fifteen billion years ago, then let matter and energy take their course?

Rather than the gradual, elegant processes that Darwin envisioned, most evolutionists now understand that there are watersheds, critical masses, pivotal times, punctuated equilibria, as Gould calls them, where change happens more rapidly, sometimes as a radical break with the past. Could it be that the evolution of our creation myth has reached that cracking point where the current version is so revised that it no longer bears

229

any connection with the original "God created heaven and earth, Adam and Eve, and on the seventh day He rested"? Doesn't "God the Great Detonator" blow too big a hole in our greatest story?

THOU SHALT HAVE NO OTHER GODS BEFORE ME

Oriana Fallaci, the intrepid Italian journalist, once remarked that when she finally decided that she did not believe in God, she was afraid God would find out she did not believe in Him anymore. Hardly a timid soul, this is the same woman who, when interviewing the Ayatollah Kohmeini in Qum, took off her chador because she found it uncomfortable and insulting. Yet even for Fallaci, after the faith had vanished, the fear of God remained. How scary it must have been to defy that bearded, stony face.

Bertrand Russell would have understood Fallaci's irrational terror, since that, in his opinion, is why people believe in God in the first place: "Religion is based, I think, primarily and mainly upon fear. It is partly the terror of the unknown, and partly the wish to feel that you have a kind of elder brother who will stand by you in all your troubles and disputes. Fear is the basis of the whole thing—fear of the mysterious, fear of defeat, fear of death," writes the Nobel laureate in *Why I Am Not a Christian.*

For the atheist so devoted that he went to jail for his convictions, the humane and rational alternative to the religion that had so benighted the world was science:

Science can help us to get over this craven fear in which mankind has lived for so many generations. Science can teach us, and I think our own hearts can teach us, no longer to look round for imaginary supports, no longer to invent allies in the sky, but rather to look to our own efforts here below to make this world a fit place to live in, instead of the sort of place that the Churches in all these centuries have made it.[10]

Russell was so dedicated to the themes of *Why I Am Not a Christian* that his first essay on the subject appeared in the 1920s, with his book of the same name written some thirty years later. For him, arguments against belief in Christianity could for the most part be used against belief in a deity of any sort. The champion atheist would have scorned today's romance between science and spirituality, and from Oriental mystics preaching physics to the budding group of whole-Earth theologians, he might dismiss it all as just a passing phase. Whenever science makes breakthroughs that outpace common sense, such as the counterintuitive conundrums of quantum physics or Big Bang cosmology, its philosophical affinity with the mysteries of religion deepens. Perhaps Russell would now argue that the converse is just as true, that as all these new enigmas weave their way into common sense, the craven need for faith in the unknown inevitably subsides.

What if Fallaci decided to replace her belief in God with, say, some other belief, perhaps in several gods? Several of the most illustrious thinkers of the postwar period have called for Western religion to forsake the solitary and overpowering humaniform deity of the Bible, not for science or rationalism but for naturalistic polytheism of ancient Greece. Much as Friedrich Nietzsche rejected the "slave morality" of Christianity and strove instead to emulate the Teutonic gods and adopt the "will to power" of the heroic *übermensch,* Michel Foucault, best known for his structuralist manifesto, *The Order of Things* and also the compendious *History of Sexuality,* championed "living beautifully," with a harmony that would emulate the noblest traits of the Greek pantheon. And in *Mimesis,* truly the sacred text of modern comparative literature, Erich Auerbach foreswore what he saw as the irretrievably ambiguous and ironic theology of the

231

Middle East, preferring the cleaner lines and values of Greek myths and legends instead.

Russell's patent disbelief was less of a heresy, by Judeo-Christian measure, than the calls of Nietzsche, Foucault, and Auerbach to worship other gods. Nowhere in Exodus does God explicitly forbid disbelief. But the first three of the Ten Commandments are specifically devoted to the terrible sins of worshipping other gods. It may be incidental to note that Russell lived to the age of ninety-eight, while both heretics may late in life have come to ponder the poetic wrath of the First Commandment: "I am the Lord thy God. Thou shalt have no other gods before me." Nietzsche died less than a hero's death, enduring a decade of lonely insanity before passing on to Valhalla; Foucault, whose prescription for the beautiful life included a proportioned amount of sexual adventuring, was cut down by AIDS. Auerbach's end was calmer, particularly compared to the years he spent in the Turkish prison where he penned his paean to Greek divinity.

The ease with which the supremacy of the biblical God the Almighty can be challenged and argued out of plausibility belies the distinct unease that many, including this writer, feel when doing so. For many of us inclined to religious belief, God is the revered and appropriate name for whatever greater spiritual goodness or oneness that exists. So to write against God is by definition profane. Not to mention foolhardy, for the same reason that there are no atheists in a foxhole—why take the chance of offending? Fallaci's faith could not be shaken even by her own decision to renounce it. An enviable quandary for as long as it lasted, especially to those who pray that their own faith in God survives their intellectual duty to put it to the test.

THE NEW COSMIC STORY

232

"Our most powerful story, equivalent in its way to a universal myth, is evolution."[11] In *The Lives of a Cell*, Lewis Thomas echoes a sentiment that has been passionately expressed by dogmatic atheists, sentimental pantheists, and all manner of theists and deists in between. "Never mind that it is true whereas myths are not; it is filled with symbolism, and this is the way it has influenced the mind of society."[12] The story of the birth and fifteen-billion-year expansion of the universe, the five-billion-year development of our planet, and the wondrous growth of life and Gaia, right on up through four million years or so of glorious humanity. Sun and Earth are equally encompassed in this meta-vision. But no God, or any other main characters.

Cosmologist Brian Swimme describes the spiritual possibilities of this latest "greatest story ever told":

> For suddenly the human species as a whole has a common cosmic story. Islamic people, Dineh people, Christian people, Marxist people, Hindu people can all agree in a basic sense on the birth of the Sun, on the development of the Earth, on the complex history of human cultures. For the first time in human existence, we have a cosmic story that is not tied to a cultural tradition, or to a political ideology but that gathers every human group into its meanings . . . we have broken through to a story that is already taught and developed on every continent and within every major cultural setting.[13]

A cheerful, entertaining exponent of the new cosmic story, Swimme colorfully envisions the day when someone's grandmother (not mine if she lived to be a thousand) gathers the children around the campfire in a hillside meadow, picks up a piece of granite, and tells the new story:

> At one time, at the beginning of the Earth, the whole planet was a boiling sea of molten rock. We revere rocks because everything has come from them— not just the continents and the mountains, but the

233

trees, and the oceans and your bodies. The rocks are your grandmother and grandfather. When you remember all those who have helped you in this life, you begin with the rocks, for if not for them you would not be.[14]

Sure, so maybe some of the boys in the back would make smart remarks under their breath about grandpa's stones. At most Swimme, the author of the imaginative new story wonder book, *The Universe is a Green Dragon*, can be faulted for having too elaborate a sense of fantasy. An avid and ubiquitous lecturer, he certainly does seem to have the fire: "Our situation is similar to that of the early Christians. They had nothing—nothing but a profound revelatory experience. They did nothing—nothing but wander about telling a new story. And yet the Western world entered a transformation from which it has never recovered."[15]

Renowned environmentalist Rene Dubos has long held that our salvation depends upon our ability to create a religion of nature. If Swimme is correct in his comparison of today's cosmic storytellers to those of early Christianity, each group compelled like the graybearded loon of "The Rime of the Ancient Mariner" to tell their story, then perhaps we are at that watershed where the vestiges and pretenses of ancient biblical creation myths fall away and Nature regains her spiritual due.

Thomas Berry, something of a mentor to Swimme, is to new cosmic spirituality much what William Irwin Thompson is to Gaian social philosophy, deeply respected as seminal by many, though a bit starched at times.

Both education and religion need to ground themselves within the story of the universe as we now understand this story through empirical knowledge. Within this functional cosmology we can overcome our alienation and begin the renewal of life on a sustainable basis. This story is a numinous revelatory

story that could evoke the vision and energy required
to bring not only ourselves but the entire planet into a
new order of magnificence.[16]

But there is no one's magnificence to imitate, is there? No
Christ or Mary to be like, no Moses, Buddha, or Muhammad to
tell about. No God, Apollo, Isis, or Thor to instill a little
healthy fear. Perhaps it is human chauvinist prejudice, but
doesn't a story, especially an inspirational, sacred one, need
more than rocks and bugs?

G. K. Chesterton saw the snag long ago:

> That man and brute are like is, in a sense a
> truism; but that being so like they should then be so
> insanely unlike, that is the shock and the enigma.
> That an ape has hands is far less interesting to the
> philosopher than the fact that having hands he does
> next to nothing with them; does not play knuckle-
> bones or the violin, does not carve marble or carve
> mutton. . . . Certain modern dreamers say that ants
> and bees have a society superior to ours. They indeed
> have a civilization; but that very truth reminds us that
> it is an inferior civilization. Who ever found an ant
> hill decorated with the statues of celebrated ants? Who
> has seen a beehive carved with the images of gorgeous
> queens of old. . . . We talk of wild animals, but man is
> the only wild animal. It is man that has broken out
> . . . it is exactly where biology leaves off that religion
> begins.[17]

Margulis and Sagan see humankind as less of a spiritual leap
than a developmental blip.

> If there is a central insight to evolution it is that
> patterns of living organization are transitory. A similar
> insight exists in the great eastern religions. The doc-

235

LAWRENCE E. JOSEPH

trine of reincarnation teaches that there is a never-
ending cycle of life and rebirth. Buddhism teaches that
Nirvana is the blissful release from such a cycle. Human beings present no exception to the law of
change. . . . "Australopithecus robustus", "Homo
erectus", "Homo sapiens", food gathering bands, hunt-
ing troops, and village life are all fleeting apparitions
on the great stage of evolution. So are Tokyo and New
York. Tool-using apes and our cities equally represent
stages in the technological development of the biosphere, just as computers and robots may represent part
of a still larger pattern.[18]

The new cosmic story of evolution may tie all creatures
together in unprecedented ways, but it does not really explain
what makes people so special that they need, like food and
drink, to tell such stories in the first place. We are sufficiently
different from microbes, plants, and tool-using apes to merit
special, even magical explanations, but not so different that our
wondrous nature can be arrogated as superior to the saga of the
rest of life and the physical world that gave it rise. Like any other
satisfying creation myth, the story of evolution needs to find its
heroes and heroines, human and non. At least it must answer
the question of to whom, or to what, does one pray?

SISTERHOOD AND THE GODDESS

Moses. Jesus. Buddha. Muhammad. Why not at least one
woman among all of these divine men? Why not a goddess?

"Contemporary feminism wants to give birth to something
new, and that something is a goddess," declared Rabbi Leah
Novick. Judging from the enthusiasm of the five hundred or so
participants attending the Gaia Consciousness conference in
San Francisco where Novick made her righteous declaration, the
birthing process is well under way. Over the course of the five-

day conference, a bewildering array of goddess and holy woman figures from more than a score of religions were presented, compared, and exalted. Their particularities were far less important than the fact that "the Goddess" had returned.

"Why are you interested in the goddess?" I asked a young woman at a recent feminist spirituality festival in New York. "Because I am the goddess," was her startling reply.

Jean Shinoda's bestselling *The Goddess in Everywoman* captures this practical appeal of goddess spirituality. The concept of the goddess within is, at its simplest, a rhetorical tool to help women engender and focus their self-esteem. Essentially a secular version of the doctrine of pantheism—which holds that divine spirit is present in everything and everyone—this form of goddess spirituality builds self-confidence by encouraging belief in the higher power that is, by definition, inside. Very much in the tradition of the motivational literature of the seventies, but eminently more graceful than most of those materialistic encomiums to the almighty *me*.

Just as Jay Gatsby sprang from the Platonic conception of himself, so too might a woman who does justice to the goddess inside blossom into her rightful magnificence. But as Fitzgerald sadly illustrated at the end of his immortal American classic, one of the dangers of flying too high is that you are likely to end up dying alone. At least as important to the goddess movement as personal empowerment is the sense of togetherness that it offers. In the goddess, the spirituality of sisterhood has found a supernal symbol, inspiring an astonishing eruption of music, dance, poetry, theater, and, particularly, sacred visual art.

Merlin Stone is without doubt the nation's leading expert of goddess art. At the San Francisco festival she gave a fascinating and extensive presentation on contemporary feminist artists using the goddess motif. The Pacific Northwest, the Santa Fe area, and New York City, particularly the New York Feminist Art Institute, seem to be the locus for much of this work, with Sandra Stanton, Regina Tierney, Buffy Johnson, Nancy Azara, Tye Grey and Cathy Freen, Carolyn Oberst and Mary Beth

Edelson all working the goddess theme. But as Merlin's frantic travel schedule attests, this renaissance has already burgeoned beyond those predictably trendy centers.

The Blue Goddess, a watercolor by Elizabeth Greenleaf, who lives and works in New Haven, Connecticut, exemplifies much of the best of the newest school of sacred art. The Earth mother, depicted in the same bluish green of the planet floating in space, is fecund and powerful, dwarfing all that surrounds her. Her physical beauty is both external and internal, ranging from a touch of hearts and flowers to a cavernous womb. She is certainly no damsel in distress but nonetheless has an enormous capacity to feel the pain of childbirth and any other importunities that may result from invasions by men. And a fat red snake coils around her body, snug but ready to strike.

THE PAGAN DEITY

Objective assessments of the goddess movement are hard to come by because its spirit is so freewheeling and anarchic; hard facts and demographic analysis seem just a bit too left-brained. Guesstimates place the number of active devotees at anywhere from ten-thousand to one-hundred-thousand in the United States, at least two-thirds of them women. While a large number of goddess adherents are drawn by the feminist spirituality, it seems that almost an equal number are attracted foremost by its elements of nature worship. By philosophy and logistics, the goddess movement is also part of a broader pagan resurgence.

The Neo-Pagan movement, and especially Feminist Witchcraft, has recently been joined by increasing numbers from the Women's Spirituality movement. These are the forces which form the core of the movement to restore the Goddess to her rightful place; a movement which has its roots in the combined studies of feminism and ecology and in the logical spiritual application of such studies. If Witches can be priestesses of feminism, then Neo-Pagans are the chaplains of the ecology movement.[19]

The above is written by Otter G'Zell, a self-described "Priest of Gaea" who is so well considered among New Age spiritualists that some claim that he, not Lovelock, is the creator of the Gaea hypothesis. Morning Glory, Otter's wife, describes herself as "Priestess of the Goddess in Her Aspect of Potnia Theron, Our Lady of the Beasts," and has gathered an exquisite collection of goddess sculptures and statues.

The quintessential pagan couple are generous teachers on all matters regarding nature worship and paganism and are ready to celebrate any and all spiritual opportunities that might come their way.

> The new Paganism encompasses many Nature-oriented groups such as Feraferia, Church of All Worlds, Madrakara, Bear Tribe, Venusian Church, Pagan Way, Church of the Eternal Source, Reformed Druids, and Holy Order of Mother Earth. The largest contingent of modern Goddess-worshippers, however, is found in Witchcraft, or Wicca. Wicca is a pre-Christian European Pagan magical tradition; European eradication of the followers of Wicca by the Inquisition can only be compared to the Jewish Holocaust of Nazi Germany (estimates of the number of martyrs run as high as nine million!), but today the Craft is making a powerful comeback on the wings of the re-emergent Goddess.[20]

The G'Zells undoubtedly place little faith in most official estimates of the number of women and men burned as witches throughout Europe and North America, which run lower by several orders of magnitude.

Certainly the finest study of contemporary American paganism is Margot Adler's *Drawing Down the Moon*. Aware that the movement's colorful eccentricity makes it fair game for those who would dismiss paganism as frivolous—or worse, as bizarre hocus pocus, Adler, granddaughter of the renowned psychiatrist Alfred Adler, takes pains to explain what paganism is not: "The Pagan movement does not include the Eastern religious groups. It includes neither Satanists nor Christians. Almost every religious group that has received massive exposure in the press, from the Hare Krishna movements to the Unification Church to the People's Temple, lies outside the Pagan resurgence."[21] Perhaps only in her blanket exclusion of Satanism, which has a certain dark affinity with some of the more malevolent forms of witchcraft, does Adler stretch her case for paganism's good name.

> The many hundreds of Pagan religious groups, by and large, stand in contrast and opposition to these authoritarian movements. The Pagan vision is one which says that neither doctrine nor dogma nor asceticism nor rule by masters is necessary for the visionary experience, and that ecstasy and freedom are both possible.[22]

Adler's grandfather, best known for his theory of the inferiority complex, might have appreciated the pagan taste for revelry, since he believed that personality difficulties derive from restrictions on the individual's need for self-assertion. For when it comes time to pay tribute to the power of Mother Earth, inhibition can be a sin.

GAIA, GODDESS, AND PATRON SAINT

More than any other deity, Gaia culminates the goddess movement because as a Greek deity she has a venerable (if tumultuous) history and is not part of any major faith's current beliefs. Christians are not forced to yield to Moslems, Jews to

Buddhists, and so on. As a spiritual figure whose domain is the entire planet, Gaia encompasses the more personalized or specialized deities the way that Muhammad provides the context for all of the other prophets or Jesus acts as focal point for the intercessions of the saints. And as Mother Earth she basks in timeless warmth and affection while at the same time appealing to vanguard ecological and feminist sensibilities.

Mother Earth also entices mainstream clerics eager to capture some of the current fervor for nature for their ministries. But the pagan goddess can play hob with doctrine. Lovelock, whose Anglican church has been the readiest to participate in the Gaia experiment, takes a creative swipe at doctrinal symbiosis:

> Those millions of Christians who make a special place in their hearts for the Virgin Mary possibly respond as I do. The concept of Jahweh as remote, all-powerful, all-seeing is either frightening or unapproachable. Even the sense of presence of a more contemporary God, a still, small voice within, may not be enough for those who need to communicate with someone outside. Mary is close and can be talked to. She is believable and manageable. It could be that the importance of the Virgin Mary in faith is something of this kind, but there may be more to it. What if Mary is another name for Gaia? Then her capacity for virgin birth is no miracle or parthenogenetic aberration, it is the role of Gaia since life began.[23]

"A Christian cannot pray to Gaia," warns Dean James Morton of the Cathedral of St. John the Divine. A master at the art of liberal interpretation, Morton knows the bounds of heterodoxy: to equate the Virgin Mary with Gaia is definitely to transgress. "Gaia is the poetic name for the Earth in all its layers, from the core to the edge of its atmosphere, and the self-corrective process that keeps the planet alive. Gaia is a localized concept, not a

241

transcendent concept. Can't pray to Gaia any more than you can pray to an ostrich egg." When asked why a Christian could not pray to Gaia in the same way that he or she might pray to a saint, Morton responded, "You don't pray to a saint. You pray through a saint to God." Morton prefers the comparison between Gaia and the angels, which he calls messenger intelligences, leaving open the possibility that the Earth goddess might serve, if not as patron saint for Earth lovers, at least as their spiritual pathway to the Almighty.

In May 1988 the Dalai Lama, the archbishop of Canterbury, and two hundred other clergy and public officials, including a number of foreign ministers and heads of state, gathered for five days at Oxford University for the Global Forum for Survival. Two scientists, Lovelock and Carl Sagan, also were invited. Sagan, far the more skillful diplomat, offered an update on his patented vision of the cosmos. Lovelock, perhaps to the slight discomfort of his good friend Dean Morton, who had helped organize the affair, proceeded to get into a bit of a row with one of the other participants—none other than Mother Teresa herself.

Their differences were clear. Essentially, Lovelock's message was: take care of the Earth and humanity's problems will start to take care of themselves. Mother Teresa expressed just the opposite: take care of the people, and the Earth's problems will come around. There are those balm merchants who would wish to smooth it all over and say that after all, the two eminences really agree on the higher goal of improving the lot of the world. But in terms of policy priorities the contrast could not be more stark. From a Gaian point of view the best way to respond, for example, to sub-Saharan famine would be to alleviate the environmental stresses causing the situation—overpopulation, fuelwood deforestation, and so forth. From Mother Teresa's orthodox Catholicism our first duty is to help the people suffering, a call that she and her Sisters of Mercy have answered on tens of thousands of occasions. In terms of spiritual duty, worshipping the Earth without expressing greater deference to the God who created it would be as silly as thanking the supermarket manager alone for providing one's daily bread. And an eternally damnable heresy to boot.

"We can be global citizens if we forget ourselves," declared the simple, magnificent woman, casting a long glance at the pomp and circumstance surrounding her. "It is not how much we give but how much love we put in the giving."[24]

Archbishop Desmond Tutu does not go so far as to include the pagan goddess anywhere in the Christian panoply. but he seems to have found a middle ground in the people-versus-nature theological debate. In *The Gaia Peace Atlas* the Anglican Nobel laureate writes:

> We find that we are placed in a delicate network of vital relationships with the divine, with fellow human beings, and with the rest of creation. We violate nature only at our peril, and are meant to live as members of one family. This is the law of our being, and when we break this law things go disastrously wrong. We know the consequences of our wanton destruction of natural resources, the ecological misadventures that follow in the train of our pollution of the biosphere.[25]

The merger of Christianity and Gaian spirituality may founder on the differences in what they offer to someone contemplating death. Christianity offers the more comforting but less believable promise of everlasting life, but the most that Gaia offers is an upbeat reappraisal of the inevitability of decay. Lovelock calls it a small price to pay for life and identity as an individual, but death is, after all, the highest price. Spiritual philosopher Joanna Macy, in her "Gaia Meditations," tries to make the ultimate purchase sound like a better buy: "Think to your next death. Will your flesh and bones back into the cycle. Surrender. Love the plump worms you will become. Launder your weary being through the fountain of life."[26]

243

CHILDREN OF THE EARTH

"You know, like everything kinda interrelates, sort of!" exclaimed the girl with the ring in her nose, waving her hand in a great sweeping circle as we all looked on in awe. In the supportive atmosphere of the New Age colloquium on Gaian spiritual philosophy, held in San Francisco's forever-flowers Haight-Ashbury district, the young lady's aha! was received with good spirits and collectively encouraged as a step toward grasping the fundamental interconnectedness of life. We began to trade stories of our first experiences of oneness with the Earth. A young woman from Nebraska told how her father first took her to the ocean and taught her to jump into the waves. Another woman remembered catching snowflakes on her tongue. We formed the inevitable circle, each hugged a Gaia globe beach ball, honored the four directions, which were symbolized by fire, water, incense, and earth, and meditated to some rather catchy New Age tunes.

It is no crime to be unscientific. Many scientists come off as the final arbiters of physical truth, stripped of all that fuzzy emotionalism in which we layfolk habitually indulge. But are they? Is a consensus of the best scientific opinion the final judgment on what is true about the physical world? Ask your lover if you're not sure.

There is a humble simplicity to the Gaian style. It is not sexy. Garments tend to be loose, flowing, and inexpensive; Spandex seems to have no place in nature worship. Women with more than the lightest makeup and men wearing ties stand out like aliens come to take the cure. There is just something retro inherent to earthiness, and, as classicist J. Donald Hughes notes, there always has been.

Athens remembered her earliest kings as sons of Gaia, so earthy that one was said to be serpent-formed in his lower parts. The more old-fashioned among Athenians gathered their long hair with golden clasps shaped like cicada, those insects that can be seen emerging from the earth in springtime, to symbolize that they were "children of the earth."[27]

In spirit and style, there is no doubt that those ancient Earth lovers would fit right in today.

The sweetly seductive, gently inclusive quality that puts virtuous reasoners on their guard is what also charms the multitudes to gather in the name of Mother Earth. In addition to the major living Earth/Earth goddess festivals that have been held in New York, San Francisco, Toronto, Amherst (Massachusetts), Boulder (Colorado), and various locations in England and on the continent, innumerable smaller seminars, discussion groups, and get-togethers, have been organized around Gaian themes. As noted earlier, the Gaia Institute at the Cathedral of St. John the Divine in New York City has been offering lectures, discussion groups, and entertainment for almost a decade.

As at most free or inexpensive public gatherings organized around a philosophy, a significant share of those who attend Gaian functions seem to care less about the subject at hand than the opportunity for finding like-souled companionship. Not unlike most political meetings, except that there the deities are power brokers and the outbursts are more often of fury than wonder. Is Gaia the latest organizing principle for people on the make or with nowhere else to go?

Could be. Unlike rowdy political rallies, where those with advantages are keen to press their points, most Gaian gatherings can be attended without fear of challenge or attack, which may be why more and more families with young children seem drawn to the budding movement. This generational mixture has a fine, pacifying effect on the swinging singles and even on the occasional cosmic kook who wanders in. Tea and cider, whole-grain sweets, storytellers, poets, and guitars, a touch of maternal feminism, enough science to keep it honest and enough environmental politics to give a body something to go out and do about it all—that is a good Gaian evening. Some theories go out and

245

grip the masses. Others create an ambience that invites them to drop by.

THE GREAT EXPLANATION

One of the most important emotional functions of a transcendent explanation is that it answer some of the mysteries of life. There are, of course, those great mysteries, like how we all got here and why hydrogen bombs go boom, but on a daily, personal basis we want answers to the smaller puzzlements: tales of dogs from Vermont tracking their masters all the way to Idaho; people who dream up the Lotto number; mothers who wake up knowing that their children are in danger; why the sun seems to come out whenever Pope John Paul II starts to speak—coincidences and circumstances that just seem to be guided by an invisible hand.

Maybe Mother Earth can explain it all away. The very fact that there is a strong scientific basis to Gaian theory, that a vast amount of hard work is being done by hard-nosed scientists who pride themselves on their cold facts, has had, perversely, a liberating effect on the lay imagination. If Mother Nature, little more than a nursery rhyme notion to most people, now proves legitimate by objective, physical standards—if she exists not just as metaphor but literally—then maybe some of those other wild, improbable fantasies and philosophies also have a chance. Perhaps it is Gaia, the infinitely integrated superorganism, who has been working in mysterious ways.

The great Greek goddess does, after all, have some experience in explaining the unknowable. Before Poseidon, Dionysos, or Apollo, Gaia was the first possessor of the oracles at Delphi, Athens, and Aegae. In *Lost Goddesses of Early Greece*, Spretnak writes, "In the Greek imagination the earth is the abode of the dead, so the earth deity has power over the ghostly world. Because dreams, which often were felt to foreshadow the future, were believed to ascend from the netherworld, Gaia acquired an oracular function."[28]

Sometimes a priestess would sleep in a holy shrine with her ear to the ground, to absorb Gaia's silent whispers of wisdom. At dawn she would awaken and erect a tripod altar at the mouth of the cave or over vapors steaming up from a profound crevice. Before mounting the altar, she would smooth rich ochre powder over the vulviform lips of the cave's mouth, methodically tracing the curves of the aperture and jabbing fingertips full of pigment into each rocky pore. Then, coiling a snake from shoulders to hips, the priestess would intone, "First in my prayer before all other gods, I call on Earth, primeval prophetess." Then she would go into a trance and talk with Mother Gaia about the dead, whom she had eaten, and the future, which issued from her body as the two women communed.

EPILOGUE

Plucked from antiquity, an obscure Greek deity has reemerged as the North Star of a new constellation of concepts about creation, life, and death. From the primordial mother goddess who bore all the creatures of the Earth, she has evolved into an organism of ideas about the power and community of life. Today Gaia lives, perhaps physically as planetary flesh, and certainly as a word that has taken on a life and character all its own.

Gaia is: a scientific hypothesis that our planet behaves as a living organism, and a biogeochemical theory of how that system has evolved; a planet-sized creature some 3.5 billion years old; a planetary patina sustained by microbial symbiosis; a necessary overstatement on the power and influence of life on Earth; a wishful trivialization of the vast mechanical power of geological systems; a profoundly erroneous supposition that nature works for the good of all; a brilliant intellectual organizing principle; an ecological world view for the twenty-first century; a romantic metaphor for oneness; a unified symbol for pantheism; a unified symbol for sisterhood; a whole lot of hot air; a travesty against both secular humanism and organized religion; and even a pop

248

star, duly dubbed by *People* magazine, which declared her one of the twenty-five most intriguing characters of 1989.

The daughter of Lovelock's and Margulis' scientific imagination is a hybrid of science, wilderness, and femininity, with preternatural charm. But charms fade. Will Gaia prove a true grande dame of the intellect, or just a New Age showgirl whose place on the marquee of modern consciousness lasts only so long as her bulbs burn bright and green?

The Gaia phenomenon may ultimately be judged as much on the attitudes it engenders as the truths it unearths. Quite in contrast to the Word that lives "In the beginning . . ." of John's immortal story, the Living Earth is more the gospel of nature than of God or man. Those who are bored with human chauvinism, perhaps weary of the way the species ties itself up in Gordian knots of psychosocial minutiae, and who long for a personal I-Thou relationship with the natural world, may find refreshment in the story of the living Earth. Dangerous, this preference for the pleasures of nature over the preoccupations of man? Thank God, yes! There is always danger in primitive passion. Pagan ecstasy of oneness with nature has always been the promise, and the threat, of Mother Earth's embrace.

Gaian sensibilities are organic and voluptuous, never macho, angular, or defiant. For example, Gothic architecture, with its triangles and buttresses and meticulous stress engineering, always seems much more a human triumph over nature than a tribute to it. Much closer to the Gaian heart are Buckminster Fuller's geodesic domes, or the fruits of the Baroque tradition, where buildings sprout like immortal mushrooms, and where gravity is no enemy but simply part of the natural curve.

If there is an enduring theme to the science of Gaia, it is this seamless continuity of life and environment—that to a vital extent all life forms adapt their surroundings to their needs and that, taken as a whole group, we biota are collectively responsible for the Earth's hospitable climate. Lovelock and Margulis thus complete Darwin's work on evolution, which for centuries has stressed, and at times overstated, the power of the inanimate

249

environment over the creatures that live within it. Gaia theory does not refute or oppose the doctrine of natural selection, but rather stands as what may be the single most important amendment to it.

Simply by challenging one hundred years of latent Darwinist assumptions that organisms adapt submissively to their environment, Gaian science should prove its worth. Not just in scientific research, but in the baseline understanding of human endeavor. For example, how many people really consider the impact they have, say, on the weather? We respond to weather conditions; weather conditions do not respond to us, right? But a lifetime of driving a car has a profound influence on the climate, in terms of pollution, acid rain and even greenhouse warming. Building a house certainly shelters one from the cold outside, and by acting as a windbreak may serve to warm the microclimate. Unless, of course, too many trees are cut down in the process.

In his lyrical lament, *The End of Nature,* Bill McKibben makes the excellent point that nowhere in the world can there be found nature unsullied by human industry, since phenomena like the greenhouse effect are by nature global and all-encompassing in scale. Earlier natural philosophers have argued that simply by exploring the wilderness man had robbed it of a certain virginity. If the living Earth theory imparts a general understanding of the impact that human beings and other organisms, particularly the livestock we breed, graze, and slaughter, have on the global environment, then the research conducted in Gaia's name may help correct some of the passive assumptions and victim mentality that are the flipside of social Darwinism.

"Love thy neighbor as thyself." Gaia expands this traditional Christian sentiment to include nonhuman neighbors and changes the punishment for disobeying the commandment from damnation in the next life to catastrophe here and now. Teamwork has become the most crucial Gaian mode. In fact, Margulis went so far as to remark recently that the planet cannot be considered a single living organism after all, because no organism can survive in its own wastes. Even accounting for all the waste products buried beneath the surface of the earth, such as the ocean sinks that precipitate carbon dioxide out of the atmosphere as the calcium carbonate of seashells, Margulis asserts that were our planet to be considered an individual creature, it would be one awash in its own excrement. So the apostle of symbiosis now preaches that the surface of the Earth is controlled by a *community* of organisms, each processing and transforming the other's wastes and carcasses. One creature's poison, after all, is another one's meat. And the team that wastes the least survives and evolves.

When I first met Lovelock years ago, I asked him what the Earth's waste product was. "Infrared radiation," he suggested. One characteristic of living organisms is that they absorb vital substances from their environment, process, and degrade them, so Lovelock reasoned that the Earth receives high-frequency, short-wavelength ultraviolet radiation, absorbs and degrades it to infrared radiation, or heat, then reflects it back into the solar system—the planet's environment. He regards the greenhouse effect as life-threatening by definition, because the Earth's waste-heat disposal process is blocked.

Whether superorganism, organismic community, or just plain orb, the planet is ingenious at converting refuse to refreshment. Ecologists take inspiration from nature's intricate recycling schemes, and umbrage at how humankind has truncated and overtaxed them. And geophysiologists wonder how the global megasystem for waste-circulation will respond. Mythologists recall that Gaia's custom has always been to eat her old children in order to make new ones, and suspect that there's a particular set of naughty progeny on whom she's getting a yen to dine. Moralists tsk-tsk at the profligacy of the human contingent, and wonder aloud at how well we deserve to fare in the species competition for survival. And homilists chuckle that it takes so exotic a creature as Gaia to remind us of the need for old-fashioned values of thrift and conservation in this era of throwaway plenty: Waste not, want not. If it's good enough for old Mother Earth . . .

Gaia theory has charged our imagination about the planet. The value of the theory is ultimately the value of our responses to the fundamental questions it raises. At this writing, Earth Day 1990 looms as a mammoth global celebration of planetary and environmental issues, and promises to shake loose an avalanche of commentary, performance, and perhaps creativity. But there's no rush to judge yea or nay. Gaia is the kind of idea that takes a century to sink in.

—New York City
February 6, 1990

P.S.: As no one yet has come up with a good, solid sentence defining life, I thought I'd take a crack. Perhaps we living creatures are doomed to miss this point, since we cannot, by definition, be objective about what is alive and what is not. So against the day when some hypersmart artificial intelligence program comes along to tell us organisms exactly who and what we are, here is my one-eyed attempt at identifying what all life forms, and only life forms, have in common:

A system is alive if it obtains energy and vital substances from a changeable environment, returns wastes and other toxins to that environment, and maintains the internal chemical and temperature conditions necessary to continue this process.

The only systems we know that are capable of fulfilling these requirements are made of carbon, hydrogen, nitrogen, and oxygen. Darwinists would insist that, except for technical exceptions like mules and some other hybrids, the definition of a healthy living organism must include the capacity to reproduce at some point in its lifespan. And Gaians might now add that living organisms tend to influence their surroundings in a manner conducive to their own existence. Please carry on.

NOTES

I am greatly indebted to three books on the subject of Gaia, and heartily recommend them as essential further reading: *The Ages of Gaia: A Biography of Our Living Earth*, by James Lovelock, W. W. Norton & Company, New York, 1988; *Microcosmos: Four Billion Years of Microbial Evolution* by Lynn Margulis and Dorion Sagan, Summit Books, New York, 1986; and *Gaia: A Way of Knowing: Political Implications of the New Biology*, ed. William Irwin Thompson, Lindisfarne Press, Great Barrington, Massachusetts, 1987.

All quotations not cited in reference below come from personal and telephone interviews and informal conversations, oral presentations, panel discussions, and correspondence over the period May 1986 through December 1989.

More than a dozen personal interviews were conducted with James Lovelock in New York City, San Diego, Los Angeles, Chicago, and Cornwall, England. Lynn Margulis gave five personal interviews, in New York City, Boston, San Diego, and Perpignan, France.

Personal interviews were also conducted with Stephen Schneider in San Diego and Boulder, Colorado; with Andrew

Watson in San Diego and Plymouth, England; with Joss and David Pearson in London; and with James Lodge in Boulder, Colorado.

The American Geophysical Union's Chapman Conference on the Gaia hypothesis, held in March 1988 in San Diego was an important source of personal interviews, panel discussions, and presentations. Those participants whose comments are cited in this volume include Robert Berner, Paul Ehrlich, James Harte, Heinrich D. Holland, James Kirchner, James Lovelock, Lynn Margulis, Dorion Sagan, Walter Shearer, Stephen Schneider, Tyler Volk, Andrew Watson, and Peter Westbroeck.

Numerous personal interviews and discussions were held with members of the Lindisfarne Association, including Reverend James Morton of the Cathedral of St. John the Divine, New York City, William Irwin Thompson, New York City, and Mary Catherine Bateson, Boston.

The California Institute of Integral Studies conference, Gaia Consciousness: The Goddess and the living Earth, held in May 1988 by San Francisco, also afforded an opportunity for a number of interviews, including Merlin Stone and Otter and Morning Glory G'Zell. In addition, Mary Clark, Ralph Metzner, Leah Novick, Philip Novak, Charlene Spretnak, and Brian T. Swimme gave presentations.

Telephone interviews were conducted with Richard Dawkins, Norman Myers, Heinrich D. Holland, Andrew Knoll, W. Ford Doolittle, and George Wald.

Introduction

1. James Lovelock, "Gaia: A Model for Planetary and Cellular Dynamics," in *Gaia: A Way of Knowing: Political Implications of the New Biology*, ed. William Irwin Thompson (Great Barrington, Massachusetts: Lindisfarne Press, 1987), 83–84.

2. William Irwin Thompson, "Gaia and the Politics of Life," *Gaia: A Way of Knowing*, 193.

3. William Irwin Thompson, "Preface," *Gaia: A Way of Knowing*, 7.

4. Ibid.

5. Morning Glory and Otter G'Zell, "Who on Earth Is the Goddess?," unpublished article, 3.

I. James Lovelock and the Theory of Gaia

1. This quotation is from a published version of the same story: James Lovelock, "The Independent Practice of Science," *New Scientist* (September 6, 1979), 714.

2. James Lovelock, *The Ages of Gaia: A Biography of Our Living Earth* (New York: W. W. Norton & Company, 1988), xvi-xvii.

3. Lovelock, "Independent Practice," *New Scientist*, 714.

4. Ibid.

5. Ibid., 715.

6. James Lovelock, "Gaia: A Model for Planetary and Cellular Dynamics," in *Gaia: A Way of Knowing: Political Implications of the New Biology*, ed. William Irwin Thompson (Great Barrington, Massachusetts: Lindisfarne Press, 1987), 89.

7. Lovelock, *Ages of Gaia*, 28, 66.

8. Ibid., 3.

9. Geoffrey Cowley, "The Earth Is One Big System," *Newsweek*, CXII: 19, (November 7, 1988), 98.

10. Lovelock, *Ages of Gaia*, 28–29.

II. Lynn Margulis and Her Microcosm

1. Lynn Margulis, David Chase, and Richard Guerrero, "Microbial Communities: Invisible to the Scrutiny of Naturalists, Most Microbial Communities Have Escaped Description," *BioScience*, 36: 3 (March 1986), 169.

2. Ibid.

3. Lynn Margulis and Dorion Sagan, *Microcosmos: Four Billion Years of Microbial Evolution* (New York: Summit Books, 1986), 106.

4. Evelyn Fox Keller, "One Woman and Her Theory," *New Scientist*, III, (July 3, 1986), 47.

5. Ibid.

6. Interview with Lynn Margulis, *Whole Earth Review*, Twentieth Anniversary Issue, 61 (Winter 1988), 86.

7. Ibid.

III. Gaia: Goddess and Theory

1. Christine Downing, *The Goddess: Mythological Images of the Feminine* (New York: The Crossroad Publishing Company, 1987), 154.

2. James Lovelock, *The Ages of Gaia: A Biography of Our Living Earth* (New York: W. W. Norton & Company, 1988), 40.

3. Dorion Sagan and Lynn Margulis, "Gaia and the Evolution of Machines," unpublished ms., July 1986, 5.

4. W. Ford Doolittle, "Is Nature Really Motherly?," *The Coevolution Quarterly* (Spring 1981), 58.

5. Harley Cahen, "Ethics and the Organismic Earth—A Skeptical View," in *Proceedings of "Is the Earth a Living Organism?"* symposium at Amherst College, Audubon Expedition Institute (Spring 1986), 13–8.

6. Richard Dawkins, *The Blind Watchmaker* (New York: W. W. Norton & Company, 1986), 9.

7. A more detailed discussion of plans being made for Martian ecopoiesis is found in Chapter 10.

8. Russell Schweikart, "Gaia, Evolution and the Significance of Space Exploration," *IS Journal*, published by International Synergy, 2:2 (December 1987), 29.

9. Sagan and Margulis, "Gaia and the Evolution of Machines," 7.

10. Jim Swan and Thomas Hurley, "Questions Raised by the Symposium: Is the Earth a Living Organism," in *Proceedings of "Is the Earth a Living Organism?"*, 81-1.

11. Lovelock, *Ages of Gaia*, 193.

IV. The Great Gaia Showdown

1. Stephen H. Schneider and Glenn E. Shaw, "Proposal to AGU to Convene a Chapman Conference on the Gaia Hypothesis," March 1986, 2.

2. J. E. Ferrell, "Gaia Hypothesis: Now There Are 2 to Wrestle With," *San Francisco Examiner* (April 12, 1988), E-1, E-3.

3. *Compact Edition of the Oxford English Dictionary* (Oxford and New York: Oxford University Press, 1971), 425.

4. James Lovelock, *The Ages of Gaia: A Biography of Our Living Earth* (New York: W. W. Norton & Company, 1988), 67.

5. Quotation from Lawrence E. Joseph, "Britain's Whole Earth Guru," *The New York Times Magazine* (November 23, 1986), 97.

6. Quotation from Richard Monastersky, "The Whole-Earth Syndrome," *Science News*, 133:24, 378.

7. Ibid., 380.

8. Stephen Jay Gould, *Time's Arrow, Time's Cycle: Myth of the Metaphor in the Discovery of Geological Time* (Cambridge, Massachusetts: Harvard University Press, 1987), 2.

9. Lynn Margulis and Gregory Hinkle, "Biota and Gaia," *Abstracts of Chapman Conference on GAIA Hypothesis* (March, 1988), 11.

10. James W. Kirchner and John Harte, "The Gaia Hypotheses: Are They Testable? Are They Useful?", *Abstracts of Chapman Conference on GAIA Hypothesis*, 17.

11. Richard A. Kerr, "No Longer Willful, Gaia Becomes Respectable," *Science*, 240 (April 22, 1988), 393.

12. David Lindley, "Is the Earth Alive or Dead?", *Nature*, 332 (April 7, 1988), 484.

13. Ibid.

14. Kerr, *Science*, 393.

15. Ibid., 395.

16. Fred Pearce, "Gaia: A Revolution Comes of Age", *New Scientist*, 117 (March 17, 1988), 32.

V. Catastrophe and the Evolution of the Earth

1. Ilya Prigogyne and Isabelle Stengers, *Order Out of Chaos* (New York: Bantam Books, 1984), 13.

2. Lynn Margulis and Dorion Sagan, *Microcosmos: Four Billion Years of Microbial Evolution* (New York: Summit Books, 1986), 55.

3. Ibid., 110.

4. James Lovelock, *The Ages of Gaia: A Biography of Our Living Earth* (New York: W. W. Norton & Company, 1988), 94.

5. Ibid.

6. Stephen Jay Gould, *Time's Arrow, Time's Cycle: Myth of the Metaphor in the Discovery of Geological Time* (Cambridge, Massachusetts: Harvard University Press, 1987), 179.

7. Walter Alvarez, "Possible Role of Large-Body Impacts in Altering Biologically Mediated Climate Regimes," *Abstracts of Chapman Conference on GAIA Hypothesis* (March 1988), 25.

8. R. Turco, O. Toon, and T. Ackerman, "Global Geophysical Catastrophes: Massive Biotic Trauma," *Abstracts of Chapman Conference on GAIA Hypothesis,* 26.

9. Margulis and Sagan, *Microcosmos,* 236–237.

10. William Irwin Thompson, "The Cultural Implications of the New Biology," introduction to *Gaia: A Way of Knowing: Political Implications of the New Biology,* ed. William Irwin Thompson (Great Barrington, Massachusetts: Lindisfarne Press, 1987), 17.

11. M. R. Rampino, K. Caldeira, T. Volk, and M. I. Hoffert, "Shiva and Gaia: The Role of Periodic Catastrophes in Terrestrial Homeostasis," *Abstracts of Chapman Conference on GAIA Hypothesis,* supplement.

12. Margulis and Sagan, *Microcosmos,* 66–67.

VI. Gaia: Models and Metaphors for the Living Planet

1. Lewis Thomas, "Debating the Unknowable: When the Scientific Method Won't Work," in *Proceedings of "Is the Earth a*

Living Organism?" symposium at Amherst College, Audubon Expedition Institute, Spring 1986, 67-3.

2. Penelope Boston, "Possible Microbial Impacts on the Atmosphere and Climate: A Catalog for the Designer," *Abstracts of Chapman Conference on GAIA Hypothesis,* March 1988, 12.

3. Stuart Brown, Lynn Margulis, Silvia Ibarra, and David Siqueiros, "Desiccation Resistance and Contamination as Mechanisms of Gaia," *Biosystems,* 17 (1985), 337.

4. Lewis Thomas, *The Lives of a Cell: Notes of a Biology Watcher* (New York: Bantam Books, 1974), 171, 174.

5. M. I. Hoffert, T. Volk, and M. Rampino, "Biological Feedbacks on the Chemical and Climate Evolution of the Earth: Does Gaia Walk the Tightrope?", *Abstracts of Chapman Conference on GAIA Hypothesis,* 12.

VII. Gaian Mechanisms of Climate Control

1. Michael D. Lemonick, "Feeling the Heat," *Time,* "Planet of the Year," special issue, 133:1 (January 2, 1989), 37.

2. Fred Pearce, "Gaia: A Revolution Comes of Age," *New Scientist,* 117 (March 17, 1988), 32.

3. Lynn Margulis and Dorion Sagan, *Microcosmos: Four Billion Years of Microbial Evolution* (New York: Summit Books, 1986), 186.

4. James C. G. Walker, "Feedback Processes in the Biogeochemical Cycles of Carbon," *Abstracts of Chapman Conference on GAIA Hypothesis* (March 1988), 12.

5. Ibid.

6. James Lovelock, *The Ages of Gaia: A Biography of Our Living Earth* (New York: W. W. Norton & Company, 1988), 124.

7. Raymond Siever, "Silica in the Oceans: Biological-Geochemical Interplay," *Abstracts of Chapman Conference on GAIA Hypothesis,* 16.

8. Tyler Volk, "Rise of Angiosperms as a Factor in Long-Term Climatic Cooling," *Geology,* 1989.

9. Ibid.

10. Lovelock, *Ages of Gaia*, 127.

11. James Lovelock, "Gaia: A Model for Planetary and Cellular Dynamics", in *Gaia: A Way of Knowing: Political Implications of the New Biology*, ed. William Irwin Thompson (Great Barrington, Massachusetts: Lindisfarne Press, 1987), 92.

12. Robert A. Berner and Antonio C. Lasaga, "Modeling Atmospheric O_2 and CO_2 over Phanerozoic Time," *Abstracts of Chapman Conference on GAIA Hypothesis*, 21.

13. Lovelock, *Ages of Gaia*, 87.

14. Penelope Boston, "Possible Microbial Impacts on the Atmosphere and Climate: A Catalog for the Designer," *Abstracts of Chapman Conference on GAIA Hypothesis*, 12.

15. Robert C. Cowen, "The Biosphere and the Atmosphere: A Global Picture," *Technology Review* (April 1986), 17.

16. Quoted from Lawrence E. Joseph, "Britain's Whole Earth Guru," *The New York Times Magazine* (November 23, 1986), 96.

17. G. Hinkle, H. McKhann, "Gaia and Salt, or, Is Oceanic Salinity Under Biological Control?", *Abstracts of Chapman Conference on GAIA Hypothesis*, 13.

18. Ibid.

19. Lovelock, *Ages of Gaia*, 106–107.

20. Ibid., 116.

21. M. Whitfield, "The World Ocean—Mechanism or Machination?", *Abstracts of Chapman Conference on GAIA Hypothesis*, 16.

22. Lovelock, *Ages of Gaia*, 134.

23. Meinrat O. Andrae, "Geophysical Interactions in the Global Sulfur Cycle," *Abstracts of Chapman Conference on GAIA Hypothesis*, 18.

24. Nancy Todd, "We Live in Interesting Times: A Conversation with James Lovelock and William Irwin Thompson," *Annals of Earth*, V:3 (1987), 7.

25. J. Lancaster, "Biospheric Energy Storage, Vertical Evolution and Gaia," *Abstracts of Chapman Conference on GAIA Hypothesis*, 13.

26. P. B. Heifetz, R. W. Schweikart and A. V. Quinlan, "The Biochemistry of Carbon Dioxide Fixaton and a Hypothesized Feedback Mechanism for Regulation of Global Atmospheric CO_2," *Abstracts of Chapman Conference on GAIA Hypothesis*, 23.

VIII. The Great Ozone War

1. James Lovelock, *The Ages of Gaia: A Biography of Our Living Earth* (New York: W. W. Norton & Company, 1988), 154.

2. Ibid.

3. Ibid.

4. Ibid., 160.

5. James Lovelock, "The Independent Practice of Science," in *New Scientist*, 83, (September 6, 1979), 716.

6. Ibid.

7. Lovelock, *Ages of Gaia*, 155.

8. James Lovelock, *Gaia: A New Look at Life on Earth* (Oxford and New York: Oxford University Press, 1979), ix.

9. Lovelock, *Ages of Gaia*, 157.

10. Ibid., 84.

11. Janet Raloff, "Ozone Hole of 1988. Weak and Eccentric," *Science News*, 134:17 (October, 22, 1988), 260.

IX. The Body of the Earth

1. Joan Price, "The Earth is Alive and Running Out of Breath," *ReVision: The Journal of Consciousness and Change*, Gaian Consciousness special issue, 9:2 (Winter/Spring 1987), 64.

2. Ibid., 63.

3. Interview with James Lovelock, *Whole Earth Review*, Twentieth Anniversary Issue, 61 (Winter 1988), 87.

4. Ibid.

5. Ibid.

6. Nancy Todd, "We Live in Interesting Times: A Conversation with James Lovelock and William Irwin Thompson," *Annals of Earth*, V:3 (1987), 9.

7. *Whole Earth Review,* 87.

8. *Annals of the Earth,* 9.

9. James Lovelock, *The Ages of Gaia: A Biography of Our Living Earth* (New York: W. W. Norton & Company, 1988), xix.

10. *Whole Earth Review,* 87.

11. Ibid.

12. *Annals of Earth,* 10.

13. Ibid.

14. Ibid.

15. Lovelock, *The Ages of Gaia,* 49.

16. Ibid., 49–50.

17. Stuart Brown, Lynn Margulis, Silvia Ibarra, and David Siqueiros, "Desiccation Resistance and Contamination as Mechanisms of Gaia," *Biosystems,* 17 (1985), 357.

18. "Forms of Gaian Ethics," Anthony Weston, *Environmental Ethics,* 9 (Fall 1987), 225.

19. *Whole Earth Review,* 87.

20. *Annals of Earth,* 9.

21. Lovelock, *Ages of Gaia,* 163–164.

22. Ibid., 164.

23. Ibid.

24. Ralph Metzner, "Gaia's Alchemy: Ruin and Renewal of the Elements," *ReVision: The Journal of Consciousness and Change,* Gaian Consciousness special issue, 9:2 (Winter/Spring 1987), 45.

25. J. Donald Hughes, "Mother Gaia: An Ancient View of Earth," in *Proceedings of "Is the Earth a Living Organism?"* symposium at Amherst College, Audubon Expedition Institute, Spring 1986, 34–4.

X. The World According to Gaia

1. Margaret Cheney, *Tesla: Man Out of Time* (New York: Dell Publishing Co., 1981), 115.

2. Ibid., 116.

3. Ibid.

4. Quotation taken from *Gaia: An Atlas of Planet Management*, Norman Myers, general editor (London: Gaia Books Ltd., and New York: Anchor Press/Doubleday, 1984), 21.

5. Lewis Thomas, *The Lives of a Cell: Notes of a Biology Watcher* (New York: Bantam Books, 1974), 170.

6. Carl Sagan, *The Cosmic Connection* (New York: Dell Books, 1975), 60.

7. James Lovelock, "Gaia: A Model for Planetary and Cellular Dynamics," in *Gaia: A Way of Knowing: Political Implications of the New Biology*, ed. William Irwin Thompson (Great Barrington, Massachusetts: Lindisfarne Press, 1987), 96.

8. Interview with Lynn Margulis, *Whole Earth Review*, Twentieth Anniversary Issue, 61 (Winter 1988), 86.

9. James Lovelock, *Gaia: A New Look at Life on Earth* (Oxford and New York: Oxford University Press, 1979), 110.

10. Ibid.

11. Dorion Sagan and Lynn Margulis, "Gaia and the Evolution of Machines," unpublished ms., July 1986, 5.

12. Anthony Weston, Environmental Ethics, "Forms of Gaian Ethics" (Fall 1987), 221.

13. Lovelock, *Gaia: A Way of Knowing*, 96.

14. Susan Meeker-Lowry, "Gaean Economics: An Economics for the Living Earth," *Proceeding of North American Bioregional Congress II*, Hart Publishing, April 1987, 63–64.

15. J. Donald Hughes, "Mother Gaia: An Ancient View of Earth," in *Proceedings of "Is the Earth a Living Organism?"* symposium at Amherst College, Audubon Expedition Institute, Spring 1986, 34–2.

16. Thomas Berry, "The Viable Human," *ReVision: The Journal of Consciousness and Change*, Gaian Consciousness special issue, 9:2 (Winter/Spring 1987), 79.

17. Johan Galtung, Introduction to "The Roots of Peace, *The Gaia Peace Atlas* (London: Gaia Books Ltd., and New York: Doubleday, 1988), 22.

18. Charlene Spretnak and Fritjof Capra, *Green Politics: The Global Promise* (Santa Fe, New Mexico, 1986), xxv.

19. William Irwin Thompson, "The Cultural Implications of the New Biology" introduction to Gaia: A Way of Knowing, 33.

20. Gaia: A Way of Knowing, William Irwin Thompson, "The Politics of Life," 205.

21. The Gaia Peace Atlas, Mikhail Gorbachev, untitled essay, 252.

22. Ibid.

23. Ibid., Ronald Reagan, letter, 253.

24. Ibid., Javier Perez de Cuellar, Foreword, 8.

25. Ibid., Pope John Paul II, letter, 249.

26. Quotation from Jacques Grinevald, "Sketch for a History of the Idea of the Biosphere," presented to the symposium Gaia: Theory, Practice, Implications, Cornwall, England, October 1987, 9.

27. James Lovelock, review of "The Biosphere," by Vladimir I. Vernadsky, New Scientist, 102 (April 12, 1984), 37.

28. Ibid.

XI. The Goddess and Her Rituals

1. Christine Downing, The Goddess: Mythological Images of the Feminine (New York: The Crossroad Publishing Company, 1987), 146.

2. Charlene Spretnak, Lost Goddesses of Early Greece: A Collection of Pre-Hellenic Myths (Boston: Beacon Press, 1978), 49.

3. Charlene Spretnak, "Knowing Gaia," ReVision: The Journal of Consciousness and Change, Gaian Consciousness special issue 9 (Winter/Spring 1987), 69.

4. Downing, The Goddess, 147.

5. Ibid., 153.

6. Quotation from Jacques Grinevald, "Sketch for a History of the Idea of the Biosphere," presented to the symposium Gaia: Theory, Practice, Implications, Cornwall, England, October 1987, 12.

7. Philip Novak, "Tao How? Asian Religions and the Problem of Environmental Degradation," *ReVision*, 33.

8. Quotation from Stephen Jay Gould, "Darwinism Defined: the Difference Between Fact and Theory, *Discover* (January 1987), 70.

9. *Bertrand Russell's Best: Silhouettes in Satire*, ed. Robert E. Egner (New York and Ontario: New American Library, 1975), 44.

10. Ibid.

11. Lewis Thomas, *The Lives of a Cell: Notes of a Biology Watcher* (New York: Bantam Books, 1974), 142.

12. Ibid.

13. Brian T. Swimme, "The Resurgence of Cosmic Storytellers," *ReVision*, 85.

14. Ibid., 87.

15. Ibid., 86.

16. Thomas Berry, "The Viable Human," *ReVision*, 81.

17. G. K. Chesterton, *Orthodoxy*, (New York: John Lane Co., 1908), 142–143.

18. Dorion Sagan and Lynn Margulis, "Gaia and the Evolution of Machines," unpublished ms., July 1986, 8.

19. Morning Glory and Otter G'Zell, "Who on Earth Is the Goddess?", unpublished article, 4.

20. Ibid., 5.

21. Margot Adler, *Drawing Down the Moon: Witches, Druids, Goddess-Worshippers, and Other Pagans in America Today* (Boston, Beacon Press, 1986), xii.

22. Ibid.

23. James Lovelock, *The Ages of Gaia: A Biography of Our Living Earth* (New York: W. W. Norton & Company, 1988), 194.

24. Mother Teresa, remarks at the Global Forum for Survival, Oxford University, May 1988.

25. Desmond Tutu, introduction to "The Struggle for Peace," *The Gaia Peace Atlas* (London: Gaia Books Ltd., and New York: Doubleday, 1988), 147.

26. Joanna Macy, "Gaia Meditations: Adapted from John Seed," *ReVision*, 57.

27. J. Donald Hughes, "Mother Gaia: An Ancient View of Earth," in *Proceedings of "Is the Earth a Living Organism?"* symposium at Amherst College, Audubon Expedition Institute, Spring 1986, 34–2.

28. Spretnak, *Lost Goddesses of Early Greece*, 45.

INDEX